High Hopes

HIGH HOPES

MY AUTOBIOGRAPHY

Ronnie Corbett

EBURY
PRESS

First published in UK in 2000

Copyright © Ronnie Corbett 2000

1 3 5 7 9 10 8 6 4 2

Ronnie Corbett has asserted his right under the Copyright, Designs and
Patents Act 1988 to be identified as author of this work.

Ebury Press
Random House, 20 Vauxhall Bridge Road, London SW1V 2SA

Random House Australia Pty Limited
20 Alfred Street, Milsons Point, Sydney,
New South Wales 2061, Australia

Random House New Zealand Limited
18 Poland Road, Glenfield, Auckland 10, New Zealand

Random House (Pty) Limited
Endulini, 5A Jubilee Road, Parktown 2193, South Africa

Random House UK Limited Reg. No. 954009

A CIP catalogue record for this book is available
from the British Library

ISBN 0 09 1873819

Design by Darren Haggar

Jacket Photography Steve Poole

All photography © Ronnie Corbett unless otherwise credited.
'Madam, I Love Your Crêpe Suzette' words by Lew Brown and Ralph Freed,
Music by Burton Lane © 1973 Chappell-Co Inc, USA
(75%) Warner/Chappell Music Ltd, London W6 8BS
(25%) Redwood Music Ltd, London NW1 8BD
Reproduced by permission of International Music Publications Ltd
'Class Sketch', The Frost Report © Roger Law and the estate of Marty Feldman
Thanks to David Frost

Other material used by kind permission of Ronnie Barker
Thanks to Mark Fox at Really Useful Theatres

Typeset by SX Composing DTP, Rayleigh, Essex
Printed and bound by Clays Ltd, St Ives plc

Papers used by Ebury Press are natural, recyclable products
made from wood grown in sustainable forests.

ACKNOWLEDGEMENTS

I would like to thank Oliver Pritchett for his gentle and caring help in the telling of this tale – he made every moment of our times together a real pleasure. Thank you Oliver for all your journeys into Surrey.

*For my grandchildren – Tom, Tilly and Dylan – in the hope that
you find as much happiness and fulfilment in your lives as
I have been fortunate enough to find in mine.*

A KIND OF PROLOGUE

To be perfectly honest with you, I am not happy with the title of this book. I have never been happy with it. No, I was dead set on calling it something really catchy, like *A Concise History of the Retail Trade*, but the publisher would not stand for it. He said it didn't have enough oomph or pizzazz. So I compromised and suggested the slightly racier *A Discerning Shopper's Guide*, but he still wouldn't agree. "Oh all right," I said, throwing up my hands, "if you want oomph and pizzazz, we'll call it *Some Notable and Less Notable Merchandising Outlets of Our Age*."

There is actually a special reason for wanting a title that would emphasise the retail side of things, which I'll explain, but first I'll have to tell you about my fantastic memory. While writing this autobiography I have discovered just how good I am at remembering things. Well, I've always known it actually – ever since I ran away from home to join a circus when I was nine and got a job reminding the elephants. Or was it the sea-lions? Or did that happen to somebody else?

So I said to whatsisname, the publisher chappie, when I started working on the book: "Don't you worry about me forgetting anything. It's all up here." And I tapped myself knowingly on the head. Which was a bit painful, because I had forgotten I was holding a large monkey wrench.

I should explain that the publisher, whose name will come back to me in a minute, had invited me round for a working breakfast to discuss the book. He had lightly devilled kidneys, fluffy scrambled egg, crispy smoky bacon and wholegrain brioche washed down with copious amounts of mochaccino – or was it toast and tea? Anyway, while he breakfasted, I worked. I was installing his new dishwasher. That's why I was holding the monkey wrench.

Where was I? Oh yes, I was talking about my fantastic memory. The important point is that I have discovered that I have this amazing gift for remembering the names of shops. The names of all the department stores of my Edinburgh childhood and the grocery shop in George Street which was beneath the drama school I went to; the cake shop and the greengrocers in St John's Wood High Street where I had a bedsit soon after my arrival in London in the 1950s; the shop in Jermyn Street that Noël Coward was coming out of when I first set eyes on him, and all the establishments where I ever bought a hat. They are all indelibly printed on my memory.

I'm so good at it, the people at Yellow Pages sometimes get in touch to ask for information. I also have this uncanny memory for telephone numbers. I can remember all the wrong numbers I have ever dialled.

The only shop whose name I've forgotten is the supermarket in Spain where I bumped into Stewart Granger. I think it might have been El Tesco.

So, anyway, this explains why I wanted to get the retailing aspect into the title. I was even prepared to put in a bit about hosiery, to make one of the "socks 'n' shopping" books which sell so well these days.

Remembering has been no problem. I can honestly say I can recall last Tuesday as if it was Thursday. Or is it the other way round? That's the trouble; I'm not so good at Chronology. In fact I failed it at O level. Three times – but I can't remember in which order. So I changed subjects and got a D in Serendipity.

The point is, if I had known when I was young that I was going to write my autobiography I would have lived my life differently. I would have organised my career into chapters and I would have met my friends in alphabetical order – to help with the Index. The dramas and the cliff-hangers would have been spaced out evenly. Unfortunately, it has not been as tidy as that. Things overlap; events occur at inconvenient times. If I had known I was going to write this book, I would have been able to say to people: "I'm rather occupied with something else at the moment, so I should be grateful if you would come back and sack me or hire me or have a passionate affair with me a little later on, maybe in Chapter Seven, which is going to be called An Unexpected Turn of Events."

So to get over this chronology problem – or, at least, I hope, to distract you from it – I have also included some passages on "themes", such as Golf and Pantomime, and this means that when you reach Chapter Twelve you discover that suddenly I am 12 years old again. Which can be quite a shock. Particularly for me.

By the way, I think I have remembered the name of that Spanish supermarket where I bumped into Stewart Granger. It was called Asda La Vista. Or was that where I first met Arnold Schwarzenegger? I let him go ahead of me at the delicatessen counter, because I wasn't really in a hurry.

My incredible powers of recall combined with my very short attention span have meant that, while writing this, I sometimes got side-tracked into telling stories about the people I stumbled across in the course of the narrative. I suddenly realised there was a way of dealing with these detours and I rushed over to see this publisher person. "I have just had this most brilliant idea," I said, bursting into the Gents, then apologising, backing out again and bursting into his office. "This will absolutely knock your hosiery off," I said. "Why don't I write an autobiography *entirely in footnotes*? No proper text, just lots of footnotes in small print at the bottom of the page. It would make it more of a weighty academic kind of thing. It could be a tome. I've always wanted to write a tome."

And, as I pointed out to thingy, the blank space above the footnotes would be very useful. People could use it to work out anagrams for their crosswords, jot down shopping lists or write their own autobiographies. This could be the new thing, I told him.

So, this publisher – chummy – said: "I'm not prepared to let you have a book consisting entirely of footnotes, but I might just see my way to giving you an enlarged Appendix."

Actually, to judge by the expression on his face, I think he really wanted to give me a ruptured spleen. This made me wonder if I might have inadvertently attached the waste pipe of his dishwasher to his oven.

We still had the problem of the title of the book. "Let's agree to differ," I suggested, but I think the publishing person, misheard me and assumed I had agreed to defer. So he got his own way. He pointed out that, if we called it *A Concise History of the Retail Trade,* the bookshops would be confused. They wouldn't know which section to put it in, Consumer Affairs, Showbusiness, or *Belles Lettres*. Or on that table marked "Any five of these for 20p."

So here it is. My autobiography. Well, of course it's my autobiography. Otherwise it wouldn't have been auto and I wouldn't be me. I'm hardly likely to write Madonna's autobiography, am I? I scarcely know the woman.

So, anyway, here it is. My tome. And I just hope it is worthy to take its place alongside such classic volumes as "Freeman, Hardy and Willis: Maestros of Tap-Dancing" and "Fortnum and Mason: The Rock 'n Roll Years" and "Harvey Nichols: A Man and His Magic".

CHAPTER ONE

In which I introduce some members of my family, including my grandfather on my mother's side, who came from Aberdeen to London to be a policeman; my grandmother, who was a housekeeper in Belgravia; and my father who emigrated to Canada and then came back after two months. The young Sean Connery is mentioned. We meet my worried Aunt Nell and get a glimpse of my exotic second cousin in Piccadilly.

I was born in the Simpson Memorial Hospital, in Edinburgh. In Lauriston Place, opposite the Fire Station. On December 4th 1930. I know I arrived in the evening, but I don't remember what time it was. My mother always could, of course. They left a swab in – so that's what made it quite memorable for her, I expect. This was mentioned from time to time in later life, almost as if it was my fault, which was not really fair as I was occupied at the time, being held upside down by my ankles and having my bottom slapped.

When she was a young woman my mother had had very serious appendicitis which developed into peritonitis. In those days they used to make sufferers sleep in a steam tent and they dosed them with pure lemon juice to clear out the poison. This peritonitis led to her losing one ovary. This was another family legend. Like the swab. It was known, but not much talked about. And, on the rare occasions, the subject was raised, the tone was grave; sometimes I thought I noticed my mother looking wistful. It was as if this ovary was a member of the family who had gone away to sea and never been heard of since.

I sometimes wondered about the mysterious absent ovary, and it even occurred to me that perhaps my mum, only having one, was the cause of her producing such a small first child. I later realised that it couldn't have been that, because my brother Allan and my sister Margaret, who both came after me, were all the right dimensions.

My first real memory, is a rather traumatic one of nearly drowning, at the age of three, in quite a deep paddling pool in St Andrews, at a part of the coastline known as the Step Rock, which is near the Royal and Ancient Golf Club. I can remember the feeling of panic, the sense of being in serious trouble. I can hear the rumbling and gurgling and see all that glittery shiny water with me underneath it . . . .When you are three years old you do not have much of a life to flash before your eyes, so it was lucky that my mother was there to haul me out just in time.

Perhaps I should say something first about my parents and my family background. My mother's parents were both from Kintore, in the north of Scotland, near Aberdeen, and they both migrated, as many restless Scots have always done, to London where my grandad, James William Main, was a London police-man. He was a station sergeant at Upper Norwood and Gypsy Hill, not far from where I live now, and I still have his desk, presented to him when he retired, with a plaque on it. It is one of those portable ones which you open and it has a sloping embossed leather surface to write on.

His wife Margaret was cook housekeeper in quite a grand house in Upper Belgrave Street. I think she worked next door to Ellen Terry or to one of those great West End ladies who, in those days, lived in some style in Belgravia. Maybe I got my theatrical leanings from my grandmother. She loved the theatre and all the glamour of it, and she would regularly go and queue up for the cheap seats in the West End theatres.

Her London life was cut short when my grandad was forced to retire early because of ill-health and they had to return to Scotland. I never met these grandparents, but from my mother's description of him, I imagine James William Main as a rather fragile, gentle, pale-skinned man. I picture him as being rather like Robert Louis Stevenson with that same wan Scottish face. He loved words and my mother told me he was a great reader of novels and poetry and was much more scholarly than you would expect a policeman to be.

My mother, Anne, was born shortly before my grandparents went back to Scotland. When I was grown up and living in London I once took her back to Bermondsey to look at the block of flats where she spent the first few months of her life. My mother was a petite, dark woman with a pretty face. Before she married my father she worked for John Menzies, the bookseller, in their head office in Rose Street, Edinburgh, on the switchboard and later in the accounts department. Like her father, she was quite bookish and she loved to recite poetry. Nobody ever said anything, but I suspect there might be a feeling in the family that my mum's side was just a little bit more genteel than my dad's.

She was in the same class in Boroughmuir School as Alastair Sim, that extraordinary sinister-looking, sad-eyed actor with the voice of a fastidious ghoul who starred in film comedies like *The Belles of St Trinians* – in which he played the headmistress. At school, the young Alastair was another great one for standing up and reciting poetry. His father was a kilt maker in Lothian Road. My mother used to point out the shop to me every time we passed it.

My mother had a sister Nell and a brother Alec who were both tailors. Alec was gassed in the First World War, and, as a result, suffered from emphysema and died quite young. I remember seeing him, with the tape measure slung round his neck, sitting cross-legged on a table in his shop window, sewing away. When his illness got worse he was taken to the hospital in Edinburgh, facing the Pentland hills where the chilly air was supposed to be good for chest conditions. To me, the place seemed half way between a prison and a workhouse. Children were not allowed inside, so when the family visited Uncle Alec on Sundays, I would have to wait in the gatekeeper's house in the hospital grounds. The patients' beds were pushed out on to balconies, to get the air, and all I could see was the bright scarlet of the hospital blankets, standing out against the distant gloom.

It was the custom in those days that each patient at the hospital had a serial number and every day the *Evening News* in Edinburgh would print bulletins on patients, giving just their serial numbers. There would be these lists of numbers to show who had gone on to the critical list, or had come off it, or had died. So you would know the serial number of your uncle or your dad, or whoever, and look for it on the front page of the *Evening News* to see how he was getting on. It was all a bit grim and impersonal.

Aunt Nell was regarded as something of a beauty, but she did not marry until late in life and then she absolutely hated it. And him. The marriage lasted less than a year and was never spoken of in the family. The thing I remember about Aunt Nell's husband is the rather strange gloves he wore; they were the sort that had started life as golden yellow shammy and then got paler and paler every time they were washed, so that they ended up like Marcel Marceau's gloves. And he wore a double-breasted tweed overcoat, rather long and very much in the style of the Duke of Windsor. That is really all I remember of him now. I have forgotten his name, which is not surprising, as it was never uttered.

Aunt Nell was a tremendous worrier. She was always pacing up and down, wringing her hands. Everything made her nervous, especially alcohol and tobacco. She was dedicated to self-sacrifice and to work. She deserved a better life than she had, but she was somehow incapable of finding it, of seizing her chance of happiness. My mum once told me that my grandmother used to say: "That Nell will let all the bonnets go by, for looking for a hat."

After the end of her marriage, Aunt Nell devoted her life to us and she was like a second mother to me. She came round to our house almost every evening with her little workbag, and she would measure something or get a bit of material and knock something up. There was always something on the go. She would come round for a cup of tea in the early evening after work, and she and mum would blether and worry each other to death. Mum was anxious all her life and Aunt Nell used to stoke up all her apprehensions.

Aunt Nell made all my clothes – or did the alterations to my trousers and jackets and coats; she did complete tailoring jobs on my school blazers because I was so tiny. She was always working on some item of clothing for one of us. One of the things I learned from Aunt Nell is that because I am small it is really important for me to be immaculately neat and well turned out all the time. She also gave me an interest in materials and the textures of cloth.

After some years she began to find that being a tailor was a physically hard and tiring job, so she decided to give it up and go to work as a buyer. I think quite a lot of our family friends were in the outfitting business, in one or other of the famous houses in Edinburgh, like Patrick Thompson, or Romaine's & Patterson. When I look back on my childhood I have a picture in my mind of a lot of brisk ladies dressed in black and these would be Aunt Nell's colleagues – the buyers at these renowned Edinburgh establishments.

Aunt Nell went to work for Patrick Thompson and then in Jenners. She also worked for Jaeger and I remember her coming to our house very excited one evening because Ivor Novello had arrived in the shop to buy some cashmere, or a camel hair coat perhaps. He must have been performing at the Empire at the time, in *Perchance to Dream* or *The Dancing Years*, or something like that.

She was a deeply affectionate soul and she had pet names for us all. I used to be called "my little Rodie-Podie". Because she had no children of her own, she took us on as a family. When she died in the late 1950s she left about £5 in a post office savings account; she cared so little for possessions herself and gave so much away. I don't think she ever had her own house; she was a paying guest with my Aunt Gammy who was a friend of my grandmother, Margaret Main, and had been in service with her. Aunt Gammy looked after Nell, making her breakfast and her tea, and Nell went out to work every day.

I think Aunt Nell must have suffered from a heart or circulatory problem because she suffered very badly from the cold and I remember she always had very, very cold hands and cold feet.

On Sundays we often used to walk with my dad to visit his father, Walter Corbett, in the Tynecastle district of Edinburgh, home of the Heart of Midlothian football team. It was a tough life in a tenement with gas-lit stairs and no bathroom, of course. You had to go to the wash-house; you would load all the washing in a pram and push it round to the steamie where you would have a good blether with the neighbours. One of my most vivid memories of those tenement buildings is of the powerful smell of tom-cats on the cold, gritty concrete stairs – or in the "entries", as they used to call them.

Walter Corbett died when I was about 10. He had run his own business as a coal merchant, but not very successfully and I think he ended up being a coalman rather than a coal merchant. I just remember him sitting by the fire most of the time, being plied with cups of tea and sandwiches. Then he would sit there, holding a solid block of tobacco, the colour of molasses, cutting slivers off it with his penknife, whose gleaming blade was partly worn away from years of sharpening. He didn't say much; he just smoked his pipe which had a metal cap on the bowl.

My dad, who was called William, had two sisters, Isa (Isabel) and Jessie, and a brother, Geordie. Dad's mother (my grandmother) died in childbirth when Isa was born. Isa died quite young of cancer and Jessie's life ended rather tragically – she was hit by an Edinburgh bus at Juniper Green and killed outright.

Dad was a remarkable man. He had tremendous energy and drive and he filled every moment. I think of him as being a very impressive, hardworking person who was dedicated to the idea of self-improvement and who had hugely high standards in everything he touched. He was a baker and he just couldn't bear it when things were not done properly. I wish now I knew more about his remarkable skills. When I bake bread or make cakes I always think of him and I try to force myself to roll up my sleeves and put my apron on and make sure everything is just right first, because that is what he always did. It is as if he is standing at my shoulder. He hated to see people starting on jobs before things were properly ready.

I learned a lot from him and I'm sure it was he who gave me the will to get on in life. He was a severe man and I always felt I wanted to impress him. But he was not, in any way, forbidding – he also had a sense of humour. It was the tough, Scottish kind of sense of humour, of seeing the funny side of the ordinary troubles of life. He would laugh at accidental occurrences, like disasters in the bake house or a suit shrinking at the dry cleaners. And he was also very gregarious and a tremendous bletherer; a man who thought street corners were for standing on and passing the time of day.

Dad was not very tall, about 5ft 6in, with a good, strong-jawed determined face. In the First World War he lied about his age, joined the Royal Scots Regiment and went to France. He actually fought in the battle of the Somme as just a boy of sixteen and a half. This is something I can't even imagine now. When he came home on leave after two or three years and he got off the train at Edinburgh Waverley station, his sisters Isa and Jessie, who had come to meet him, did not recognise him. They walked down the platform looking for him and walked right past him. He had gone away a wee boy and come back as a man.

He came back from the war physically unscathed, but how could I tell what other effect it had on him? I was born 12 years after it was over and I don't suppose I asked him all that many questions about it. He was a reticent man and would speak only occasionally about the terrible things he had seen. I know he had vivid memories of certain people and over the bravery of some of the officers and the sense of camaraderie. He was always proud of his connection with the Royal Scots Regiment.

So, after the war, he returned to his apprenticeship at McVitie and Guest, one of the four very good bakers in Edinburgh at the time. One effect of going to France was that it made him restless, tougher and bolder. Having survived the war, he was ready to take a gamble in the world, so, after he finished his apprenticeship, he decided to go to Canada, to set up his own baking business in Toronto.

But love changed his plans. He stayed only two months in Canada before returning to Edinburgh and going back to work at McVitie and Guest. He had met a girl one night at a dance hall in Edinburgh shortly before he set sail for Canada and before he had time to settle down in his new life in Toronto he realised that he had to go back and see that girl again. That was my mother, Anne Main. And she certainly didn't want to go to Canada, so that was that.

I happen to know that the bandleader on the night they met in that Edinburgh dance hall was Sidney Lipton. He later came to London and had a big band at the Grosvenor House hotel where he was also responsible for booking the cabaret acts. I worked for Sidney as a comedian at a number of balls and functions in the 1970s and I always remembered that his music played some indirect part in putting me on this earth.

Mum and dad got married and lived in a flat in Warrender Park Road, in Edinburgh, near the University. It must have been quite daunting for my mother being married to a man who was such an accomplished housekeeper himself and I think it sometimes dented her confidence. As he was a baker, it was quite intimidating to cook in front of him. On Sundays, after church, we would have a lunch of pot roast, a bit off the aitch bone, and there was always an argument about whether or not there should be milk in the Yorkshire pudding mix. My mum said her mother – the cook housekeeper in Upper Belgrave Street – always maintained that there should be a little dash of milk, but dad said no, adding milk made the texture leathery.

This debate was one of our Sunday traditions. (On Sundays there was always tinned fruit – tinned pears or tinned peaches. Lovely, glistening, golden yellow, slimy peaches. And Carnation milk.)

In 1937 my dad went to the opening of the famous Portobello Baths in Edinburgh and caught a very severe chill. They were going to be the biggest swimming baths in the whole of Europe, open air, with even an early version of a wave-making machine. They were hugely spectacular in their day, but pretty cold. These were the baths, by the way, where Sean Connery was a lifeguard early in his career.

As a result of the chill, my dad developed diabetes and, because insulin was in its very early days then, he had to take great care in balancing his diet, weighing everything, measuring everything. He became very skilful at it.

It is an example of the kind of man he was that, finding he had diabetes, he immediately became interested in the subject and wanted to know more. He realised that he was going to have to be much more aware of the food values of his intake, so he took a course in dietetics at night classes at Edinburgh University. On two evenings a week he would be doing classes on dietetics and on another two evenings he would be giving classes at another night school, on baking and confectionery and decorating cakes. And after that, late at night, he would go on to his job at the bake house.

In the way of families who are comparatively poor, there was sometimes speculative talk in our house about a rich relative, a small, distant ray of hope. It was usually Aunt Nell who raised the subject, or perhaps my mother. The relative in our case was a self-made Scottish industrialist named Sir Alexander Roger who came from Aberdeen and was wealthy in that monumental

Scottish way, like Andrew Carnegie, the great steel baron. It was said that he was some sort of cousin of my grandmother on my mother's side – her name had been Annie Roger before she married the policeman.

Sir Alexander was a great benefactor, but never, alas, to us. I don't expect he even knew of our existence. Sometimes, Aunt Nell would murmur "Perhaps Ron might drop him a line and look him up when he is in London," but I never did.

I did, however, come across one of his sons, Bunny Roger. He was a very gay, dandified wit who walked about the West End of London in magnificent suits and very curly bowlers, set right in the middle of his head, and a lilac tie with jewelled tie-pin, very narrow drainpipe trousers, hand-made Lobb shoes, an umbrella and a high-buttoned waist coat.

Bunny Roger, whose real name was Neil, was the second of three sons of the wealthy – and disappointingly dour – Sir Alexander. It was not surprising that the father and son did not get on all that well. The three brothers were sent to Loretto, the Scottish public school, and, the story goes, the father offered Bunny a reward if he was picked for the rugby first XV. Bunny made it into the team and, as his reward, he asked for a doll's house. And he got it.

Bunny lived in grand style, in Walton Street, and he looked amazing. Heads would turn as he walked through Burlington Arcade. He was really one of the sights of London, extremely camp and very sweet, and he had also been very brave in the war, in Italy with the Rifle Brigade. When he died in 1997 one of his obituaries said: "Typically, he claimed to have advanced through enemy lines with a chiffon scarf flying as he brandished a copy of *Vogue*. He also said that being in no man's land at least gave him a chance to repair his make-up." I'm sure Aunt Nell would have worried a great deal about all this if she had known.

Years later, in London, I used to see Bunny Roger in the

street, but at first I never dared to approach him. Then, when I felt I was doing well enough, and my suits got good enough to rub shoulders with his, I went up to him and introduced myself. He was really very kind and friendly and said, yes, he thought we were related. After that we would bump into each other from time to time, usually at the theatre, and he would introduce me to his friends, saying "This is my second cousin, the clever little comedian."

CHAPTER TWO

An account of my childhood in Edinburgh. Holidays to St Andrews; visits to the bakery where my father worked; swimming lessons with the terrifying Jimmy McCracken. My school days. Aunt Nell worries about my height and decides to take steps. I devise a method for working out how tall girls at dances are, when they are sitting down.

We nearly always went to St Andrews for our summer holidays – joined, eventually, by my brother, Allan, who was born six years after me and by my sister, Margaret, four years later. All our luggage would be packed into trunks and roped up 10 days before, then sent on in advance to the digs where we were to stay. Then, on the day, we took a taxi to Waverley station. It was the only taxi we took in the whole year. We caught the train to St Andrews, changing at Leuchars.

We usually took our holidays with other families; the fathers would play golf in the morning and then join the wives and children on the beach in the afternoon. I have a photograph of myself at St Andrews in one of those embarrassing knitted swimming costumes which used to get longer and wider and saggier as the stitches separated with stretching.

When I look at this picture it reminds me of the time on the West Sands when, much to my dad's annoyance, someone gave me a big round boiled sweet, the sort you used to have those days with very strong fruity flavours, and I swallowed it whole and it got stuck in my throat. My dad had to lift me up, hold me upside down, like a rabbit, by my legs and thump the middle of my back until the sweet fell out and lay all sticky in the sand.

At night in St Andrews we would always take a wee walk round the old town, maybe buying a penny poke of chips to eat on the way back to our digs, and the fathers would go and make their booking for the round of golf the following day.

My father walked everywhere. Much later in my life, when he got a car he actually garaged it a good three miles away from home, so that every time he used it he had a three-mile walk there and a three-mile walk back. The garage was in the Churchill area of Edinburgh, opposite the excellent Dominion cinema which has remained there, pretty well unscathed for 50 years. I sometimes take amazed friends back to where the garage was, just to show them how far away it was from our house. There is also a very good cooking utensil shop in the area, which is another reason for the pilgrimage.

Oddly enough, my dad and I both learned to drive at the same time, when I was 18. Dad's brother Geordie gave us both lessons. I passed my test at the first go, but my dad didn't. So this was an unusual situation, a reversal of our normal father–son relationship, with me driving the car or sitting beside my dad, trying not to look too smug, as he drove with his Learner plates on.

One evening when we went out for a drive with the L plates on and I was in the passenger seat, a policeman stopped us and asked to see my dad's driving licence. Of course it was a provisional licence, and the only other person in the car was me, in the passenger seat, looking like a wee laddie of 14.

The policeman took it slowly. He looked at the car, he looked at the provisional licence again, he looked at my dad and then he looked at me. "And what about the lad?" he asked.

You don't get many moments like this in your life, so you have to treasure them. With studied nonchalance – because at that age I was a keen student of nonchalance – I reached into my inside jacket pocket, took out my proper licence and handed it to the policeman. He took less time to look at that one, passed it back to me and then had to walk away, rather shamefaced. I was quite pleased about that.

Anyway, back to my childhood. I was eight years old when the war began and shortly after that I was evacuated. My mother took my brother and me and three other children away from Edinburgh. It was really a ridiculous evacuation because we only went 45 miles south of the city, to the Borders.

We went to an estate called Newton Don which was owned – and still is – by the Balfour family and we lived in the gamekeeper's cottage. We children quite liked it, but mother hated it. I enjoyed the farm life, running around the fields, playing games of hide and seek in the hay lofts and finding hens' eggs in secret places. Then, after six weeks, we went back to Edinburgh.

So that was it. We were issued with our gas masks in cardboard boxes; had those labels tied on our coats; travelled 45 miles, and then just came back again. Actually, Edinburgh was not badly bombed in the war, but Glasgow was, and sometimes the Germans bombed Edinburgh as an afterthought on the way back from Glasgow. We got the leftovers.

During the war we still had our summer holidays in St

Andrews, except for a couple of years when holidays by the sea were banned. Once even St Andrews was bombed. That was just because the German aircraft were unloading what they hadn't dropped on Clydebank, which was the place they were really after – Clydebank and the shipbuilding. I remember my father going to help clear the rubble of the damaged buildings in St Andrews the following morning.

My earliest public performance was in aid of the war effort. It was in a concert for the Spitfire Fund which I think probably raised about £9. I wore a dressing gown and carried a candle and sang a Christopher Robin song, while standing on the flat roof of the air raid shelter in the communal garden behind our tenement. I like to think I helped to undermine German morale.

On Sundays in my childhood we would all walk to church, my father in his best Sunday suit and us boys in our Royal Stuart kilts, lovat green sweaters and the black brogues. In the afternoon, if we were not visiting my grandfather in Tynecastle, we would go on our Sunday walk, still in our best clothes, usually in the south of Edinburgh, over the Braid Hills, near the Pentlands. I can remember the smell of the grass as we walked there, looking down over the Firth of Forth. The smell of grass and the feel of it under my feet are still a special comfort to me, and a reminder of those Sunday walks. It is also one of the best excuses for playing golf. One of the great relaxing feelings for me these days is walking over a newly cut fairway in the evening.

Those walks would start at about two o'clock in the afternoon and we didn't get back home for our tea until about half-past five. Then my father went for the second time to the church where he was an elder and a member of the choir, and my brother, sister and I would go off to Bible class.

Much more than the Sunday smell of grass, the sweet warm

aroma of baking bread and cakes wafted through the whole of my childhood. I was brought up with a knowledge of the bake house and a feel for it. In those days the bake house would close down on Sundays, but somebody would have to go in on a Sunday evening for "spongeing", or preparing the doughs, which would then be left to stand overnight.

I used to love to go with my father at these times. It was a paradise, a sweet treasure house. There was a loft full of glacé cherries and sultanas and muscatels and walnuts and tubs of butter and demerara sugar. I could have as many glacé cherries as I wanted, and then maybe a wee bit of marzipan or frangipane as well.

And there was always a bakery cat, or usually three or four of them, and there would be kittens. My father would take me to the corner of the loft to see the three day-old kittens curled up in an old sultana basket with some jute sacking.

My father would change into his baker's outfit, a chef's white jacket and check trousers, thick pale grey woollen socks and big leather boots. Bakers wore boots with no laces in them – I suppose it was to keep their feet cool – so they tended to shuffle about, not lifting their feet properly. The bakery had a concrete floor and there were big carved wooden tables which had been worn down from the great handfuls of dough being crashed down on to them.

Because of his job, my father was away at night time for most of my childhood. He would come back home after seven o'clock in the morning, usually have a sleep and then take me for a walk or have a game of golf.

When he left McVitie and Guest, where he was baking manager, he went to run Mackie's bakery. He could start work later in the evening then because they were producing pastries and delicate cakes and eclairs and things that did not have to be ready early in the morning like baps had to be. You would go out early for your rolls, but people didn't want their vanilla slices and iced buns till later in the morning.

Every different sort of cake was known as a "line", so the bakery would produce a line of vanilla slices, or a line of eclairs, or whatever.

There was nothing my father could not turn his hand to. He could bake cherry cakes, mille feuille pastry, charlotte pastry, rough puff pastry or rich rough puff pastry. He used to bake the wedding cakes for all our relations and friends. And chocolate cakes and beautiful Madeira cakes. I can picture him now, preparing little individual sponge cakes which would be baked in small metal cups. He would have the cake mixture in a bowl beside him and he would take precisely the right amount of it in his right hand and then flick it into the metal cup from a distance of about five or six inches. I used to marvel at the elegance and economy of his movements.

Throughout his life, my dad could never stop himself judging the work of other bakers. If we were on a family holiday – and even much later when he visited me in London – he would always find a reason to go to the local baker's shop and he would buy a couple of cookies or a couple of rolls or maybe a loaf, and cut them open to see what they were like inside. When he judged what he called "tea bread" (something that was part cake and part bread, like a plain bun with raisins inside and crystallised sugar on top) he squeezed it between his fingers to see if it sprung back. If it stayed down and was doughy in the middle it showed that the bread was not properly proved, or risen.

When he left Mackie's, with his knowledge of dietetics and his baking skills, he got a job running the Lothians schools meals service. The cooking centre was in the Fountainbridge area of Edinburgh and it used to prepare school dinners for thousands of school children and send them out all over the Lothians.

I was about 14 or 15 when my father worked there and the cooking centre was a wonderfully glamorous place for a child to visit, with those vast vats of custard and gravy and ladders going up, so that I could climb up and peer into them and watch the custard heaving and throbbing like a great yellow volcano on the point of erupting. I gripped the ladder more tightly as I imagined myself drowning in the gravy.

Then, for some reason, the Lothians school meals service was re-organised, the cooking centre disbanded and my father was made redundant. It really hurt him. They offered him a job as caretaker at a big school and he did that to fill in the time until he retired, but his spirit was rather broken.

I wish I had learned more from my dad about baking. It was tragic, but he became so disillusioned in the end that he destroyed all his recipe books. There were 28 of them which he had written up in his own neat hand, a record of his career and all he had learned. One day he just ripped them up or burned them. He never showed much emotion, but he must have felt terribly bitter to do this. For most of his time as a baker he had to work from 11.15 at night till seven in the morning and he was paid about £8 a week. It was slave labour for a man of his skills. Destroying the recipe books was a gesture of protest. Even after he gave up, he kept on going into bakers' shops to examine the bread and, if he ever went missing, we could be pretty sure we would find him at the nearest cake shop having a blether and finding out how many lines they were doing.

I remember my first day at school and I remember not liking it much. I cried a lot and I think I disgraced my mother. It was the James Gillespie School for Boys and I wore a maroon and grey uniform. My first teacher was Miss Sandilands, who looked very stern and had her hair in a very severe bob, but was actually quite kindly.

Muriel Spark, the author of *The Prime of Miss Jean Brodie*, went to the James Gillespie School for Girls, so that might give an idea of what it was like. However, my years at James Gillespie were not the prime of Master Ronald Corbett. I seem to remember being good at very little. I don't think I had any close friends and I was not even particularly naughty. I was just one of those pupils who could be trusted to sit at the back of the class. I seem to have made an art of being unremarkable. I recently found a school group photograph, with me seated on a chair, fourth from the left in the front row. I am the only one of the boys in that row whose feet do not touch the ground.

There were bus trips to the Pentlands and there were swimming lessons. We would form a long maroon and grey crocodile and march once a week to Sciennes School where we were taught to swim by a very stern and famous swimming instructor called Jimmy McCracken. He was famous because in the summer holidays he used to teach the toffs in North Berwick to swim. These were the grand people who used to have holiday houses on the front there, or near the golf course. In a way, he had the status of a skiing instructor today.

You were considered very lucky if you managed to book a swimming lesson with Jimmy McCracken. He had a little military moustache and wore a white shirt, white flannels and white pumps and he had a large whistle on a cord round his neck. He was quite a bully and quite frightening, but he got me to swim and to dive off higher boards than I really wanted to dive off.

It was quite a jaunt, going to swimming lessons. We walked in crocodile along Warrender Park Road, along Sciennes Road, and past the Royal Sick Children's Hospital, where I have a rather horrendous memory of my tonsils being removed and where I was taken on a number of occasions to have stitches put in my head or my arm or my leg, because I was accident-prone as a child and tended to fall over quite a lot. I remember those rust-red thick rubber sheets they put on the trolleys. They smelled rubbery and there was something brutal about them; they made me think of gallons of blood sloshing about and a surgeon waiting outside in the corridor with a saw.

After swimming we would be marched back. As a special treat we were given a penny by our mums on swimming days because we were allowed to buy what was called "a shivery bite." This was a warm sausage roll or a cream doughnut; something to stop the teeth chattering and bring back the breathing and the circulation. I can still see those cream doughnuts. Dusted with icing sugar. Standing on the too-high diving board looking down into the unfriendly pale blue water below, with a hollow feeling in the chest and Jimmy McCracken shouting "Get on with it, laddie," the thing that kept me going was the thought of those sugar-dusted doughnuts. They were to dive for.

Talking of shivering, I used to go to the cinema to give myself a fright. I went many times to see *Dr Cyclops* and then to *The Mummy's Hand* just to prove to myself that I could take it. As the mad scientist pursued his vile and dastardly scheme to miniaturise a party of jungle travellers I would miniaturise myself, sinking deeper and deeper in the cinema seat. And as the high priest of the evil sect used a revivified Egyptian mummy to kill off members of an archaeological expedition I would glance along the row for the reassuring sight of the illuminated Exit sign just in case I needed to leave in a hurry.

I have wonderful memories of the times we went to Patrick Thompson, the store where Aunt Nell worked as a buyer, to get a new school coat or a pair of trousers and afterwards we would go to the tea room on the third floor. People sat round the balcony and looked down on the string quartet playing on the floor below. We would have a wonderful high tea – which is something they have always done very well in Scotland. There was always beautiful fish and quite the most memorable chips, which I can still almost taste to this day. They were big, fat and deliciously chunky.

There was a cake stand in the middle of the table and we worked our way up it, from the slices of bread and butter at the bottom, to the pieces of cake and the tea bread or fruit bread, before we finally reached the summit and the iced cakes. Tea at Patrick Thompson was always really something.

I went on to the Royal High School and I don't think I did much better there than I did at James Gillespie. But I did at least take part; I was always a great joiner. I went to the literary and debating society every week and didn't speak. Or I would go to the school dance and not dance all night. Then I used to play rugby for a very lowly school team and keep score for the cricket XI. I always seemed to be slightly in the shadows, hiding in a corner, peeping out, observing, gathering information, building up a kind of dossier on life.

Oddly enough, I don't ever remember being particularly troubled about being small. My mother worried about it, and this was reinforced by Aunt Nell who worried about it even more, which drove my mum to greater anxiety, which caused Aunt Nell to fret some more. They both suspected that I must be worrying about it too, although I could never compete with them in that department. It is possible, although I didn't say anything about it, that I may have sent out some slight signals of concern, round about the age of 13 or 14, at a time when you would expect to go into long trousers. So Aunt Nell paid two guineas and sent away for a course on How to Become Taller. I remember it consisted of a few glossy white sheets of paper with blue print on them.

The secret of adding to your stature, according to this course, was positive thinking combined with stretching exercises. So I had to recite: "Every day and in every way I'm getting taller and taller." Which I wasn't. Then there were exercises in which I had to stretch up the bedroom wall, trying to reach pin marks, while my mum and Aunt Nell watched, willing me to grow.

Even with the concentrated thought-waves of my mum and Aunt Nell, we had to admit eventually that I was still the same size and all the course had achieved was a few more marks on the bedroom wall. So my mum took me to a specialist in Moray Place to see if there was something wrong with me and he said there was nothing to worry about; I was just a tinier sort of person. Fortunately, they did not embark on any special treatment, because that has since proved to be quite dangerous. So I reached the height of five feet one and a half inches and that is where I stopped.

I never had a hard time at school because of my size, which surprises me now, considering how cruel schoolchildren can be. There was a boy in my class whose father was a big fishmonger down the road from us and he was always called Stinky Thomson or Fishy Thomson, and there was another boy who had dermatitis and always had to wear bandages and was given a hard time by some of the others. Then there was a boy called James Elder who was obviously severely dyslexic. We would hug ourselves with pleasure and pull secret gleeful faces at each other when there was reading round the class. We waited for it to get to Jimmy Elder, and for it to be his turn to stand up and not be able to read.

We could be awful little beasts, but I don't remember ever being hurt or being called names. Perhaps I was a better talker than I thought, or perhaps I was more funny than I realised, and that gave me some protection.

The scoutmaster made me a troop leader and that was a great

encouragement to me. And later when I did my National Service in the RAF I was given a commission, which also did my confidence a lot of good. It's not easy to pick a tiny person and give them authority, so I was always grateful to the scoutmaster and the RAF selection board.

When I was round 14 or 15 I had a phase when I used to go on tough and demanding holidays in Scotland. After about a day and a half, I realised I wasn't really the hardy type, but I kept on persevering. One winter, four of us rented a miner's cottage on the bleak and deserted island of Raasay, off the east coat of Skye. All we did was stoke the fire with peat, walk to the post office to buy a day-old newspaper, go back and stoke the fire with peat, put paraffin in the lamps, then huddle round the fire for the rest of the day eating hot buttered toast.

I also went on a rugged skiing course in the Cairngorms, long before skiing was a popular pursuit in this country, and I went youth hostelling. Actually, I gave up youth hostelling after I had problems with my bike which was so heavily laden at the back that I had great trouble keeping the front wheel on the ground every time I went up a hill.

I was aware of being uneasy with girls. I defy anybody of my height to meet a girl of about 5ft 10in in the foyer of the Regal Cinema, in Edinburgh, and not to see something funny about it. A little man with a taller lady is basically comic, and you have to have a lot of *savoir faire* and *élan* not to let it be so.

That is why I remember those school dances – and especially the ones I didn't dance at. Which was most of them. We used to sit round the walls of the gymnasium while the band played. I developed a way of working out a girl's probable height before the moment she stood up.

If she was sitting down and her shoulder was up to the dado or up to the lower parallel bar I knew that when she stood up there was every chance that her shoulder would be up to the next parallel bar. So I had a pretty good idea, before I went up to a girl, how tall she was going to turn out to be. The whole thing could be expressed as a sort of algebraic formula:

$$s = (pb +3) = rt$$

Here, *s* stands for shoulder; *pb* + *3* indicates that it is three inches higher than the parallel bar, and *rt* stands for rather tall.

Or I might get a case where the equation was:

$$s = pb + 6 = de\ ci.$$

Here, the shoulder is six inches higher than the parallel bar and *de ci* stands for "don't even consider it."

I became quite an expert, but sometimes it did not work, because the girls would introduce awkward variables into the equation; for example, their backs might be unusually short in proportion to their legs and all my calculations would be thrown out. On some occasions I might get the sums wrong because I had not made enough allowance for the slump factor when the girl was not sitting up straight.

I made these calculations to help me decide whether I should get up and go across and ask the girl to dance, and, more often than not, I decided not to. And, when I did, the answer very often was "No, thank you." And that was very hurtful. I still remember that walk across the floor towards the target, my courage draining away, as I imagined the mutterings of the group of girls on the other side, saying "He's coming this way."

I would be well into no-man's land now and I couldn't turn back. The girl in the lavender frock (a promising *pb +2*) would be whispering to her friend: "Oh God, I hope he's coming to ask you." And then when I finally stood in front of her I would feel that I could actually hear her murmuring: "Oh, I don't *believe* it."

Still, I kept going to those dances and I kept measuring the girls against the wall and I kept taking that long walk across the floor.

I left school at 17 with seven Higher Leaving Certificates. I also took the Civil Service clerical officers exam and the executive officers exam and passed them both. I applied and went to interviews for all the sorts of jobs you would expect a boy in Edinburgh at the time to go for – the Norwich Union, the Britannic Assurance, the Union Bank of Scotland. I was filling up the forms, putting on my best brown suit and going to see the managers of banks, publishing houses, animal feedstuff suppliers – interviews for all sorts of jobs – none of which I wanted.

These places didn't interest me at all, because, by that time, something had happened which had made me absolutely determined to be an actor.

CHAPTER THREE

I become determined to go on the stage and am frequently seen at the stage doors of Edinburgh theatres, hoping to escort visiting actors back to their hotels. I lose my Scottish accent – or most of it – and I learn to play the organ. Sean Connery is mentioned again and we learn the significance of the Scotts lightweight felt hat.

I played the part of the wicked aunt in the St Catherine-in-the Grange church youth club production of *Babes in the Wood* and that was what changed everything for me.

I was 16 at the time. Although I went every Sunday to the College Street church with my family, my friends living in the Marchmont area were all members of the youth club and scout troop at St Catherine-in-the-Grange so I used to join them there. That was where I was made a troop leader in the scouts.

The pantomime was written by Elizabeth Urquhart, who was a member of the youth club, and it was produced by Mrs Ritchie, a very large and bouncy blue-rinsed lady with rosy cheeks, a pale violet suit and fur stoles. We always addressed her as Mrs Ritchie, but I think her first name was Muriel; she certainly seemed to be a Muriel sort of person when I think of her.

Immediately, I discovered that everything I had to do in *Babes in the Wood* seemed to suit me down to the ground; I felt at home; I took to it like a dame to panto. Suddenly I was no longer the small boy in the background at school, going to the debating society, but never speaking; keeping score for the cricket XI, but never going in to bat; going to the dances in the gym, but hanging back and making calculations. Suddenly I was centre-stage and no longer in the wings, and I was astonished to discover that I loved it.

This was my first real performance. I had done a little bit in a revue at school before and had a small success playing the part of a slightly comic troubadour, but I knew this was really special.

It must have been noticeable at the rehearsals, because the minister, a very kindly man called Tom Maxwell, came round to visit my mum and said: "I think you ought to know that something quite remarkable is going on at the rehearsals. Little Ron is being wonderful as the wicked aunt."

When the show went on, my mum and dad came to see it and I rose to the occasion. I really put everything into that wicked aunt; never had a female been so villainous and so droll. I was elated. I was aware of being strongly in touch with the audience and I felt them responding to my performance, taking on board everything I offered. I knew it was working. All I can remember now about the part is that I sang a parody of the Eddie Cantor song "Margie".

When I came off after the final curtain call, the minister, Tom Maxwell should by rights have been standing there in the wings, holding out a telephone to me and saying: "There's a call for you, Mr Corbett. It's a Mr Orson Welles in New York." That didn't happen, actually. The youth club at St Catherine-in-the-Grange was not on the phone. I imagine the operator saying: "About your person-to-person call to Mr Ronald Corbett, Mr

Welles, I'm afraid we don't have a listing for that Edinburgh youth club." And Orson Welles would have heaved an enormous sigh and said: "Well, if I can't get Corbett, I'll just have to play the part myself."

In truth, everyone just went home for their tea. I don't think I was particularly heaped with praise for my performance in that pantomime, but the experience had been enough to convince me I had been given a very clear message about what I should do with the rest of my life. I realised that I had felt comfortable in what I was doing that evening in that church hall and I knew I had discovered some skill inside me. It may sound presumptuous for an undersized 16 year-old, but from then on, I never doubted for one moment that I would be an actor, a comic actor, and I never faltered in my ambition.

It was stronger than simply being stage-struck, as boys and girls of that age often are. I can honestly say it was a vocation. I was aware of the contrast between being on the stage and leading the grey everyday life at school and I knew I had to grab this opportunity with both hands. I never turned back. I had lots of setbacks and discouragements, but I never lost that resolve I first found as the wicked aunt, although it took many years before I was chosen to play the dame again.

From then on, I went to the theatre every week, to the Lyceum or the King's Theatre, to see whatever was playing. Usually, I would go on my own. By this time, I was also quite musical. I took piano lessons from the age of 11 to about 18, with Freddie Holmes, at Greenbank, going there by bus once a week. I actually got quite good and started to play the organ in church.

I shared the organist's duties at a church in Stockbridge, in the north of Edinburgh, with a chap called James Lockhart who later went on to be the organist at All Souls, Langham Place, next door to Broadcasting House in London, and then became a very successful conductor with opera companies all over Europe.

Jim and I would do the occasional oratorio with the choir, with Jim conducting and me playing the organ. Between the ages of 16 and 18 I became quite versatile – I mean in a denominational way. Stockbridge was Church of Scotland, but I also played in a very, very high Episcopalian church in a deprived area of Edinburgh called Niddrie Mains.

At the same time, I was obliging at the keyboard in a Methodist chapel where they had a very basic instrument, more like a harmonium, which you had to pump with your feet. So it would be "When the roll is called up yonder" with me pedalling away like anything, and then pedalling some more for "O far whiter than the snow, washed in Jesus's blood I know. . . ." Very bracing.

There was an awful lot of church music in my life and I went through quite a religious phase at the time, but, to be honest, I think it was the theatricality of it all that attracted me. My father used to take me to a performance of Handel's *Messiah* every New Year's Eve. The Glasgow Orpheus Choir was a very big thing at that time and we never missed the concerts they gave in Edinburgh.

Sean Connery was an exact contemporary of mine in Edinburgh. There we were, both with our dreams of becoming actors, but never meeting, although Sean was actually stepping out at one time with my cousins, Ella and Maisie Corbett, who lived quite near him in Fountainbridge. Before he worked as a lifeguard at the Portobello Baths, Sean was a milk delivery boy for the Co-op and a French polisher. He was a bit of a bodybuilder and it was while he was a lifeguard that he got the part of one of the strapping seamen in the touring production of *South Pacific*.

I knew him early in his career when he came to London in

that musical and, in fact, we had bedsits in the same area. Later on, he often used to invite me over for a bit of pasta when he lived in a mews flat near St John's Wood. This was about the time he had been spotted by Bob Goldstein, the London boss of Twentieth Century Fox, when he appeared in the Sunday night TV play *Requiem for a Heavyweight* after Jack Palance had to drop out through ill-health. So he was then on the brink of his career in films. I have always had a feeling of closeness with Sean and every so often we meet for a bit to eat and blether about Edinburgh and those days.

Sean fascinates me; he is so sweet and he is such a nomad. He hires the most reasonable car, like a little Vauxhall Nova, and he travels very light. If he needs a shirt for the evening he just goes somewhere and buys one. I often have a call from him early in the morning or a message on my answering machine if he is passing through Heathrow airport or if he is going to Scotland for the day. On my machine, I'll find a message from him in his slow, laconic growl. "Ronnie Corbett . . . Sean Connery here . . . I'm in Scotland, briefly . . . for the day, and I'm wondering how you are . . . . .and wishing you all the best for the year 2000 . . . . I'll speak soon . . . All right."

I get a lot of these little messages and they're very warming, really. Just as he passes through the area I think memories of the past strike him. It's all to do with what Robert Louis Stevenson called the hills of home.

And so, back to Edinburgh in those days. After I decided that I was going to become an actor, my mum and dad encouraged me to enrol in the Glover Turner Robertson School, in George Street, up some stairs above a smart grocers called Dymock and Howden. The school was run by two rather stately ladies with silver buns at the back of their heads and they gave private classes in drama and verse speaking.

And that was the start of my Scottish accent going, because these ladies used to teach you how to speak Shakespeare and the classics. They got me to round the vowels, push the voice out, take the burr out of the Rs, just slowly turning it into something closer to a BBC newsreader's voice. So it was how now to brown cow and goodbye to the broon coo. Sometimes my former voice comes back to me; when I get worked up I can hear the clues to my Scottishness flying off my tongue.

In those days you would have to hammer out the accent unless you wanted to be a broad Scottish comic like Harry Lauder, or Will Fyffe, the man who used to sing "I Belong ta Glasgae". I didn't see myself like that; I wanted to be in the straight theatre. I saw myself as a light comedian, a sort of cross between Bobby Howes and Jack Buchanan and I would do whatever it took. No, I didn't see myself as the wee one in the kilt; I wanted to be suave.

Often when I went to the theatre I would go round to the stage door after the show and loiter with my autograph book. Sometimes I would even manage to walk quite well known actors back to their hotel. I remember tagging along with Kenneth Connor (later to be one of the stars of the *Carry On* films) although, in the euphoria of my ambition and my high hopes, I preferred to think of it as *escorting* him. In the same mood, I also walked Harold Warrender from the King's Theatre, in Edinburgh, back to the Caledonian Hotel which was right down the Lothian Road. All the way, I was blethering on about how I was going to be an actor. I wonder now how I had the nerve to do these things, but it did not seem at all odd to me at the time.

I do remember that the walk with Harold Warrender was the longest one and he was one of the friendliest actors I met at the time. I wonder that he put up with his uninvited hanger-on. It's just possible, I suppose, that he saw something a little special in me that he felt deserved helping. A few years later, when I first arrived in London, the actress Helena Pickard and the musical comedy star Evelyn Laye were both far more helpful to me in my career than I could dare to expect, so it is possible that all three of them saw something in me that was worth encouraging.

On that long walk down the Lothian Road with Harold Warrender, I remember he was carrying a set of golf clubs on his shoulder, because he had been playing that day and had taken them back to his dressing room. When we finally got to the hotel, he turned to me and said: "I don't know why you don't want to be a little comic – you've got the build and the shape for it." That wasn't the advice I was looking for. I saw myself playing in *Private Lives* or *Present Laughter*, and I wasn't going to allow the word of one of the theatre's most successful romantic leads, to put me off.

My father, who was always a bit of a natty dresser, used to talk of the Scotts lightweight felt hat as the height of sophistication. It was made by Scotts, the famous hatters in Bond Street, in London, who also had a branch in Edinburgh.

This hat became an important symbol to me. One evening I went to see Peter Graves and Margaret Lockwood in *Present Laughter* and there was Peter Graves, wearing one. Although it seems the most unlikely thing for me, that is how I always saw myself at the time, wearing a Scotts lightweight felt hat.

The biggest stars used to come to Edinburgh in those days. I used to see them getting in and out of taxis. I remember the time when the great cinema swashbuckler smoothie Stewart Granger and Jean Simmons appeared in *The Power of Darkness* in 1949 with Freddie Valk. I saw them getting out of a taxi in George Street and going into the Roxburghe hotel. Stewart Granger was wearing one of those swish camel coats with a belt that you knot at the waist and Jean Simmons was in an expensive fur coat.

★

I didn't get the chance to take Stewart Granger for a walk – somehow he managed to elude my escort service – probably by jumping into a taxi and lying on the floor – but I did have a strange encounter with him in Spain many years later.

It was in about 1972 and my wife Anne and I were on holiday in Spain with our daughters Emma and Sophie who were then around seven and six years old. We were in a Spanish supermarket and suddenly the girls came tearing round the corner to us whispering excitedly that the man from *The Virginians* was over there by the tinned vegetables. A moment later we came face to face – just next to the special offer on instant coffee, I think it was – and it was Stewart Granger.

"My God, it's you!" I said.

"My God it's you!" he replied, in that wonderfully smooth voice of his, which seemed to conjure up the rich aroma of freshly granulated Arabica coffee beans. He had seen me in something on television, so that's how he knew it was me. Once we had established that we both were who the other one thought we were, he said: "I'm building this hacienda up in the hills near here, so why don't you come tomorrow or the next day and have a bit of dinner?" I think when you live in these places abroad and you bump into someone who has a little bit in common with you, you really can't wait to ask them home, to have a bit of a gossip.

So we went to his hacienda where he was looked after by two very sweet oriental girls who cooked for him and ran the house for him. Granger, who was then I suppose about 60, looked marvellous. He looked absolutely the part . . . of Stewart Granger.

He was dressed almost exactly as he had been when he was the colonel of the Raj in the 1956 film *Bhowani Junction*. He had the khaki shirt, the safari jacket with the patched pockets; he wore the elephant's hair bracelets round his wrists and a sort of silk choker round his neck. And, of course, he had the sleek silver hair. Only the jodhpurs were missing. I was expecting Ava Gardner to arrive at any moment, slinking across the moonlit verandah. But she didn't. Probably still at the supermarket.

Anyway, he was being wonderfully urbane and he was shaking the most stylish cocktails and I was thinking about the time, more than 20 years earlier, when I was a youth with dreams of being someone like Jack Buchanan and I had stood in George Street, in Edinburgh, and watched this same man in his camel coat getting out of a taxi.

One other thing I remember about that dinner in Spain with Stewart Granger is that the girls brought *two* legs of lamb to the table for us to eat. Two legs for three people, was overdoing it a bit, I thought. I guessed it was so that we could all have the best cuts. And I suppose he must have had it cold for the rest of the week.

CHAPTER FOUR

*My brief career in the Ministry of Agriculture. National Service
in the Royal Air Force, where I get a commission. The beginning
of my lifelong friendship with Edward Hardwicke. A love affair
and the poignant story of the train that divided at Carlisle.*

The West End theatre had to wait, as farrowing sows were to
occupy much of my attention for the next year and a half.
Somehow the West End theatre got over this disappointment.

I joined the civil service as a clerical officer in the Ministry of
Agriculture, working in a little office in Palmerston Place, in
Edinburgh. I took the job because I knew it would stop my
mother worrying, seeing me in regular, sensible employment. I
also knew that it could not last for too long because I was due
to be called up to do my National Service in 18 months' time.
That would be my wonderful release and my escape from
Edinburgh. I was looking forward to the adventure of doing my
National Service in the Royal Air Force, finding new interests
and friends, having new experiences. My theatrical career was
making no progress, but I was prepared to be patient.

I suppose my parents secretly hoped that once I got into the
Civil Service that would be it. After National Service I would

sensibly put my theatrical career out of my mind, return to Edinburgh and go on and on and up and up in the Ministry of Agriculture. In those days it was considered very important to have a career where there was a nice pension waiting at the end of it.

There was no special reason for choosing the Ministry of Agriculture, although I think my parents hoped, if I wasn't mad enough to go into the theatre, I would do something with a bit of a rustic flavour to it. Maybe in the veterinary service, or perhaps in the animal feedstuffs or fertiliser trade. Being brought up in the Lothians, it was fairly natural to go in for something connected with farming.

In those days there was still rationing of animal feedstuffs and I was in the ministry department which dealt with that. We issued the coupons for protein and cereal for the farrowing sows and for the milk herds in the Lothians. I received monthly returns from the pig breeders and records of the milk yield from the dairy farmers and in return I issued these coupons.

Our office also organised the wages for the Polish ex-servicemen who lived in camps in the Borders and helped the farmers there with the harvest. The department which dealt with marginal land subsidies, was downstairs.

It was better than it sounds. In fact, I rather enjoyed it. The office had the feeling of not quite being an office. It was one of the grand houses in Palmerston Place which had been converted but it still retained some of the original atmosphere with its fine staircases and floor to ceiling windows. The desks and chairs were arranged in these rather grand salon rooms and the gilt mirrors were still there on the walls. It made the job more palatable; I felt I was working in fairly civilised surroundings. It was nice to have the sort of staircase I could "ascend" rather than just "go up".

The romantic side of me also liked the feeling of being in touch with the land in some way. Farmers would come into the office sometimes to see the labour officers upstairs and they would often bring us a few eggs or some fruit and vegetables from their farms. I can remember the excitement of my pay packet on the first Friday, taking the little brown envelope home and giving it to my mother. This was the weekly ritual; she would take the pay packet and then give me back a little money. Mothers and sons were doing this all over the country. Friday was a good day. That was when we went home with the presents from the farmers; sometimes vegetables and eggs or a bunch of flowers, but if you were lucky you might get a bit of chicken or a pigeon or a pheasant which had been shot in the Borders.

Every day I would walk home for my lunch. At this time I was still going to the youth club and to the Glover Turner Robertson school once a week, and still going to the theatre and loitering by the stage door. I joined the civil service amateur dramatic society and was assistant stage manager for a production of *Hay Fever* which was staged at the Cygnet Theatre in Edinburgh. That theatre is now called the Pleasance and it is, as it happens, the place where a lot of the comics perform on the Edinburgh Festival Fringe these days.

My one worry was that I would not pass my medical for National Service. I have always had a deviated septum in my nose. If you don't wish to know that this is something to do with the bit that separates the two nostrils, look away now. Actually, it's not something you would notice, but the Ear Nose and Throat doctor was worried that it might affect my breathing. It looked as if they might turn me down, so I went to the RAF doctor and I said that the last thing I wanted was for me not to do National Service. I knew people would say: "He's just far too weedy. He says it's his nose, but the real reason they're not letting him in is his height. Deviated septum, my foot." I actually pleaded with the man and, to my huge relief, I got in.

I first went for a fortnight to RAF Padgate, near Blackpool, to enrol and to be issued with the uniform and the boots. It is an odd thing when you leave home for the first time. There is a moment when you empty your suitcase on your bed in front of a lot of strangers in the barracks and your life tumbles out. You are all furtively casting your eyes over other people's luggage. Something about your background, maybe your mother's or your father's influence, is laid out on the bed for everyone else to see.

There's a pair of pyjamas, maybe two pairs of pyjamas, and you think you might hide one of them because some of the people around you have no pyjamas at all, and sleep in their vest and pants. Simple objects, like a hairbrush or a pair of slippers, which you took for granted at home, now look alarmingly intimate in the impersonal setting of that barrack room. We tried to be casual as we unpacked, but we knew we were being observed, weighed up.

Some of us had sponge bags. I remember mine; it was black and white check and had a draw string. And I remember I had a leather writing case with a zip all the way round and a little compartment for the stamps and a pad of Basildon Bond.

After Padgate, they sent us to Weeton, in Lancashire, for square bashing. I don't remember being persecuted because of my size and I wasn't given a nickname. I don't even recall any cruelty from the drill sergeant jumping on me; I think he had a lot of other recruits to jump on before he got round to me. There were a good many parade merchants who were more inept than I was.

I also did a bit of baby-sitting for the flight sergeant at Weeton. This may seem an unusual kind of National Service training, but I can see that it might have it uses. If the Russians ever invaded we could rush the Royal Corps of Babysitters to the front to shush them. The Russian corporal in the leading tank would shout "Look out! It's the new secret British weapon – the lullaby!"

Well, anyway, I can still picture the little married quarters at the camp and the kitchen where the wife would leave out a plate for me, with two uncooked sausages, a tomato, an egg in its shell, three slices of bread and butter and a packet of tea. I was quite content, catering for myself and it was a refuge from the barrack room. I could get out my Basildon Bond and write to my parents.

I applied to be trained for a commission, but I didn't say anything to my mum and dad about it. I said nothing to them until I had gone through all the stages and finally been accepted for officer selection. I suppose I was nervous of raising their expectations and then not living up to them. Eventually I passed out as a pilot officer at Spittalgate, near Cranwell. I was then posted to Bircham Newton, in Norfolk, for secretarial training. I never actually took to the air in the RAF except on a couple of occasions when a fellow officer took me for a ride in a Tiger Moth.

We did rather well at Bircham Newton, because it was near the Royal estate at Sandringham and we often dined in the mess on pheasants from the Sandringham shoots. They would send us their spare birds.

Then the RAF changed its mind about me and decided to train me in personnel selection. After a course at the War Office, in London, I was sent back to Weeton, this time as an officer. It was a good feeling to find myself in the officer's mess which I'd gazed at from a distance in my square-bashing days. I liked the idea of coming back in a different guise and meeting some of the men I had known in the early days of my National Service.

Shortly after my return I was called in to see the RAF station commander. There was one small problem, he explained – and he put it as tactfully as he could. At that time, quite a number of former RAF men were returning to Weeton from civilian life as "re-entries" and the station commander thought that some of these experienced old hands might get the wrong idea about me. Seeing me striding about in my battledress, reaching up to my full five feet one and a half inches, they might mistake me for a cadet. He suggested that at all times I ought to wear the full number one dress, as it was called – that's the peaked cap, the brass buttons, the works – as much as I had going for me, in fact. So I spent the rest of my time at Weeton in a state of splendour.

While I was there, I had this wonderful and very diligent flight sergeant who used to run the department. His name was McCabe. I used to arrive a bit early at the office, at about 8.40, and then I would go to my desk, open the drawer and there, waiting for me inside, would be toast, bacon, egg and sausages. Flight sergeant McCabe had got it all organised. Getting things organised was his talent and his mission in life. Between the full English breakfasts I managed to fit in other duties. I was also in charge of the entertainments and I was responsible for setting up a production of *The Shop at Sly Corner,* the murder play by Edward Percy. I gave myself just a small part.

McCabe was a bit of a rascal, but very enterprising. He always had his feet under the table with a lady who ran a 17-bedroom private hotel in Blackpool. He had organised things rather well for himself so that there was somewhere for him to go in the evening.

More than 20 years later, in 1972, I was in pantomime in Bristol and on Sundays I used to go out for a little lunch with my wife Anne and our daughters and on this occasion, we were going to a very good restaurant called Thornbury Castle. We were driving up the road and we stopped to ask the way. Anne wound down the window and asked a passer-by, and although I could only just see the middle section of him, I immediately recognised the voice.

"Flight sergeant McCabe!" I said. There he was, in another part of the country, living in another private hotel with another lady. Flight Sergeant McCabe had still got it all organised.

I always think it's rather awful, actually, that once you've known someone in the Services, their rank stays with them for ever. It's always flight sergeant This or wing commander That, or "Good God! It's Colonel Smethurst." You can't rub it out. In fact, you can't help sounding like a character in one of those two-hander sketches in *The Two Ronnies*.

Back to RAF Weeton. But not for long. I had been troubled in my teens by asthmatic bronchitis and this came back to me in the RAF. It could be quite serious and I found myself in the sick bay a number of times, with an oxygen mask over my face. There was talk of posting me abroad, to a better climate, but, in the end, they sent me to Hornchurch, in balmy sun-drenched Essex. Oh well.

First, perhaps, I ought to mention that when I was in the sick bay at Weeton I had a little bit of a romance with a nursing sister. I'm embarrassed to confess that I don't actually remember her name. Was it Sheila? Or Jennifer perhaps? I don't know. I suppose if I bumped into her today, I'd blurt out something like "Good God! It's nursing sister Smethurst!" What I do remember is that she had auburn hair and she looked very fetching in her uniform. I always thought that the white starched head-dress with the Air Force blue cape and the white stockings and white pumps looked glamorous.

We had quite an innocent romance, but it was an emotional time for me. I don't think anything had happened to me in that way before, although I had been attracted to a lovely girl in the youth club in Edinburgh who lived in a rather grand house down the road from St Catherine-in-the-Grange. I still remember that girl saying to me "If you weren't so small you'd be quite handsome." I also remember one night standing on her doorstep talking and perhaps trying to pluck up the courage to have a cuddle, and the light going on in the hall – which was probably her mother or father coming to the door – and me just sprinting, at once, away from the scene, helter-skelter down the road.

Of course we were all much less confident about things like that than kids are today. I can remember walking a girl down a lane one evening, after the cinema or something, and thinking "In three lampposts' time I will take her hand," then ducking it on the third and saying "No, I'll make that four lampposts." Then: "All right, *definitely* after the ninth lamppost – and maybe just past that second big tree."

Anyway, to get back to my RAF romance There was one occasion I went home on leave and the auburn-haired nursing sister went home on leave at the same time. We travelled on the same train to Carlisle, where it divided up and my portion went to Edinburgh and her portion went to Blackpool. This was more poignant than Trevor Howard saying goodbye to Celia Johnson in *Brief Encounter*; this was Ronnie Corbett saying goodbye to the nursing sister in *Uncoupling at Carlisle*.

I can remember the emotion and the terrible sense of loss as the train split in the middle and we parted. I went home and told my mother all about the agonies I was suffering and I wasn't able to settle down for four or five days.

Some time later when I was posted to London for a brief period I arranged to meet her after she came down representing Queen Alexandra's nurses in a large parade which was taking place in front of King George VI in Hyde Park. I had booked tickets for the London Palladium and managed to get a little box. It was 1949 and Danny Kaye was top of the bill.

As happens with a holiday romance when you meet up again, it is never quite the same. Our reunion was a disappointment. I enjoyed the show and it was lovely to see her again, but it was the end of the romance. She didn't live up to my memory of her and I don't suppose I lived up to hers either.

Since then, when I have performed at the Palladium I have often thought of that occasion and of being in the box watching Danny Kaye. I remember seeing him go off for the first break in his act and having his dresser waiting for him in the wings with a glass of water and a shammy leather with cologne on it, to cool him down. I have sometimes thought "I am standing on the spot where Danny Kaye stood that night in 1949 and I am looking up at the box where I sat with the auburn-haired nursing sister. Whose name I can't remember."

When I saw Danny Kaye at the Palladium that time in 1949, I was very struck by one of the songs he sang, which began:

> I don't mean to be rude
> But I'm not in the mood
> For food.

And the chorus went:

> Madame, I love your Crêpe Suzette
> I think your Crêpe Suzette is wonderful
> But, for the moment, let's forget
> All about your Crêpe Suzette.

I wanted to find out more about this number – I expect I imagined myself, on stage and singing it – and, even though I was barely 20 years old, my determination to get into showbusiness gave me the boldness to telephone the Dorchester hotel where I knew Danny Kaye was staying. I wasn't as pushy as to try to speak to Mr Kaye himself, but I asked to be put through to his manager. I found myself speaking on the phone to some charming American man. I mentioned this song and told him I couldn't find it in any of the music publishers in London. He told me the history of the song and how it had been written by Burton Lane and Roger Edens for the film version of the Broadway musical *Du Barry Was a Lady*. We had a very friendly conversation about it and just the fact that this member of the Danny Kaye entourage was prepared to take the time to talk to me like that, fortified my ambition.

Away from the dreams of Broadway, and back to the reality of Hornchurch. This was the place where I made my first really close friendships which have lasted for the rest of my life. Up to then I had been a bit of a loner, feeling I had my own private timetable for educating myself, listening, being aware, preparing myself for my career on the stage. Being commissioned was part of my social education; dining in the mess, passing the port, having a mess bill, having tailor-made clothes. A representative of Gieves, the military outfitters, used to visit the camp once a month, selling the sort of clothes a young officer might like to wear. I was learning all the time, soaking up a lot of private information for myself.

At this time I was beginning to adjust or refine my ambition. I decided now that I really wanted eventually to be a comedian, doing sketches and revues. I admired the work of monologists like Jack Benny, Bob Hope and Max Wall and I realised that you won a sort of independence by being able to stand up and just talk to people, maybe for 15 minutes, or maybe a whole hour. All you had to do was take a dress suit and a pianist with you. It meant that you weren't at the mercy of the fads and fashions in the theatre.

When Edward Hardwicke and Alan Fenton arrived in Hornchurch there was a bond straight away. Edward was the son of Sir Cedric Hardwicke, the great theatrical knight who went on to be a star in films and on the stage in America.

I had heard about Edward before I met him. There was a sort of National Service grapevine and when I was at Padgate I had heard about this chap called Hardwicke who was going to be an actor. He was planning to go on to RADA after National Service and then to a career on the stage. Alan had been at Oxford and wanted to be a writer.

All three of us achieved our ambitions, although it took us some time. Edward became a successful actor, playing, among many other parts, Dr Watson to Jeremy Brett's Sherlock Holmes, and Alan started out doing some television work, like writing the *Dickie Henderson Show*, before going into the City and making a great deal of money, then giving it all up to write novels.

Edward had an Austin Ruby Seven called Charlie and we all used to drive out to the cinema or the theatre or to have a meal. One day he asked me if I would like to come up to London to meet his mum. They lived in a quite beautiful double fronted house in Avenue Road, Swiss Cottage, where there are mostly embassies these days. I had never before been to a house where a chap answered the door in a white coat, morning suit trousers and black tie.

Edward's mother was the actress Helena Pickard, known to everyone as Pixie. She and Cedric Hardwicke had been together at the Birmingham Repertory Theatre with Laurence Olivier and Ralph Richardson in the great days when it was run by Sir Barry Jackson. Now they were separated and they were divorced in 1950.

All this was an amazing new world to me. The butler opening the door, the grand house, the elegant hostess; these were things

I had only seen imitated on the stage on my nights at the theatre in Edinburgh. On this first visit to Avenue Road I had no idea that this house would soon be my home and that Pixie was to become such a tremendous support to me in my early days in London, helping me find jobs and sending me to see people she knew who might help me in my career.

I went back to Hornchurch for the final months of my National Service and when I came out of the Air Force in 1951, I could look back and see that I had made some progress. I had progressed from Edinburgh to Padgate, to Weeton, to Spittalgate, to Bircham Newton, and finally to Hornchurch, so I had been gradually getting closer to the West End all the time. Well, geographically, at least. And I never went back to the Ministry of Agriculture office in Palmerston Place.

CHAPTER FIVE

In which I arrive in London and try to embark on a theatrical career and find myself pursuing several non-theatrical careers. Lessons in singing and dancing and how to sell advertising space in the ABC Coach Guide. After a serious setback in Margate I set sail on a perilous journey to France. I return and place large bets on some greyhounds at a Glasgow racetrack.

One of the first people I bumped into when I arrived in London was Noel Coward. Well, when I say I bumped into him I mean I caught sight of him. No collision occurred. He was coming out of Floris the perfumery in Jermyn Street. He then stepped into quite an ordinary Hillman Minx – which was a bit of a disappointment to me – but I suppose he was just popping about doing his shopping. Not long after this I did actually meet him in the Café de Paris, thanks to Edward Hardwicke's mother, Pixie.

I came to London with £97 in my post office savings account and with no thought of going home to Edinburgh. I loved London right from the beginning, no matter what sort of place I was living in. Actually, I have always found that, whatever my circumstances, I have always managed to find something about every day that is worth looking forward to.

My circumstances, to begin with, were very comfortable. For the first six months I lived in the basement of Pixie's lovely house in St John's Wood. She really was my saviour at that time in my life. She tried to launch me on as many people as she could. She knew impresarios like Prince and Emile Littler and Bert Montagu and she would send me off to their casting people, to see if somebody was directing a play or if there was a little job for me in a pantomime.

She used her influence to get me my very first proper acting job which was a part in the film *You're Only Young Twice*. I played the part of the president of the Glasgow University students' union. The film was an adaptation of the James Bridie play, *What Say They?* and the script was written by a very funny actor called Reginald Beckwith who was a friend of Pixie. Duncan Macrae, Charles Hawtrey, Patrick Barr, Diane Hart and Robert Urquhart were in it. It was mostly notable for being the first non-documentary film produced by John Grierson, whose Group 3 production company was responsible for *Night Mail* and *Drifters* and other famous documentaries. It was not notable for immediately launching me on a successful acting career.

It looked, in fact, as if I was doomed to a long career in short trousers. My next film part was a small one as a schoolboy in the film *Top of the Form* which came out in 1953, was directed by John Paddy Carstairs and starred Ronald Shiner, with Anthony Newley, Harry Fowler and Gerald Campion, who made his name as Billy Bunter on television. Ronald Shiner was a well-known cockney actor on the West End stage, in plays like *Seagulls Over Sorrento*, and he was also a huge box office success in British films – although a rather unlikely one.

After that, I continued my cinema education at an even worse school. I got a part in an amazing film – not amazingly good, just amazing – called *Fun at St Fanny's* – a sort of Carry On in Short

Trousers. This first burst on to cinema screens in 1955 and was directed by Maurice Elvey. It had a most extraordinary cast which included Freddie Mills, the boxer, Cardew ("The Cad") Robinson, Fred Emney, Johnny Brandon (who was known for some reason as "The King of Zing"). Gerald Campion was in it too, and also "The Francis Langford Singing Schoolboys". I have no idea if the film still exists, but, if it does, it must be a collector's item. That is for people who collect weird films about schooldays.

The Francis Langford Singing Schoolboys did quite a lot of touring and performing in music halls. They used to have to stay in theatrical digs, four or five of them to a room. While we were filming, one of the schoolboys told me that on their previous tour they returned one night to their digs, after doing two shows, to find that their landlady had prepared them a supper of potato crisp sandwiches. Somebody must have told her about school dinners at Dotheboys Hall.

Edward's mother was petite with fair hair and blue eyes – pixie-ish, but also extremely chic. I can picture her now, breakfasting in style off a smart tray; going round the house arranging the flowers, dressed in a handsome trouser suit with a cravat round her neck, knotted at the side; setting off for lunch with actress friends, wearing a beautifully tailored suit and with a hat set rather jauntily on the side of her head.

She also introduced me to the society life of the theatre; there was much more of that sort of elegant theatrical life than there is now. She used to entertain important writers and actors to dinner. I remember Ralph Richardson coming to the house, and J.B. Priestley and Clive Morton and his wife Frances Rowe – and the American cabaret star Hildegarde when she was performing at the Café de Paris. Ralph Richardson had worked in Birmingham with Cedric Hardwicke, and that was where they put on some of the Priestley plays. I have only a vague memory of J.B. Priestley at the dinner table, just of his 'presence'. I think Edward and I were rather frightened and just sat and listened. That's really all you had to do with him – listen.

Pixie would have these people round to dinner and save a couple of places at the table for Edward and me. I always used to love going to say hello to them, but Edward, having been brought up with this sort of thing, was a bit more shy and had to be pulled from some cupboard and rather cajoled to come downstairs to meet his mum's friends. I couldn't wait, because it was all so new and refreshingly exciting to me.

Another member of the household was Pixie's brother, Walter Pickard, who had a flat at the top. He had been in the RAF in the war, was rather bluff and usually had a pretty lady on his arm. I was very impressed by him because he had a part-time valet and that seemed the height of sophistication to me. This chap came round once a week for about two hours. He had his own key and would let himself into the flat, polish Walter's shoes, check all his shirts, sew on any buttons that were needed, and press his suits.

Walter had a strange verbal mannerism. Whatever he was talking about was always "what I call". So when he was talking to his sister he would say things like "You don't understand, Pixie, what I call an army officer is . . . ." Or: "This man is what I call a managing director." It even got to the point of "what I call *The Queen Mary*". I don't know what everyone else called the ship, but it was always "what I call" with Walter. Years later he used to show up regularly at Winston's night-club when I was performing there and he always had what I call a pretty lady on his arm.

One night Pixie took Edward and me to the opening of Noël Coward's show at the Café de Paris. I think this was the first time he did a complete cabaret act as a late supper entertainer. Norman Hackforth played the piano for him and he also had the Sidney Simone orchestra. It was Noël Coward's first stab at doing a big major solo act. It was pretty shrewd of him to do it, because he was immediately snapped up to do more, and was soon performing in Las Vegas. So when we went to see him that night at the Café de Paris his career was just about to take a new turn.

There was a lot of good intimate revue in London at the time; the Lyric Revue, the Globe Revue, *Penny Plain*, shows by Alan Melville and Herbert Farjeon. Pixie used to pass on tickets she didn't want to Edward and me.

In those days the Café de Paris was run by Mecca and they operated a scheme called the Guinea Pig Club which meant that young people of 18 or 19 or so, who paid a few pounds, could go and sit in the balcony on quiet nights, have some smoked salmon and a glass of white wine and watch the cabaret. The Guinea Pig Club was the special responsibility of Eric Morley, an up and coming young executive in the Mecca organisation who, years later, made his name running the Miss World contest. In those early up and coming days he was also having elocution lessons – which don't seem to have worked.

Thanks to the Guinea Pig Club, I was able to see some terrific performers in this way; not just Noël Coward, but Marlene Dietrich, Jack Buchanan, Elsa Lanchester, Hildegarde, and also Dwight Fiske, a rather risque American piano entertainer who sang songs full of *doubles entendres*. These people were all part of my education.

The butler, opening the door in his white coat when I first visited Pixie's house in Avenue Road with Edward, was called Bill Turner and he had a very mongrel dog named Trottie, named after the main character in a film of the time called *Trottie*

True, starring Jean Kent. Bill Turner had a lovely wife called Vera and the two of them ran the house as a couple. Eventually, they (and Trottie) left and were replaced by a remarkable chap – and obviously a pedigree – named Burr.

He was called Burr and was a little bit of a toff. It seemed that his mother had a good bit of money and a large house in the country. Burr was rather grandly camp and he enjoyed his tipple. He drank very strong martinis in the kitchen and smoked incessantly. Good cigarettes, hand-rolled and probably with his name on them. He cooked quite delicious meals if you caught him early enough, but later on in the evening he tended to be a bit out of it as the martinis took their effect. He did a lot of things in aspic and this tremendously impressed my mother and Aunt Nell when they came down to London once to visit me and Pixie invited them to lunch. Burr was grander than most of the inmates of the house he worked in, but really quite sweet. I know Pixie liked him and found him very entertaining.

The great musical comedy star Evelyn Laye – known to everyone as "Boo" – was a friend of Pixie and a great help to me. Her own theatrical education had been assisted by C.B. Cochran, the famous showman, and so she believed in helping young performers.

She booked a few hours in Dinely's, the rehearsal rooms off Baker Street and near to where she lived, so that she could coach me in some numbers, showing me how to perform them, how to move properly and how to develop a stage presence.

You could hire a rehearsal room with a piano in it at Dinely's for about three guineas an hour. There was a whole block of them, so when you got near you heard a terrific cacophony of coloratura sopranos and tenors and crooners and of song and dance men practising tap.

I would sing songs like "Tiptoe Through the Tulips" or Bobby Howes numbers like "Have You Met Miss Jones?" and Boo would get me moving about, so I didn't just stand there looking like some band crooner. She would get me to place my feet properly, or do a schottische or a little turn, making sure that when I put my hands out to gesture they went right out, as far as my arms would go, and that I held them there for just a bit longer, for effect.

It was part dancing lesson, part presentation lesson and part music lesson. She was helping me to walk on, to gesture, to make everything look big.

Even with Boo's lessons and all Pixie's support and introductions to the world of the theatre I had to spend eight or nine struggling rootless years before I found any security as a performer.

After six months in Avenue Road, I moved to a house in Carlton Hill, also in St John's Wood. I paid 37 shillings a week for a room. The house belonged to Mary Merrall, who was a successful character actress. She was a handsome lady in her early 60s and her aristocratic appearance went rather oddly with her communist views. She was the stepmother of Valentine Dyall who was famous as the Man in Black in the radio series, *Appointment with Fear*, having been married for a while to his father, the actor Franklin Dyall. She now had an Irish rogue lover, called Chris. He was tall and heavily built and had a rather daft haircut; the hair was brilliantined with a false wave, like a whirl of meringue, at the front. He also had a very lazy right eye.

It was a stormy relationship, and Mary really deserved someone much better than Chris in my opinion. I once had to separate them in a fight in the middle of the night. Mary was in her night-dress and Chris in his dressing gown and there was a lot of screaming and shouting. I skipped about on the fringes of the battle, trying to grab Chris or dart in between the two of them.

Chris told me he had been a fighter pilot, but I couldn't imagine him being much of one with that very obvious lazy eye of his.

It was a mad theatrical household. Mabbie Lonsdale, daughter of Freddie Lonsdale, the playwright lived there with her play-wright husband Rodney Ackland. Rodney was very, very gay and Mabbie knew all about his boyfriends, but didn't appear to mind, even when he stayed out all night. They seemed to have a very happy marriage.

The best room in the house, apart from Mary Merrall's, was occupied by a grand piano and a very grand and camp cabaret artist called Mischa de la Motte whose speciality was singing operatic arias in a very high coloratura soprano voice with a mantilla on his head. He was a close friend of several other camp people, such as the actor Ernest Thesiger and Francis L. Sullivan the enormously fat actor who went to Hollywood and specialised in playing villains.

Mischa's great dream and ambition was to deceive a whole theatre full of people with his operatic performance as a woman. He didn't keep very busy, so his soprano voice could often be heard ringing out on the stairs of that house in Carlton Hill.

You might think that, as a young man from a good Church of Scotland family from Edinburgh, a regular attender of Bible class, a former member of the St Catherine-in-the-Grange church youth club *and* a troop leader in the scouts, I might be startled to find myself in this sort of company, but actually I seem to have settled in very easily.

While still struggling to get started with my theatrical career, I made one not very happy return to the RAF station in Hornchurch where I had spent the final months of my National Service. I went with Edward Hardwicke, his then wife, Anne and a very pretty girl called Jane Downes. We formed a quartet and sang songs from old fashioned musicals, not particularly well. So we gave a performance in the officers' mess at Hornchurch. The audience reaction was mixed – a mixture of hoots and jeers. And the odd howl. Some of this may have been due to the general rowdiness of officers' messes, but, in any case, the quartet did not stay together for long after that. I still see quite a lot of Jane Downes, who became a big success at the National Theatre and married the actor Terence Alexander who played the part of Charlie Hungerford, the Yorkshire millionaire, in *Bergerac*, the television series set in Jersey.

Edward and I would sometimes take a straw boater each and go to a party and be the cabaret. We even made a record (one of those do-it-yourself affairs at HMV) of the Noël Coward song "Don't Make Fun of the Festival, Don't Make Fun of the Fair" – about the 1951 Festival of Britain, which was mocked, in its day, as much as the Millennium Dome is now.

I was too proud to go back to Edinburgh and still determined to stay in London until I fulfilled the ambition that first came to me in the St Catherine-in-the-Grange church youth club, so I didn't have much contact with my family, except for the occasional visit at Christmas and the occasional letter home. But Aunt Nell came down to London, very bravely and all on her own, to visit me. She stayed at an hotel somewhere behind Selfridges and I remember going to visit her one evening. I was late, arriving about 40 minutes after the time she was expecting me, and I knew she would be anxious. I knocked on the door of the room, went in straight away and discovered her kneeling at the end of the bed, in her inter-locked directoire knickers and her slip, offering up a prayer to the Almighty for my safe return.

So, there I was, the answer to a maiden aunt's prayer, in a way. As I have mentioned, Aunt Nell was world class when it came to worrying.

Pixie's brother, Walter Pickard, was a director of Mecca, the big entertainments group. Their father had founded Mecca tea rooms which then took over dance halls and eventually turned into this huge enterprise. So, through Walter, I got an introduction to the man in the organisation who was responsible for hiring casual labour. It meant I did no end of odd jobs for Mecca.

I was the Stores Manager in the Victory Club, the ex-servicemen's place in the Edgware Road. Sometimes I ran the canteen where they served things like cod's roe on toast, or beans or poached egg on toast. Sometimes I worked in the bar next to the canteen. I got on very well with the chefs and they would tip me off when they were about to bring a joint of beef or pork out of the oven, so that I could pop into the kitchen and get a slice for myself. Then I would return my empty plate and get a slice of freshly baked apple pie, so I did pretty well.

One summer in these eight lean years I had the job of looking after a very grand house in Hamilton Terrace, acting as caretaker and keeping the maid company while the owners were away. So I was living in style in this house where most of the rooms were spread with dust sheets. Then I would set off every day, walking to Regents Park where I was employed to look after the tennis court reservations. I spent the summer sitting in a kiosk with my phone and my large and impressive reservations book, selling a few Mars Bars and Crunchies. We did a limited range of confectionery.

It was quite a long solitary day in the kiosk, from 9 a.m. to 8 p.m., with a break for lunch and tea when I would go to the park cafeteria. Quite a few actors used to come and play tennis. You could say they were my only theatrical bookings.

I enjoyed observing the outbreaks of polite hostilities which always occur at park tennis courts when the next people due on court arrive to find that the people already there show no sign of ending their game.

There was a lot of eloquent body language, a lot of pacing the perimeter, a lot of swinging of racquets and a lot of elbow work as wristwatches were ostentatiously looked at.

"Will you be much longer? Only we booked this court from three o'clock."

"OK. Just finishing the set."

"Only its nearly ten past."

"Sorry, partner. I was distracted, and I've forgotten the score. Is that forty-love or thirty-fifteen?"

The newcomers would then start fiercely bouncing balls on the ground, the players on court would stick at deuce for an extra long time, and I would stare hard at the reservations book, making mental notes on ways of conveying well-bred exasperation.

Another job I had was selling advertising space for the ABC Coach Guide whose office was in Victoria Street. I had a little car, a Standard Eight, a £5 a week guaranteed wage and quite a percentage of the money from the space I sold to people who wanted to attract coach parties to their businesses.

So I would go round the country in my car, visiting big cafes on the motorways, and pubs and entertainment complexes, like the Kursaal Gardens at Southend – I always remember that one because I managed to sell them a whole page which was a bit of a coup.

I had been coached by the advertising manager of the ABC Coach Guide who had been a salesman so he knew all the tricks.

The secret, when you walked into one of these establishments was to have all the leaflets and literature hidden about your person and not to carry a briefcase or anything which might suggest you were trying to make a sale. The process also helped me develop my acting skills.

I would walk in, with my hands in my pockets, holding my overcoat tightly round me so that the paperwork inside didn't rustle, and say: "Excuse me, is the manager that I saw last time, Mr . . . er . . . um."

"Smith," they would say. That is, if all was going to plan.

"That's it. Smith. Is he about?"

"I'll see if I can get him for you. Who shall I say is calling?"

"Oh, just say it's Mr Corbett."

When the manager appeared, I would say: "I understand you look after coach parties . . . ."

"Yes, we do quite a lot of that . . . ."

Then I would pounce, whipping out copies of the Coach Guide, order forms and leaflets from every pocket.

Another old trick I learned was that if I had a really good day with two or three sales, I would write down only one of them in my daily report and keep the other ones up my sleeve for another time, so that I wouldn't need to go out at all the next day. By pacing myself I could organise things so that I did only three and a half or four days a week. That left me more time for auditions. It was a time when I was getting quite a few rebuffs – from the people I was trying to sell advertising space to – and at the auditions. I was not deterred.

One Saturday I agreed to drive to Peterborough to pick up Boo Laye who was touring in a show with the comedian Sandy Powell and I was to take her back to London. It was a bad time in her life because she had expected to get the leading role in the first British production of *The King and I* but it went to Valerie Hobson instead. I think she was deeply hurt by this and she went on tour to keep herself occupied.

Sandy Powell was a wonderful comedian who made his name on the radio and was known everywhere for his catchphrase "Can you 'ear me, mother?" On stage he did a very funny act as a hopeless magician and a disastrous ventriloquist. When people, who didn't really get the point, criticised his ventriloquist act and said they could see his lips moving, Sandy would reply: "Yes, but only when the dummy's talking."

It might have been considered a bit of a comedown for Evelyn Laye, the great lady of musical comedy, to go on a tour with Sandy Powell, however brilliant he was, but I think it was an example of her courage and her determination to carry on after the setback over *The King and I*.

So I went to Peterborough, watched the matinee, had tea with her, saw a bit of the evening show and then drove her home. I remember she was wrapped up in a rather smart coat with a fur collar and wore a sort of toque turban and these knitted lisle sporty socks to keep her warm on the journey.

We were getting very low on petrol and we stopped at a garage which had just closed. Boo said: "Let me speak to him and see if I can persuade him to open up." It was no good. I don't think the man at the garage realised that he was turning away the great Evelyn Laye.

I'll never forget her saying on that journey: "Some people *think* they are star performers and some people *know* they are. Inside themselves. You must never forget that you *know* you are. And you must never let people touch that inner part of you, your confidence. Whatever happens to you, and however much people try to damage it, you must keep it safe." It was good advice, but I think she was also addressing herself and talking about her own recent experiences.

★

My own career was showing little sign of taking off. The jobs were few and rather too far between. There were two or three concert parties and the odd out of town pantomime, but nothing substantial. I was not discouraged; I was still prepared to be patient. It was all part of my education and a time for me to improve my skills.

With all the casual work, I was just making ends meet and I wasn't getting into debt. Mecca were very good, because if an acting job did come up and I needed to get away to do a summer season they would release me. Then, a fortnight before the summer season came to an end, I would drop them a card. I would ring up Mr Self, the man in charge of casual jobs, and he would find me something to do.

Putting on my Scotts lightweight felt hat and carrying a cane, I did an audition in 1957 for Clive Dunn (later of *Dad's Army*) for a concert party he was putting on at Cromer, in Norfolk. I went along to the audition in a rehearsal room off Shaftesbury Avenue and sang "When you're in love, when you're in love, when you're in love, you're walking on cloud lucky seven." Clive liked some funny bit of business I did in my act and he invited me to do the show with him.

It was an eight-handed show called *Take it Easy*. There were four programmes and you changed every Thursday, the idea being that, if people came on holiday to Cromer for a fortnight, they could see all four shows. I played the small comic parts. Everyone in the show had their own spot for four or five minutes, so with four programmes, that was about 20 minutes of material altogether. I got together some little jokes, little bits of parody and other things which were probably all terrible. Unfortunately, the pier had blown down in a storm, so we performed the whole summer season in the church hall.

The principal comedian in the show at Cromer was Graham

Stark, a very successful performer on radio and in films and a great friend of Peter Sellers. He was the last-minute replacement in our show for John Hewer who suddenly got a big break and went to Broadway with Julie Andrews in *The Boy Friend*. John Hewer is now Captain Birdseye in the fish fingers commercials.

Aunt Nell made the journey by coach from Edinburgh to Cromer to see me perform. For her, it must have been an arduous and worrying trip, but it was typical of her affectionate nature that she made it. I think she stayed to see all the shows.

I had a very good deal with a Cypriot restaurant in Cromer. It had rooms upstairs, some of which were occupied by waiters, and they let me have a room for about four guineas a week, with food. So I had breakfast, a light lunch and supper after the show – a diet of steaks, kebabs and moussaka, for the 11 weeks it lasted. I was paid £8 a week for *Take it Easy* and I remember coming home having saved up £24. Actually, the show was reckoned to have been a pretty big success; it won a Bucket and Spade Award from the Concert Artistes Association in the category of best Eight-Handed Summer Show.

The following year, Clive Dunn included me in a similar show, called *Good Evening,* at the Victoria Pavilion in Ilfracombe, but immediately after Cromer, I went through another patch of unemployment and I went to live in cheaper digs, in a house in King Henry's Road, in Swiss Cottage. It was one of those awful five-storey mid-Victorian houses made of grey brick and I had a bedsit which was fairly grim, with cold linoleum on the floor. Another lodger, next door to me, was an Indian man who worked at Euston station and cooked curries in his room – which wasn't really allowed – but I found the smell of curry on the landing rather comforting. In the communal bathroom there was one of those terrifying geyser things for producing hot water. You put your shilling in and it rumbled and moaned for a while, then it suddenly exploded into life, spewing soot, hot water and steam. One thing it was important to remember was, the longer the pause before anything happened, the more ferocious the bang would be, giving you just enough time to run away and cower in the corner. For all this sound and fury, the amount of hot water it actually produced was meagre. Over the years, it had left a depressing rusty stain on the side of the bath, and there was a black scorch mark on the enamel of the geyser, left behind after what must have been a particularly memorable explosion.

I found it better to go to the local public bath house in Swiss Cottage where you could get generous amounts of hot water, if you shouted for it over the wall of the cubicle, and there were very good rough towels. This was a more appealing way of getting clean, and it reminded me of the bath house, or the "steamie", of my young days in Edinburgh. I particularly remember those great chunks of rust-red carbolic soap and the way the people at the bath house would cut you off a slice.

Meanwhile, being well scrubbed and fragrant with carbolic, I was still trying to get my career moving. I decided to consult a comic called Charlie Stewart whom I had seen when he performed in Edinburgh in a show called *Five Past Eight*. He had a pekinese dog in his act. When he later appeared in the *Fol-de-rols*, the famous seaside show which moved for a while to the St Martin's Theatre in the West End, I wrote him a note asking if I could come and see him for some advice. We met in a little coffee bar behind the St Martin's. Charlie Stewart advised me to go through the newspapers every day and through magazines like *Reader's Digest* and cut out any funny bits I saw and stick them in a book, and slowly, like a stamp collection, I would amass a lot of little remarks and observations which I could use. This is what I did.

At the time I was starting out, or trying to, the Windmill

Theatre was the place where a lot of comedians, like Tony Hancock, Peter Sellers, Harry Secombe and Jimmy Edwards got their first break. I auditioned at the Windmill several times and got turned down several times.

Boo Laye came with her husband Frank Lawton to see me in a show at the Stork Club, in Streatham, written by Alan Fenton, the friend I first met when I was doing my National Service. It was probably dreadful; I sang a few numbers and did a terrible patter. And then somebody started throwing these quite hard dinner rolls at me. First one roll was lobbed in from a dark distant corner of the room, and I pretended to ignore it, then three or four more followed. They were Viennese rolls with a crusty exterior, which, in other circumstances I might enjoy. It was a cruel fate for the son of a baker.

I just about managed to get to the end of my act, and then Boo Laye stood up and really tore into the audience. "I've come here to see a young artist, in his early days, struggling," she said, "and I have never come across such an ill-mannered lot as you." Then she sat down, finished her drink, stood up again and swept out of the room. This little drama was actually recorded in the "In London Last Night" column in the *Evening Standard* where they reported all the social goings-on.

There were countless auditions and the big American musicals were the things we all wanted to get into. When the first production of *Guys and Dolls* was coming to London I went to several auditions for the part of one of the four gamblers in the "Tin Horn Fugue" at the beginning when they sing "I've got the horse right here/ the name is Paul Revere." For the first call, probably 480 people showed up, then they whittled it down. I got down to the last 28, but I didn't get the part.

Strangely enough, I had a job with the estate agents Druce and Co, helping them rent out flats to people coming to London for the Coronation. Later, with the same firm, I let about five houses to members of the American cast of *Guys and Dolls*, so, although I never got a part, I got to know them extremely well and went to see the show over and over again.

After leaving Mary Merrall's house. I moved to another part of St John's Wood, to a house in Clifton Hill run by a generous Irish lady. There were probably 11 or 12 bedsits in the house and we used to get our breakfast and an evening meal which you went down and collected on a tray.

The people who lived there were much more commercial types, less arty, more everyday. And the food was a bit everyday, as well. Rather lumpy. I used to wrap most of it up in newspaper and throw it away.

There was one interesting character in these digs. He was a very sweet man who had a badly damaged leg and drove a drophead XK 120 Jaguar. He used to illustrate the romantic stories in *Woman's Own* with all those splendidly handsome men and full-bosomed ladies. For years afterwards, I used to pick up copies of the magazine and look for his illustrations.

The Irish lady in Clifton Hill was the only person I remember owing rent to. When I moved on I owed her £11, so I gave her my portable radio.

I then moved in with Mrs Wilson in St John's Wood High Street, above a very good fishmonger and an excellent cake shop called Jacquot, and opposite a greengrocers called Salamone's. Phil Salamone, the son, ran a garage where he tuned rather racy cars, like Mini Coopers.

With my memories of my father's baking, I would always pause and look in the window and admire the cakes in Jacquot. Even now, when I pass a baker's shop I can't help looking in and making judgements, just as my father used to. I'll notice if the bread has been too highly fired or if the pastry is too soggy, or if they have used too much fat.

My jobs for Mecca were gradually becoming a bit more responsible. I was even sent to be relief manager, no less, of a pub on the seafront in Brighton called the Arlington, which had accommodation upstairs. I was there for about six weeks, running this pub.

While I was there I used to think about the man who managed the pub I usually went to in St John's Wood. He wore big brown double-breasted suits and two-tone shoes and looked like a character from a Ben Travers farce. He would come down from upstairs at precisely quarter to seven every evening, looking immaculate, tweaking his tie and greeting the regulars.

At the Arlington I acted the part, coming down in my blazer, tweaking my tie and saying things like "Hello, sir. Nice to see you. Having your usual?" Regulars loved to see their drinks being prepared for them as they walked from the door to the bar. If there was someone who annoyed me I could use this to get my own back.

"Good evening, sir, and what will it be?"

"The usual."

"Ah, the usual (*tweaks tie*) – and what would that be?"

"Same as I always have."

"Worthington E?"

"What I had yesterday evening, when I was standing in this very spot."

"Ah, yes a Bloody Mary, no ice and lots of Worcester. No, of course, that's someone else – one of our regulars."

"I'm a regular and I want my usual."

"Ginger wine? Brown and mild? Campari? Let me know if I'm getting warmer."

One of my favourite jobs was working at the Buckstone, an

actors' club which was in a basement opposite the stage door of the Haymarket Theatre. It was one of those places that verges on being scruffy. There was a bar and a small, rather poky dining room, with banquettes, where you could get very good cheap food at lunch, tea and dinner. All the actors went there – Emlyn Williams, John Gielgud, Donald Wolfit. Really, the whole of the West End came to the Buckstone. They would come in for cheap suppers on their way home. It was also a very popular place for teas. Actors would come in after the matinee and before the evening performance; they would come with *The Times* or the *Telegraph* crossword, have a poached egg, some brown toast and raspberry jam and a nice pot of tea.

At the Buckstone I got to know people almost as well as if I had worked with them in the theatre. Kenneth Tynan, the critic was never out of there, and Elaine Dundy, his wife at the time. Two Stanleys – both Baker and Baxter – Joan Greenwood, André Morrell, Glynis Johns – everyone. There were two wonderful waitresses; an Irish lady called Nancy who lived in Camden Town and an Austrian lady called Bianca. They were really the stars of the place. And I worked behind the bar. The Buckstone Club was very important to me; it was where I carried on most of my courtship of Anne Hart, who was to become my wife.

At the same time as running the bar at the Buckstone, I was *also* working in the stores in the Victory Club. I would be there from half past eight in the morning until five in the evening. The storeroom was my own little world and I could even nod off at my desk if I needed a rest. At 5.30 I would get in my little car and drive to Suffolk Street, where the Buckstone Club was and I would set up the bar, wipe down the top, get the ice out, and so on.

The car was a bullnose Morris which I had bought from the stage door keeper at the Manchester Palace for £75. I had been doing a summer season there with Jon Pertwee and Stan Stennett. The stars of the show were Jimmy Young (who had a big hit with "Unchained Melody" and, indeed, a number of other hits as a crooner) and Joan Turner, the soprano. And Pertwee and Stennett.

Jon and Stan helped me refurbish the engine of the Morris, changing the spark plugs and the distributor and doing all sorts of things to make it go faster, but it didn't make a lot of difference.

Late one night, as I was leaving the Buckstone Club, I had only driven a few yards when I heard a strange grunting noise coming from the back of the car. I turned round and discovered a tramp asleep on the back seat. I stopped and asked him kindly to get out of the vehicle. It might be only a £75 Morris, but it had its dignity.

I had now left St John's Wood at last and was living in a bedsit in Notting Hill Gate. It was a satisfactory arrangement. I would get my lunch and my tea at the Victory Club and my supper at the Buckstone. I did not need to eat at home, but if I wanted a little extra something I would have a glass of milk, ice cold from the fridge, and a plain chocolate digestive. I have always loved McVitie and Price's plain chocolate digestives.

And if I wanted a change, there was a very good bakers across the street where they did very good cakes and pies and quite delicious iced cookie buns with jam centres. This bedsit in Notting Hill Gate was my most glamorous home since I had left Pixie's house in Avenue Road. The most luxurious thing about it was that it actually had a fitted carpet – pale beige. It was the first fitted carpet I had enjoyed. The lady who owned the house was rather grand and let out two rooms to help pay her son's boarding school fees.

After I had done two summer seasons with Clive Dunn, he

recommended me as a light comedian to Greatrex Newman who happened to be his godfather and, more importantly, the producer of the seaside show, the *Fol-de-rols*. (It was the 1951 London run of the *Fol-de-Rols* that Charlie Stewart was in when I went to see him to get his advice about being a comedian.) I auditioned with Greatrex (or Rex, as he was more conveniently known) and I signed an agreement to go for 22 weeks with the *Fol-de-rols*, in Margate. Bill Pertwee (later with Clive Dunn in *Dad's Army*) was in the company but the most important member was Jack Tripp, one of this country's top pantomime dames who was, at one time, understudy to the great music hall comedian Sid Field.

At last, this was a big break for me. This would mean the end of the struggling and the odd jobs, because the *Fol-de-rols* was just about the most famous concert party going at the time. The show was already running and I was to join it in Margate and do two numbers and various other bits and pieces in it. I couldn't wait to join the party. I got all the clothes made, the coat cut down and I got the top hat – for the "Help Yourself to Happiness" routine. I rehearsed my two numbers and my photographs went up outside the theatre.

I did my first night and everything seemed to go all right. The next day there was a rehearsal call at 10 a.m. I was sitting there in the stalls, waiting to be called to rehearse, when Rex Newman came down the aisle behind me, tapped me on the shoulder and said: "Can I have a word with you in the dressing room?"

I followed him to the dressing room and he shut the door, turned to me and said: "I'm afraid I've made a terrible mistake." I had no idea what was coming next. I just looked at his solemn face and his rather prim wire-framed spectacles which didn't seem to go with his more daring bow tie and his extrovert check jacket. "It's not your fault," he went on and it dawned on me that I was about to be sacked. Those three words "not your fault" usually mean bad news. Rex ploughed on. "It's as if I had booked two tenors when what I was really looking for was a tenor and a bass," he explained. So that was it. Basically, I suspect I was too like Jack Tripp and I think Jack Tripp may have also thought I was too like Jack Tripp. Anyway, somebody had said something and I had to go. So I did just one night with the *Fol-de-rols*.

Of course, I had said to all my friends at the Buckstone Club: "Come down and see me, I'm at Margate for 22 weeks." Two nights later I was back. I had to pick up all my stuff and collect my photographs from the front of the theatre and put everything in the car and drive away. It was a deeply gloomy drive back to London; I was bitterly disappointed and hurt. I felt I had been unfairly treated and I didn't understand why. Years later Rex Newman thanked me for having taken it so well, but at the time I had just felt too shaken to take it badly. At least I got a month's money out of the management, so they were quite generous in that way.

The night I got back from Margate I went to a pub I used to go to called the Star, in a mews in Belgravia. It was run by a man called Paddy Kennedy and a wonderful mixture of actors, villans, bohemians and burglars went to drink there.

In the pub that night I met a good friend of mine called Jimmy who was half a bit of a smart operator about the West End. Jimmy, as you might say, lived a short distance from the edge of the law. Or certainly in that vicinity. He was very successful at whatever it was he did. When I knew him he was already well off and had a villa in Spain. He had originally come from the hard part of Shepherd's Bush, but was very handsome, smooth and charming. In fact, he was more kindly than he would ever like to admit, and always good for a laugh.

He was involved in greyhound racing and owned a lot of

dogs. He was also a great friend of Eddie Chapman, the famous safe-cracker who worked for MI5 in the war.

Eddie Chapman had been in jail in Jersey during the war, waiting to be sent back to Scotland to face trial for a job he had done in Glasgow, when the Germans arrived and occupied the Channel Islands. They let him out of jail and, after training, sent him back to Britain to carry out acts of sabotage for them. Obviously, his experience with explosives and blowing the doors off safes, was just the right qualification.

When he arrived in England Eddie Chapman reported to the police and was hired by British Intelligence as a Double Cross agent, codenamed Zig-Zag. He worked for MI5 in the war, but they eventually had to drop him, apparently because he boasted too much to his underworld friends about his secret exploits.

Anyway, back to Jimmy and me in the bar of the Star in Belgravia. Over a drink, I told Jimmy about the farrago with the *Fol-de-rols* and he said, "Would you be interested in crewing a boat with me?" He had bought a boat, a motor cruiser about 27ft long, and it was being delivered to Kew Bridge the following week. He was planning to take it to the south of France, going across the Channel, up the Seine and through the middle of France down the Canal de Bourgogne. He said he would pay all my expenses and for my food and drink. I liked the idea. In earlier times, after the disappointment I had just had, I might have signed up with the crew of a tea clipper going away on a long voyage to the Indies; crewing a motor cruiser to the south of France was a more convenient alternative.

I said yes. The next week Jimmy and I set off across the Channel, neither of us ever having done anything like it before. We got stuck on a sandbank and our idea of navigation was to say "Shall we follow that boat?" And "Try to steer to the left of that church spire on the coast ahead." And we said nautical things, like: "Do you think we're pointing in the right direction, me hearty?"

I always remember that, at one point when we were crossing the Channel, Jimmy said: "I'm getting a bit peckish. Can you knock something up for me in the galley?" So I went below and came back a few minutes later with a brown bread banana sandwich. He seemed to think this was very strange and rather repulsive, which is odd because I still rather like brown bread and banana, but he still remembers it as one of the most horrid snacks he'd ever had.

We got to Paris somehow and stayed there for four days because Jimmy had friends there from the war. I slept on the boat, which was very difficult because the river is very busy in Paris, and if you are in a little vessel, however well tied up, there are a lot of big bumps as other boats go past.

We went down the Canal de Bourgogne, and, with all those hand-operated locks, we soon got very strong and fit. It was a wonderful way to see France and observe the canal life as all the big barges sailed past, loaded with all sorts of cargo including chickens and dogs. It's wonderful, the way you can exchange long, lazy, curious stares with the people on the other boat as the vessels slide slowly past each other. We would exchange curious stares with Frenchmen all morning, then, in the middle of the day we would stop at a lock and buy a bit of bread and cheese and a glass of wine and perhaps half a charentais melon. Then we'd cruise on lazily, staring some more, through the rest of the afternoon.

At seven o'clock in the evening we would tie up, have a swim in the canal, walk into the town and ask to be directed to the best place to eat.

We carried on down the Rhone, which you are not really supposed to do without taking on a pilot because there is a 17–

knot current there, but we survived this somehow and then came out at Marseille and made our way along the coast. We got caught in a mistral (the cold northerly wind which is a speciality of the region) and had to go back. Finally, we delivered the boat to Cannes, after a journey that had taken seven weeks. The idea was that Jimmy was going to spend the summer on his new vessel. However, the petrol engine blew up with him on board and he was nearly very seriously injured. So, after all our efforts in getting it to the south of France, the boat was lost, and Jimmy did not have quite the holiday he'd expected.

It was a very memorable trip after my major setback in Margate, and a godsend because I had been so depressed about it.

On this long journey in a small boat, Jimmy and I had only one argument. I can't remember what it was about, but we were in some town and it was a big holiday for Bastille Day, July 14th. We walked around the town, going our separate ways, sulking. Every so often we would catch sight of each other in the street and have to turn round and stalk off in the other direction.

I returned to the boat at about eleven o'clock that night. The water was lapping against the hull and there was a light on in the bows. As I stepped on to the deck I heard this very small voice calling "Is that you, Ron?" It was so funny to hear this faint, weak, un-tough sound of Jimmy welcoming me back from my sulk. Neither of us was really living up to the gnarled old sea-dog image. Still, we managed to continue the rest of our voyage in that boat without falling out. In both senses of the word.

As I mentioned, Jimmy had lots of interests and among them he had several greyhounds in training, and because he was a trainer, I suppose, he always seemed to know – or he had a better idea than most – when these greyhounds were going to oblige. I used to put on bets for him, and quite often put on a bit of my own money and, more often than not, it was profitable.

The bookies must have got to know about Jimmy's winning streaks so it wasn't so easy for him to put the money on, because he was recognised. So I, being totally unrecognisable, placed his bets for him, often visiting several betting shops throughout the day and spreading his cash around between them. This was another role for me, the betting shop habitué. I like to think I gave a rather fine performance as a man who knew his way about the betting shop, but wasn't all that well informed about the dogs. I managed to look faintly surprised when I picked up Jimmy's winnings.

On one occasion, after our voyage to the south of France, Jimmy asked me to go to the White City dog track in Glasgow with a large sum of money – I forget exactly how much – and put it on two dogs. I don't know why he chose me for this important mission; I suppose he thought I could sound a bit Glasgow and look the part. One dog belonged to Jimmy and the other was owned by a friend of his. I remember hearing Jimmy talking to his friend on the phone and saying: "I'm sending up my top man." I felt rather good about that and mentally I tipped my trilby hat forward a couple of inches, turned up the collar my raincoat and gave him one of Humphrey Bogart's calculating, watery stares.

With my pockets full of banknotes, I made my way to Glasgow and went to the dog track. I had to put two or three hundred pounds on the first dog, and it won comfortably, at about four to one. The trouble was that I then had to back a dog in the very next race. So now I was going to have to go and collect my winnings – several hundred pounds – and try and look nonchalant as I put the cash in my raincoat pocket, while in the other raincoat pocket I had the other wad of money ready to put on the next dog.

As I walked through the crowds to the line of bookies at the back of the stadium I could feel the eyes of everyone were on me. I handed over my ticket, like a man passing a state secret to a spy, but that didn't help, because the bookie made a great flamboyant performance of counting out the notes and handing over my winnings. They always like to do it with a bit of a flourish.

By this time all the bookies were watching me, wondering who I was, waiting to see which dog I was going to back next. They were poised, with their dusters close to their blackboards, waiting for me to make my move, ready to change the odds. It seemed as if everybody in the stadium had stopped. It was so quiet I felt I could hear the dogs whining in the kennels beneath the stands. I carefully took the money from my other raincoat pocket and put it on Jimmy's second dog, then I walked away and tried to get lost in the crowd.

And the second dog obliged. Disaster! So now I had to go and pick up another thick wad of winnings and watch while the bookie went through his big counting-out performance. I plucked up my courage, turned up my raincoat collar and made my way once again to where the bookies were. This time there was a good deal of muttering, then a bit of chanting, then suddenly the people all around me started singing "Robin Hood, Robin Hood, riding through the glen . . . ." I was being serenaded in heavy Glasgow accents. Perhaps they thought I was robbing the rich bookies to give to the poor punters, but I don't think so. I think there was a good deal of Sauchiehall mockery in it.

I left White City stadium in a hurry and I hailed a taxi – because money was no object now – and I went to the St Enoch hotel for a cup of tea, to get my breath back, recover from the excitement and to wait for my flight back to London. I was hugely relieved that my one-man betting coup was over.

So that night I got on the plane at Glasgow and settled in my seat. Then I casually looked around at my fellow passengers and, to my horror, I saw that nearly all the bookies who had been at the White City earlier were now on the same flight as me. It was like some sort of nightmare. I discovered, during the flight, that Glasgow Rangers were due to play Moscow Dynamo at White Hart Lane the following day, and the bookies were on their way to watch the match. They looked at me, with my raincoat pockets stuffed with cash and they must have wondered: "Where has this wee bugger come from?"

CHAPTER SIX

Mostly about night-clubs and Danny La Rue. But also about filming in the Hebrides, meeting a soccer referee in Majorca, and about how I nearly became type-cast as an ape. Some mention of Royalty. Also the Great Train Robbers. David Frost puts in an appearance. Most importantly it is about how I met Anne Hart and how she became my wife – eventually.

Have I mentioned how I met Laurence Olivier and how I came to play Othello? No? How extraordinary. I suppose you could say it all started when I was working behind the bar at the Buckstone Club one evening and Harry Fowler, the cockney actor who was a friend of mine, was there, talking to Digby Wolfe, a rather smart patter comedian who worked in the West End clubs.

Digby happened to mention, quite casually in the course of conversation, that he reckoned that he could get anybody on to television if they were clever enough. So Harry Fowler said: "How about Ronnie?" I just stood there, behind the bar. Polishing a glass. Rather expertly, I like to think. You know, giving it a bit of a polish, holding it up to the light, then giving it another little polish.

Anyway, Digby took on the challenge and he did get me into television, but, more importantly perhaps, he got me into Winston's night-club in Mayfair. Danny La Rue was the resident star of the club, but he was going away for a couple of months to do a pantomime. While he was away a new show was being written by Digby Wolfe and he put me in it. The singer, Anne Hart (who is to become my wife later in this chapter) was also in the show, taking over a lot of Danny's numbers while he was away.

So Digby got me into Winston's and he also got me into a show he did for BBC Television called *The Digby Wolfe Show*. After that, just to rub it in, he also got me on *The Yana Show*, on Saturday nights on the BBC, where I played small comic roles. Digby was having a romance with Yana while writing the show. It was something he did a lot of – romancing and writing.

Yana was the glamorous blonde singer who specialised in plunging necklines and was a tremendous success in the 50s and 60s. But her career had its ups and downs – unlike her neckline which mostly had its downs. By the 1980s she was working in Boots, the chemists, in Marylebone, London, where she was re-discovered, rescued from the toiletries counter and given the role of the Good Fairy in *The Wonderful Wizard of Oz* at Crewe. She died in 1989 and her last job was demonstrating a slimming machine in Harrods. It is a sad story and one that is repeated often in showbusiness.

So anyway, Danny La Rue returned to Winston's from pantomime, saw the show and decided to keep me on. The writer of the show then was no longer Digby Wolfe, but Bryan Blackburn – who now does a lot of Jim Davidson's stuff – and he was followed by Barry Cryer.

Winston's was run by a wonderful character called Bruce Brace. He had been in partnership with Harry Meadows, running Churchill's, but they had a fall-out, a major bust-up, so major, in fact, that I can't remember what it was about. Bruce walked out in a fit of pique and set up a rival club nearby, which, in a feat of imagination, he called Winston's. Churchill's was in Bond Street, between Aspreys and Hermes, Winston's was in Clifford Street and between them was the Celebrity, run by Paul Raymond who later went on to own most of Soho.

It was a time when there were lots of night-clubs in London – like Rico Dajou's and the Wardroom, run by Eustace Hoey, and Siggi's, Al Burnett's Stork Club and the Edmundo Ros Club. It was the heyday of a sort of post-war nightlife glamour which might appear unsophisticated by today's standards, but which we found tremendously exciting at the time. They were the sort of places you could go to dine out in an ambience of plush and soft lighting, dance, see a cabaret, or talk to a hostess who would usually try to look interested. Or at least pretend to listen.

Working at Winston's meant I had a bit of financial security at last, although it was always advisable to cash your pay cheque quite quickly after you got it. Bruce Brace, who ran the club, was very sweet and always extremely well dressed in silk shirts and hand-made shoes, but sometimes tradesmen had to wait rather a long time to get their accounts settled. Bruce tended to be out quite often when suppliers came in to discuss their bills.

Winston's was one of those places where everybody knew a man who knew a man. You could get hold of just about anything on the cheap. If you had a Rover car and you gave it to a certain chap for a couple of days he would get it to the Rover factory, which was somewhere near Wormwood Scrubs, and you would get the car back with a new engine in it. All you had to do was slip somebody £20. I never understood how it worked.

There was another man who knew how to get hold of

Wedgwood china. You told him which pattern you liked – with your second and third choices, just in case there was a problem – and he would deliver the goods. I got a complete set for eight people – coffee set and tea set – for £75. I think if you wanted to replace just the teapot nowadays you would have to pay about £400. I also got a double bed for my flat in Camden Town through contacts at Winston's. I just signed a chit and gave somebody in the club a tenner and the bed arrived the next day. I suppose all this was part of the culture of the post-war years and people used to love to show off about how they could "arrange" things.

When Bruce Brace retired from the club he ran a stationer's and newsagent's shop in the Pimlico Road, near Victoria station – a most unlikely thing to do and not really his scene at all. For a start, it was the opposite end of the day to when he was used to working. He had always been a late riser before. He told me he couldn't help losing his temper in his shop when people came in first thing in the morning to buy a *Daily Mail* and a packet of Polo mints and then handed over a £50 note.

In 1957 I went to Barra, in the Outer Hebrides, to make the film *Rockets Galore,* which was a sort of sequel to *Whisky Galore*. I got the part after touring in a play called *Love's a Luxury* with a very lovely girl called Melissa Stribling. She was married to Basil Dearden who was directing *Rockets Galore*. A lot of the Scottish actors who had been in *Whisky Galore* appeared in this sequel. The stars were Donald Sinden and Jeannie Carson, and they were supported by people like Roland Culver, Duncan Macrae and Gordon Jackson. I played the part of a West Highland fisherman and, while we were shooting the film, I shared a croft with Duncan Macrae.

I was paid £75 a week. I remember this because work on the film meant I could afford to buy a carpet for my flat – I was living in Camden Town at the time – and buying your first carpet is an important milestone in any actor's career. I bought it in a Liberty's sale and the colour was called "Empire Gold."

On location on Barra we were pretty well cut off from the fleshpots and we had to make our own entertainment, as they say. There were lot of games of charades in the evenings and also a ceilidh. I had found a man who wrote me a very funny parody of a terrible, boring Gaelic song which I sang in a nasal whine. I can still remember some of the words:

> Sing me a Hebridean song, laddie,
> One about 40 verses long, laddie,
> That will reduce my embonpoint.
> Sing of the wild waves, something, something sailing,
> Sing of the washing that hangs on the paling,
> Sing till the neighbouring dogs stop their wailing,
> Sing me a Hebridean song.

Duncan Macrae, my croft-mate, was a wonderful actor who made a career out of looking craggy in scores of films and was also in the first film I ever appeared in – *You're only Young Twice*, back in 1952.

On Barra, Duncan and I decided to give a dinner party for the rest of the cast. We had great help with this because the daughter of the croft where we were living was a student at the school of domestic science in Glasgow. We had raspberries and fresh cream and lamb specially flown in from Glasgow for the dinner party, so our life was a lot less bleak than the words of my Hebridean song would suggest.

When I returned to London, and to Winston's, at the end of filming I brought back a roll of tweed which had actually been hand-woven in the croft where I was staying. Melissa Stribling (who was the wife of Basil Dearden, the director, remember? Try to keep up) told me her sister was married to a tailor and that is how I came to meet Doug Hayward. He worked as the sort of front of house man for Robbie Stanford, a very good tailor in Shepherd's Bush who had quite a number of showbiz clients. Doug introduced me to Dimi Major who, at the time, was an out-worker for Robbie Stanford and Dimi was the one who used the tweed to make me a splendid raglan coat.

Anne (who really is going to become my wife later in this chapter) always hated that coat. A few years later I lost it when my Mini Minor was stolen from outside Danny La Rue's club. The car was recovered, but the coat was gone for ever. I am not actually accusing Anne of being the mastermind behind this crime, just noting that she had the motive. Someone was going round London in my raglan overcoat – wearing it as a jacket perhaps. For a few months I gave hard looks at anyone I saw wearing tweed.

One interesting thing about Robbie Stanford, by the way, was that he worried a lot about his height – or his lack of it. He was small, but not by my standards, and it troubled him so much that he even had lifts in his golf shoes.

After his triumph with my raglan coat, Dimi Major went into partnership with Doug Hayward in Fulham where their clientele included film stars like Kirk Douglas and Gregory Peck. Later on, Doug moved on to set up his own business in Mount Street where he became an even greater success and Dimi stayed behind in Fulham where he still makes suits for me. Doug might easily have taken umbrage at the fact that I have never been back to him for suits since he introduced me to Dimi Major, but in fact we still get on as well as we ever did and he's never even mentioned it – and I always think that's big of him.

★

My grandparents, James and Margaret Main, from Kintore, near Aberdeen. He became a London policeman and she was a cook-housekeeper in Belgravia.

My father in his World War I uniform with his father and his younger brother Geordie, and his sisters Isa (left) and Jessie (right) who didn't recognise him when he came home on leave.

I think I was about four when this was taken, and slightly worried because the kilt was not a perfect fit.

My first day at James Gillespie School for Boys. I cried a lot and disgraced my mother.

At home with my brother Allan and my sister Margaret. I'm the debonair one on the left.

Looking very cold on holiday with my mother, brother and sister at
Cellardyke, near St Andrews. If you hold the picture up to your ear you can
hear my teeth chattering.

James Gillespie's School for Boys – not the prime of
Master Ronald Corbett, seen here in the front row, fourth from the left,
with feet not quite touching the ground.

National Service in the RAF at Weeton in Lancashire where
I did my basic training and also did a bit of babysitting. I'm third from
the left in the front row.

Anne, a really thrilling singer, in *Annie Get Your Gun* on tour in New Zealand. Kiri Te Kanawa was a member of the chorus.

Anne, as leading lady with the Crazy Gang. Teddy Knox would sometimes send out to Overton's fish restaurant and order a portion of scampi to be delivered to her on stage.

That's me as a cygnet in the *Swan Lake* fiasco which was first devised for Stanley Baxter and me when we were the Ugly Sisters in *Cinderella* in Glasgow.

Portrait of the artiste as a smooth young man about town. I think it was taken in the days when I was appearing at Winston's nightclub. The suit's nice, too.

There was always a party at Danny La Rue's Club. Here's Danny cutting his cake and having it. Jenny Logan, who was David Frost's girlfriend for a time is on Danny's left and Toni Palmer is on his right, then that's me in the foreground. Barry Cryer, in dark rimmed glasses, is at the far end of the table and Anne is on the right with a bow in her hair. The waiter with the pile of plates, by the way, was called Angelo.

This is *Rockets Galore* in which I played a character called Drooby. I shared a croft on the isle of Barra with Duncan Macrae, who is on the left.

The young John Cleese with the young Ronnie Corbett in the days of *The Frost Report*.

The famous Class sketch from *The Frost Report*, with John Cleese and Ronnie Barker.

From *The Frost Report*. David with Julie Felix, the folk singer and (at the piano) Tom Lehrer the composer and performer of such tasteful numbers as *Vatican Rag* and *Poisoning Pigeons in the Park*. Nicholas Smith, later of *Are You Being Served?* is on the left with the newspaper, and Nicky Henson is on the right, in uniform.

With Arthur Lowe in the 1962 film *Some Will, Some Won't* which was a remake of *Laughter In Paradise*, about people who have to perform out-of-character tasks in order to gain inheritance.

With Joanna Pettit in the James Bond spoof *Casino Royale*.
I was sort of robot villain named Polo.

Me, giving it my all, during the first run of *The Two Ronnies* at the London Palladium.

Getting to grips with my role in the 1973 film *No Sex Please, We're British*.

No Sex Please, We're British. I played the part of Brian Runnicles.

In the 60s Doug Hayward was one of that group of people like Michael Caine, Roger Moore and the photographers Terry O'Neill and Terence Donovan, all trendy working class boys who had done very well with flair and style. They were the sort of people who would be seen at Stamford Bridge when Chelsea was in its heyday with players like Peter Osgood, Charlie Cooke and Alan Hudson.

Actually, I had a bit of a soccer career at the time, playing for the Television All-Stars and Showbiz XI, with gifted ball players like Tommy Steele, Anthony Newley, Lonnie Donegan, Harry Fowler and Mike and Bernie Winters. We used to gather in a bleary huddle outside Broadcasting House on a Sunday morning to be picked up by coach and driven to the match which was always in aid of charity. I was the nippy one on the right wing. Actually, for a bunch of comedians, we took it extremely seriously. Tommy Docherty, who has been manager of just about every football club in the country at one time or another, used to be our trainer, or sometimes he played for us and sometimes he was referee. And knowing him, sometimes he did all three at once.

In fact, I did know Tommy Docherty quite well because he had been in the Scotland side in the World Cup in Sweden alongside my cousin, James Murray. James, who played for Hearts, was my famous relation when I lived in Edinburgh. If I wanted to impress people I could casually drop his name into conversations. "I don't know if I have ever mentioned this," I would say, "but James Murray is, in fact, a cousin of mine."

In 1962 Doug Hayward and I went on holiday together, to Sitges in Spain. On the first night we sat down to dinner in our hotel and when the pudding came and it turned out to be sliced Wall's ice cream, we realised we had picked the wrong hotel.

We checked out and moved into a smaller place which was much more Spanish and much less package touristy.

Doug and I got on very well, but on this holiday it soon became clear that we were both anxious to meet up with someone else. We've often teased each other since about this, but you can't help wondering if we found each other's conversation totally fascinating, because when we bumped into one particular very charming chap, we were both thrilled to have his company. I think it was really because you can lose a sense of proportion on holiday and develop an exaggerated interest in your fellow tourists. So many murmured conversations begin "Isn't that the couple from our hotel?" and the speculation follows. "Do you think he's coming down to breakfast?" or "Perhaps they've gone shopping" or "I wonder if they've discovered that little bar behind the church."

Anyway, for some reason, we thought this chap was wonderful. And, as he was in Spain on his own, he was just as happy to latch on to us. It turned out that he was a Second Division football referee from Birmingham. Quel glamour – as they say in Smethwick. But he was good enough for us.

The three of us went to a bullfight in Barcelona. It lasted a whole day and, looking back on that bloody marathon now, I feel slightly queasy and ashamed. Something like 21 of Spain's greatest bullfighters took part – the Peralta brothers, Dominguin, all the *crème de la crème,* some of them coming out of retirement specially for it – because it was in aid of the people who had been made homeless in the Barcelona floods. I used to have the poster for that bullfight. Let's face it, *everybody* used to have a bullfight poster at some point in their life.

In Barcelona we went for a meal at a fabulous restaurant called Caracoles, with open fires in the middle of the room for barbecuing the food. I think it is still there. Our Second Division football referee decided that he wanted some chips with his meal, but the waiter, who was obviously not as impressed by him as Doug and I were, pretended he had no idea what he was getting at.

"I'd like some chips with that."

Blank stare from the waiter.

"Chips. You know, cheeps."

Faint sign of movement in the waiter's left eyebrow.

"Me. French fries."

Even the referee's subtle Andalucian lisp on the "s" of "fries" failed to get through to the waiter.

"Los cheepos."

Affecting resignation and incomprehension, the waiter turned and started to move away from the table. Suddenly, the referee was struck by inspiration. He half rose, held up his hand and shouted after the retreating waiter:

"Chipolatas!"

I stayed at Winston's for about five years in the late 50s and early 60s, performing in the shows that were put on there. It was there that I was first spotted by David Frost. He used to come to the club quite often because he was going out with a girl from the show called Jenny Logan. After his great success with *That Was the Week That Was*, he did tend to swish about the West End quite a bit with attractive ladies. David became a hero of the 60s because of *That Was the Week that Was* – or *TW3*, as it was called – and was one of the creators of the so-called "satire boom". On Saturday nights, parties used to be suspended as the guests went into another room to watch *TW3* on the box. David was the anchor man. Cultivating an amiable snarl and speaking rather through his nose, he conducted a look-back at the week's news – a sort of "nasal review". Millicent Martin was the resident singer, and Willie Rushton, Kenneth Cope and Lance Percival were among the performers who made their names on the programme.

As well as David Frost, another person who first spotted me at Winston's was the comedian Jimmy Tarbuck. He used to come into the club and laugh loudly at the show, and particularly at my performances. When he took over as the compere of the television show *Sunday Night at the London Palladium* he gave me lots of little parts in the sketches on the show. This was before I was at all well known and before David Frost gave me my first big break. So Jimmy Tarbuck was the first to recognise my talents and I think it was brave and generous of him to give me those opportunities.

The good thing about night-clubs was that they ran 52 weeks a year and it meant that I could do television at the same time and even be in a West End show. At one time I was doing four jobs a day. It was a wonderful confection. I was in the matinee of *Noddy in Toyland* at the Shaftesbury Theatre, then I was in the evening performance of *The Famous Five* at the same theatre. After that I did some cabaret at the Cote d'Azur club in the West End, then on to Winston's where the show started at about one in the morning.

I can't now remember whether I was Whiskers or Big Ears in the Noddy thing, but it was something fairly grotesque; then in *The Famous Five* I was a member of the celebrity quintet. The plot revolved round somebody being locked up and trapped inside a gypsy caravan. One evening the whole performance was blown when the door of the gypsy caravan swung open fairly early on in the performance. This left us rather at a loss and somebody had to creep across and push it shut again.

While working at the night-club, I was also able to get away, in the course of a year, for a summer season in Ilfracombe, say, or to do a pantomime in Bromley, then I could go back again to the club.

Winston's consisted of a long room with a small stage at one end. It looked a plush and posh place with red velvet and chandeliers, but the backstage conditions were not quite so glamorous. The men's changing room was downstairs and you had to dash through the kitchens to get to the stage upstairs and there was never time to get back downstairs while the show was on, so you had to slip in and out of your costumes behind the curtain.

The girls' changing room was also downstairs, next to the cold room, and there was another little room for the hostesses where they would sit and do their *petit point* or whatever, and the manager would come down and say something like; "Suzie – table 14." This rather peremptory call to duty meant that the girl had to go and sit with one of the tired gentlemen in the club upstairs.

As well as the cigarette girl and the coffee boy there would be girls going among the tables selling teddy bears and negligees and pyjamas. They were pretty ordinary teddy bears, I must say, but very expensive. And I suppose the customer thought that the negligee and the pyjamas he bought might just have a chance of seeing each other later on in the night. The hostesses were usually in league with the girls selling these things, so if they were bought a teddy bear or a negligee they gave it back afterwards.

The clientele were mostly groups of people who had come up to town, perhaps to the Motor Show or the Dairy Show. I used to have a friend called Ron Waverley who came from Kelso, in the Borders, and he would talk of folk being "fresh in frae' fair oot", which could be translated as "newly arrived from the country".

You could imagine these people getting off the bus in the square in Kelso on a Saturday, with their new Harris tweed caps on and their best new boots, and the family with them, all having come in for the shopping.

Many of the punters who came to Winston's were also fresh in frae' fair oot and everybody then proceeded to take them for something – cigars, negligees, pyjamas or teddy bears.

The other customers were West End chaps who were friends of Bruce Brace, plus a few sleek and prosperous members of the underworld. These were the sort of people who were swanning round the West End in drophead Aston Martins at that time. I used to enjoy socialising in the room after the show and got to know quite a lot of villains who, I thought, were rather attractive in a Runyonesque sort of way.

In the early hours of the morning I would find myself chatting with a cat burglar or blethering to some villain or other. Of course you had to steer a careful course on conversation with these people. It wasn't a good idea to ask, "And what do you *do* exactly?" I knew some of the Great Train Robbers before they robbed the train. I used to see Bruce Reynolds in the club and also a chap called Charlie Mitchell who was at one time an associate of the Kray brothers, who then gave evidence against them at their trial and died much later in mysterious circumstance on the Costa del Sol.

In the late 50s and early 60s, when I worked at Winston's and later at Danny La Rue's own club, there was a sort of West End community. Smart people from Chelsea liked hobnobbing with villains and found them rather dashing. I think some of the villains were social climbers, in their way, and enjoyed being seen around with the upper classes. They used to go to pubs like the Star, in Belgravia, the Scarsdale, the Angelsea and the Queen's Elm where they would gather in the evening or at Sunday lunchtime, before going on to the Lyons Seven Stars restaurant or a curry place. In the Star, you might see Bruce Reynolds come in with a pretty girl, or you might spot some model who was famous for a time, or maybe Terry-Thomas, the gap toothed comic actor who specialised in playing rotters, would pop in after riding in Rotten Row.

When you worked at Winston's or Danny's you felt that, although you might not be a big name in the wide world, you were a big name in the West End. These were the places where the toffs and the big spenders came for a bit of late-night bacon and eggs or some bubbly. Anne and I both felt, in a way, that we were brought up in the West End. Even now, when we go out at night, we often meet some figure from that past – a doorman from Winston's, say, who is now a doorman at one of the West End hotels. That is another community that survives – the community of doormen.

One of my friends in those days – and ever since – was Bobby McKew. Bobby and the amateur jockey Michael Caborn-Waterfield (another famous figure of the period and better known as Dandy Kim) had a bit of a brush with the gendarmes in France in the early 1960s over the small matter of £25,000 which went missing from a villa on the Riviera. It was Bobby McKew who introduced me to Jimmy, my shipmate on that strange cruise to the south of France, and the man whose bets I put on.

Bobby was a very dashing fellow, a member of the breed known by the newspapers as "West End playboys". He was charming and elegant and, when he was around the West End, he was always immaculately dressed in suits by Tony Sinclair who was a most fashionable tailor of the period and made all Sean Connery's clothes for the first James Bond film.

I sometimes used to see Bobby in his little mews house in Swiss Cottage on a Sunday. He was quite different then, in these homely and cosy surroundings, wearing an old dressing gown and eating his Sunday lunch off a tray. Terribly domesticated.

There was a very eccentric creature, and Irish lady called Madge, who used to do all Bobby's bits and pieces of cooking and tidying the house. She had been a great beauty in her youth and had been rescued from her Irish peasant life by the director Gabriel Pascal for a role in a film. When she worked for Bobby she had a little Yorkshire terrier bedecked with red bows and she used to wheel it in a little baby's pram round the Swiss Cottage shops.

The shows at Winston's were very good and, besides Danny himself and Anne Hart, people like Barbara Windsor, Victor Spinetti, Barry Cryer and John Junkin were in the company. The material was good; fairly rude, always topical and often satirical, in the spirit of the times.

There were always attractive girls, very good dancers, and also four very tall very lovely showgirls who paraded in big feathers. They were not topless, they were just pretty gorgeous girls who knew how to move beautifully.

Danny was also gorgeous. He always had the glamorous roles, playing beautiful ladies, like Elizabeth Taylor or Sophia Loren. Danny would appear as Sophia Loren arriving at London Airport and would swish in with a splendid hat on and everyone round about would play rather bedraggled underprivileged friends. Anne, who was also extremely glamorous, always joked that in this sort of sketch she would almost certainly be cast as "air-sick passenger".

With Danny, the great priority was never the words, it was the outfits. When we were going to do a new show, Dan would say "We've got this wonderful number. I'm coming on in this or that and I've got this magnificent picture hat and this big cape . . . . and you're going to be dressed up as a chimney sweep."

And we'd say: "Yes, but what are we actually going to be *saying*, Danny?" and he would reply: "Oh, I don't know, but I know I've got this big hat, these extravagant furs and these amazing gloves . . . ."

But we would all get our turn; we all had a little single to do, and Anne would do a big number, like an impersonation of Shirley Bassey or someone like that. Anne was a really thrilling singer, and she also had this air of being very worldly and confident – which made me hesitate about asking her out, although I really wanted to. A lot of her confidence, I learned later, was a facade. She has always looked so assured when she acts and sings that it is extraordinary to discover that she suffered terrible stage-fright every time before she went on.

At the same time as being the leading lady at the night-club with Danny, Anne was also the leading lady with the Crazy Gang at the Victoria Palace, next to the terminus in London. She would do two shows a night with Flanagan and Allen and Nervo and Knox and Naughton and Gold and "Monsewer" Eddie Gray and then come on to Winston's. Then on Sundays she would do a show at Butlins with members of the Crazy Gang, doing her own act and also acting as "feed" to Eddie Gray, or Bud or one of the others.

Anne always had to be on her toes when she was with the Crazy Gang because you could never tell what they would get up to next. Sometimes, if he thought things were going too smoothly and he was getting a bit bored, Teddy Knox would send out to Overton's the famous fish and oyster restaurant across the street, and order a portion of scampi to be delivered to her onstage while she was appearing in some set-piece, for example, seated at one of the tables in a Western saloon.

Anne's father was Marvin Hart, a light heavyweight boxer until he broke his elbows in a car crash and had to give up. He was a bit of a West End laddie and he would sometimes take friends to see the Crazy Gang, showing off a bit, walking in late and arriving in the middle of the opening or just after the opening. Then Bud would stop the show and say: "Evening Mr Hart. We've got your daughter here. Now say hello to your dad, Anne."

At Winston's if they ever called for customers to come on stage to take part in some silly game, like riding a race on wooden toy horses, you could be pretty sure that Marvin would be among them. After giving up boxing, he dabbled in all sorts of things, making a bit of money and buying big houses which he couldn't quite afford, then he ended up running a printing business in Caterham which did very well.

Anne told me that when she was a child he had a wonderful 1928 Rolls Royce and he used to run her to the local council school in it, with her lying on the floor in the back, hiding. It was one of those embarrassing contrasts – like Marvin having this absolutely splendid Rolls Royce and his wife having no tea towels.

When I first met Anne, she was married to a very nice chap called John Padleigh who was a member of the singing group the Jones Boys, but the marriage wasn't going well and he had moved out of the house she owned in Riggindale Road, in Streatham. The Jones Boys was a very strong vaudeville act; there were quite a number of groups like them at the time – the Bachelors, the Hi Los, the Four Freshmen, and others.

These groups were so good that it sometimes made it hard for the person who was top of the bill to come on and follow them. I think the Jones Boys, like the Bachelors, used to finish with "The Lord's Prayer" or "I Believe" or something like that; some huge number which would bring the house down, and then it was up to the poor comic to come on and try and follow that.

I remember going to see the Hi Los give a concert at the

Gaumont State Theatre, in Kilburn. It was a weird evening, actually. I went with Clive Dunn, who was in the process of getting a divorce. In those days the whole business had to be carefully arranged so that a private detective would surprise the husband with some lady at an hotel. Of course, there wasn't much of a surprise element about it because it had all been arranged, and usually paid for, in advance. Anyway, Clive had found the lady who had agreed to be surprised with him, then he surprised me by bringing her along to the Hi Los concert. Actually, I was very nearly flabbergasted. I think he thought the whole being-caught-in-a-hotel business was a bit of a charmless but necessary hypocrisy – as it was – so he thought he would make it more of a social thing by inviting her to the concert as well. I went along, I suppose to help make the atmosphere easier. Actually, she was a very nice lady and she enjoyed the concert.

Now, I'm nearly getting to the bit where I invited Anne out for the first time. First, I just want to say the Hi Lo's were amazing. They came on stage, two from each side, dressed in their neat cutaway black jackets, their striped trousers and buttoned down shirts and each one of them must have held their note in their head all that time until the applause died down, because they then hit it in a wonderful explosion of close harmony. It was thrilling. Even the private detective who was due to surprise Clive and the lady would have enjoyed it. If he had been there. Which would have been really surprising.

Anyway, one day I summoned the courage at last to ask Anne what she did to fill in the time after the Crazy Gang finished in the evening and the show started at Winston's. She said she usually just went out for a coffee or a bowl of soup somewhere. She was a great friend of Celia Kentone, a member of the singing group The Kentones, so she sometimes went back to her place in Battersea for a snack. So, anyway, I took the plunge and said: "Why not come down and meet me at the Buckstone Club and have an omelette?"

That is where it all started. We got on very well, I was very taken by her and it grew from there. Well, that's not quite right. I wasn't very taken by her, I was totally bowled over. She was – and still is – a stunning looking lady, and I was deeply attracted to her. I had never felt an intense, heart-stopping attraction like this ever before and I knew that this was the real thing.

After that, we used to meet at the Buckstone Club every night. In spite of my hopeless infatuation I was a cautious suitor at first. I was a bit nervous, among other things, that my lack of height might put her off. Anne, you could say, had a great deal of height – five feet and eight inches of it. And being in a precarious profession, I didn't dare commit myself until I was sure I was properly established. A bit of my Scottishness came out there.

Danny was such a success at Winston's that he went on to open his own club in Hanover Square. Danny La Rue's club immediately became a really hot ticket in London. His reputation had gone before him. The new club seated only about 150 and everybody wanted to go there.

For his first season in his new club, Danny took all the cast from Winston's, as well as the writers, but, for some reason, he didn't take Anne or me. Anne was very busy with the Crazy Gang anyway and I didn't seem to be offended at being left behind at Winston's. I don't know *why* I wasn't offended, come to think of it. I think it was probably because I've always wanted to preserve my independence as a performer and I wanted to show that I could manage perfectly well away from Danny and the others.

So I stayed at Winston's and did a show, written by Barry

Cryer and John Junkin, which was not as glamorous as the things we did with Danny, but perhaps was stronger on content and a bit more satirical. There was more of a flavour of intimate revue about it.

One fine day, in 1961, I was driving down Tottenham Court Road, in London, in my Austin Healey Sprite . . . . Before anybody interrupts to say I was going the wrong way down a one way street, I'd just like to say that in those glorious days you could travel up *or* down Tottenham Court Road, as your heart desired. So, I was driving down the road when a taxi overtook me, with a passenger in the back seat waving at me frantically. After a lot more waving, I realised that the frantic passenger was Terry-Thomas.

I pulled into the side of the road and the taxi drew up in front of me. I walked up to the taxi and Terry-Thomas leaned out of the window. "I've just had, dear boy, the most wonderful idea," he said. "I just can't believe how lucky I am to bump into you. How are you, by the way? Jolly good. I'm about to make a film and I've got an idea that there is a part in it for you. Just the thing. It's so fortunate I've met you, dear boy. Here is my number – give me a ring tonight at home." Then he drove off in his taxi.

I was on my way to lunch at a Greek restaurant with Robert Urquhart whom I had known since I had made my first film, *You're Only Young Twice*, so I told him about my momentous bumping-into with Terry-Thomas and I said that it looked as if I was about to get a nice job.

I knew Terry-Thomas from the Star pub and I also knew him through his girlfriend who was a nightclub singer. And a couple of years before he had seen me do my act and paid me an unusual compliment. I was doing a spot in Al Burnett's Stork Club, near Piccadilly Circus, on a Sunday night when young artistes were auditioned and he was in the audience. Afterwards he invited me to join him at his table. Although my material probably wasn't up to much, he said he recognised me as being comic. "It's just the way your feet are placed on the stage," he explained. "It's just the way you stand – there's a comfort in your stance." I think I understand what he was getting at; there was some kind of calmness in the way I worked which started simply with the placement of my feet.

Anyway, not feeling so calm, I telephoned Terry-Thomas that evening, after our encounter in Tottenham Court Road, and he said he had spoken to Robert Day, the director of the film, and Robert Day wanted to see me. By now I was convinced that something really good was being lined up for me; I would be playing Terry-Thomas's brother, or his cousin or his room-mate or his next door neighbour.

So, I was excited when I went to see Robert Day at his office in Wardour Street. "We're making a film called *Operation Snatch*," he said, "and it's about the British occupation of Gibraltar during the war, and about the fable which says that as long as the Barbary apes inhabit the Rock it will remain British territory."

This all sounded very promising and I was waiting eagerly for him to get to the bit about my role in all this.

"So, in this film," Robert Day went on, "in order to convince the Germans that the Rock is well populated with Barbary apes, the authorities are going to dress up small British soldiers as apes."

So that was it. Far from being Terry-Thomas's best friend or brother, I was about to be cast as a little soldier who could dress up as an ape. It almost made me nostalgic for my days in short trousers in *Fun at St Fanny's*. Still, I needed work, so after a bit of hassle about the money, I agreed to take the part.

They cast quite a lot of short people in the film – I remember there was someone from the circus with the exotic name of Bobo Rexano – and we did get a few moments when we could actually remove our artificial heads and speak as human beings. So we weren't apes all the time, but all the same it was a humiliating experience, because actors like James Villiers and Dinsdale Landen were playing captains and majors, while people like Ronnie Corbett were apes. We even had a teacher in movement, who gave us lessons in how to walk and move about like primates.

One day, during a break in filming, we were having a game of football, having first removed our ape heads, but still wearing our skins which were extremely hot, when the assistant director came to call us. He shouted "Apes!" across the football pitch and waved us over to him. This made me get on my high horse. "Excuse me," I said. "I don't answer calls like that. I do not respond to 'ape'. I'd like to be called 'artiste' at least – or, preferably, you can use my name." I suppose the situation made me sensitive – and my ape costume was itching.

I sometimes think I had a narrow escape from being type-cast as an ape. One Monday morning, after I had been appearing in *Sunday Night at the London Palladium* – when Jimmy Tarbuck was compere and was a great support to me, as I have mentioned – I got a mysterious telephone call. It was from Stanley Kubrick's office and they asked me to go along to see him, without saying what it was all about. So I showed up, full of optimism. This was when he was in the early stages of planning his film *2001: A Space Odyssey* which was eventually released in 1968. Stanley Kubrick had seen me in *Sunday Night at the London Palladium* and thought I might make an excellent job playing some sort of role in his film as a part-ape part-human, a primate but one which was capable of laughing and crying.

There were several weeks of arduous tests after this when I

was sent along to try out various kinds of hairy skin costume, some peculiar angora body suits and things like that. After that I was sent to see the man who was head of make-up for MGM at Ealing Studios because they wanted to make a plaster cast of my head. The idea was to create a sort of primate mask which would also fit my head perfectly.

It was a horrible experience. They put two straws up my nostrils so that I could breathe and then they covered my whole face, including my eyes, with warm plastic.

I was given a pencil and pad, so that I could communicate. After they had covered my face like this I had an attack of claustrophobia and I scribbled on the pad: "Take it off, I can't stand it." Then I pulled myself together, crossed that out and wrote "No, it's all right, I'll be patient. Leave it on." Moments later I was scrawling "Get it off!"

After this frightening ordeal I never did get the part in the end, but I can't remember why not, or what happened next. If I had got it, my career might have gone in an entirely different direction. Way out into space probably. With a plum part in *Planet of the Apes*. Actually, I'm extremely grateful that it didn't happen. I have been much happier playing homo fairly sapiens.

After Danny La Rue had been at his new club for a year, Anne and I went to join him. There was a terrific atmosphere. Every night, somebody like Princess Margaret or Nureyev or Noël Coward would be there. There were always parties, with Judy Garland or Barbra Streisand or some huge star. The villains were not welcome.

I remember Princess Margaret arriving one night with a bunch of friends, like Robin Douglas-Home and Jocelyn Stevens, who was then editor of the glossy *Queen* magazine, and her usual gang, and Danny and I were invited to join them at their table. In the course of conversation I pulled a packet of ten cigarettes from my pocket and took one out, and they all found that frightfully amusing. A packet of ten! How quaint! They didn't know such things existed; they only knew about fresh packets of 20, or even bigger boxes which they used to stock up their silver cigarette cases.

Another time I met Princess Margaret in the club, Danny and I had been doing our ballet sketch and I was limping about a bit and all strapped up because I had a badly sprained ankle. Princess Margaret said: "What sort of accident did you have?" I had to make up a pretty glamorous accident on the spot. I think I said: "Fell off my horse, actually," or it might have been: "It's nothing, really. The old wound I got in St Moritz is playing up a bit." The real cause of it was that I slipped on the step going to the outside loo at my house in New Cross, but I didn't think she would understand what kind of accident that was.

One friendship I made in my days at Winston's and Danny's which has lasted ever since was with Simon Parker-Bowles (the brother of Andrew Parker-Bowles) who when I first met him was in the Guards and a very good customer at the nightclubs. I am now godfather to his youngest son, Sam. Throughout the years he's been a sort of social counsellor to me, a good friend, who has invited Anne and me to very smart places and has always done everything to make us feel at ease.

At Danny's club, the show would finish at about 2 a.m. but often we would stay on and Danny would talk – generally about the show or about plans for a new show or about show business, because this was his whole life and he put everything into it. Then we would all have fried egg, bacon and chips from the kitchens – the chef was always very kind.

Noël Coward came to see the show at Danny's club. We were doing a special Coward finale, so he probably thought he had to come and check up on us. I was singing "Poor Uncle Harry" and Anne did "I'll See You Again" and "Mad About the

Boy". This must have been in 1965 because Noël had just come from seeing John Osborne's play *A Patriot for Me* at the Royal Court theatre and he hadn't enjoyed it very much. The new playwrights were producing a lot of hairy stuff which wasn't really his cup of tea and I think he felt rather out of fashion – needlessly as it turned out, as today, he is as popular as ever. He came round to the dressing rooms afterwards and was friendly, urbane witty and charming – everything you would expect him to be, and more. Just as he had been when Helena Pickard had taken me to see him perform in cabaret at the Café de Paris all those years ago and he had come to talk to us afterwards.

Danny was – and is – a wonderful performer and has always looked fabulous. He is a very handsome man and a very beautiful lady – theatrical, stylish and classy. The business is his entire life; he thinks about it all the time. It must be a huge effort to keep up his work schedule, touring and moving all his outfits and everything from place to place, yet he always seems fresh and bubbly. He's also a very kindly good soul, and godfather to our daughter Emma who was born in 1967.

Acting is really physical, almost a branch of athletics. It is all about stamina, "physicality" and fitness. People sometimes think of it as being a rather arty, emotional exercise, but it is even more a matter of energy, adrenaline and concentration. I think about Dan and the astonishing stamina he has, not just for performing, but for *preparing* to perform. Even the process of putting on his make-up is demanding; he has always been patient, meticulous and exacting and he has never done it in a slapdash way. When you just think of the wigs he has to use in one night and all the careful fixing them in place with spirit gum, you just have to marvel at the trouble involved. Then there is the actual weight of all those magnificent gowns he wears. Here he is, past 70, and he will still go on stage and do eight or nine changes a night in his show. That is real strength.

Anne knew him at Churchill's when he was also a window dresser in Regent Street. He "fed" a wonderful comedian called Ted Gatty and he played his extremely beautiful, glamorous, stupid assistant. His real name was Danny Carroll. He went to do a revue with Ted Gatty at the Irving Theatre and he saw this big sign up outside the theatre saying "Danny La Rue". He asked: "Who's that?" And Ted said: "That's you."

Anne really found her niche in 1962 when she was cast to play Dorothy in *Gentlemen Prefer Blondes* with Dora Bryan at the Shaftesbury Theatre. She was sensational in it, the role was made for her and she loved it. She was brilliant with the Crazy Gang and in the show at Winston's and Danny's, but this was her true métier, this was where she really belonged.

It was at this time that our romance really started in earnest, when Alyn Ainsworth, the musical director of *Gentlemen Prefer Blondes*, gave a New Year's Eve party.

As a result of *Blondes*, she was offered a tour of New Zealand as Annie in *Annie Get Your Gun*. She still has a programme which lists the names of the members of the New Zealand Amateur Operatic Society who were in the chorus of the show and among them is Kiri Te Kanawa.

Anne really was a thrilling singer – and she still is. Just recently we were sent a cutting from *The New York Times* Book Review where there was a notice of a book about Broadway musicals, discussing people like Ethel Merman and Mary Martin and Howard Keel. The book, apparently, refers to Marilyn Monroe "the world's most magnificent woman" who is rivalled only by "the spectacular Anne Hart". I'm sure that Anne could have been a huge star if she had not chosen to devote her life to the family and our girls, Emma and Sophie.

★

Back to our courtship. Anne was in New Zealand for six months and, while she was away, a tremendous correspondence went on between us. I think the separation, and all those letters, confirmed even more strongly what we had begun to feel about each other. When she came back the romance continued. After that, she was offered a tour of Australia with *Annie Get Your Gun* for a shorter season, and the letter writing resumed.

Eventually we got married in 1965, on May 30th at Brixton Register Office, with just our mums and dads and two witnesses present. Then we went back to Anne's house in Riggindale Road for champagne and sandwiches and returned to Danny's club for the show that night.

I was still doing other work as well as the show at Danny La Rue's. About this time I got a part in the film *Casino Royale,* the James Bond spoof. Absolutely everybody was in it, from David Niven to Orson Welles, from Deborah Kerr to Ursula Andress, not to mention Peter Sellers, Woody Allen, Peter O'Toole, Jean-Paul Belmondo and many others who would also probably rather you didn't mention it. I played the part of Polo, a nasty, Peter Lorre type of villain who was battery-operated.

Most of the critics described it as the sort of wacky extravaganza where the audience has much less fun than the cast did when they were making it. One of the kindest comments came from Donald Zec who called it "The worst film I ever enjoyed". I spent six weeks doing my bit in *Casino Royale*. I would get home from the studio at about six o'clock in the evening, go to sleep for four hours, then go to the night-club, get back from there at about two in the morning, then sleep for another four hours before going to the film studios. Whenever Anne woke me up I would ask : "Is this for the night-club or the film?"

★

Some time after Anne and I were married, my mother and father came to the club to see the show. Danny made a tremendous fuss of them, gave them champagne and put them at the best table. After the show, when they were being entertained by Danny, my father turned to him and said in his Scottish way, "You're wasting your time here, son."

Of course in this exotic company my dad was just way out of his depth – although he didn't think he was – and he got very excited and nervous. He was not used to the ambience, let alone to meeting an exotic flower like Danny, and he was actually trying to pay him a compliment, meaning that, with his talents, he should really be in a bigger and more glorious place than this little jewel box of a club.

As I became more successful my mum and dad used to come down occasionally to stay with us. They usually drove down from Edinburgh which made my mum nervous, because of my dad's diabetes, although he was so good at balancing his insulin he only ever had two hyperglycaemic attacks in his life.

In the days before Chinatown had grown up in Soho, we took my parents for a Chinese meal in the East End, to the Old Friends which was the place to go to at the time. It was up some narrow stairs in a poky little house in Limehouse, but the food was marvellous. The place was a shock to my father's system. "Dearie me," he kept saying. "What kind of place is this? Dearie me." Then the food came up and he realised how tasty it was and he scoffed all of ours.

On another occasion we went to another East End Chinese restaurant, to the Young Friends, and this was the only time I ever saw him have a hyperglaecemic attack. This time he misjudged his insulin and it was made worse by the fact that there was a delay in the food coming to the table. He went outside for some fresh air and collapsed in the gutter and split his head open. Of course, mother and I didn't know about this and we were just waiting for him to come back to the table. We went out to look for him and found that he had wandered into a pub, bleeding, and the man behind the bar was treating him as if he was drunk. We got him to a hospital in Plumstead where they patched him up and said they would keep him in for the night.

I drove my mother back to Norwood, in South London, where we were living at the time, and, as we got into the house, the telephone was ringing. We immediately thought my dad had taken a turn for the worse, but it was him on the phone. "I'm not staying here the night," he announced, so we had to drive all the way back to Plumstead and bring him home, all bandaged up and rather sheepish.

My dad always called me Ronald. He was not the sort of person to show he was impressed by things, but it didn't matter to me, because I just knew that he was pleased I was doing well and everything was, as he would put it, "on the right footing". And he adored Anne. My mum was very proud of everything I did and probably showed off to everyone.

Anne and I had a little boy called Andrew who was born in April 1966, but, very sadly, we lost him when he was still a very young baby. He had a serious heart defect, which nowadays the doctors might possibly be able to do something about. He had several holes in his heart and it was also on the wrong side. Andrew was born in St George's hospital, in Tooting, in South London; it was clear that something was wrong with the little soul and they took him to St George's hospital at Hyde Park Corner to monitor his progress. After that they let him come back to our home in Upper Norwood, but it was clear that he was struggling. It was an awful time. I was going to the club at night, desperately trying to concentrate on my work and thinking all the time of poor Anne and the baby. You just don't know how you can carry on at times like these, but somehow you do. That's the tradition is our business; sometimes it sounds corny and sometimes it seems callous, but you steel yourself. It wasn't easy telling other people what was happening.

Anne was being supported at home by her sister. After a few days, Andrew had to be taken back to hospital and operated on, but it was no good. He died when he was six weeks old. I still think about him a lot; by now he would have been a young man in his thirties.

Anne had worked at Danny La Rue's club right up to Andrew's birth, and, after his death, she went back, but only for a short time. Our first daughter Emma was born the following April and then, neatly, Sophie arrived the April after that, in 1968. Thank God they were both all right. The dreadful experience with Andrew made Anne a very protective mother and she decided to give up her very successful full-time career and concentrate on bringing up the children.

Anne didn't just give up a very promising career, she also set aside a remarkable talent. I can appreciate what she sacrificed every time she sings today; she just thrills the room, because she has such a sensational voice. As well as being a caring mum to the girls, Anne has made a tremendous contribution to my life as a very supportive wife.

Having worked with all the great comedians of her day, like the wondrous Max Wall, the quick-witted cockney, Tommy Trinder, the popular Derek Roy and with the Crazy Gang, of course, she is a good and sound judge of what is funny and has all-round appeal. She can sniff out anything that is rarefied or chi-chi, so she can be a terrific help to me. We have had a very, very happy and wonderful life together.

Almost from the day Anne and I got together my life changed entirely and my fortunes turned. I was with her in her house in Riggindale Road, during our courtship, when I got the phone call from Joan Littlewood asking me to be in *Twang!*, and although that show did not turn out so well, things were different for me from that day on. She has been the cornerstone of my life for all these years – in a business where there aren't many cornerstones.

Every so often, Anne has been tempted out of retirement to perform again – mostly with me, but once in an amazing double act with Max Wall when he was doing his famous Professor Wallofsky sketch and recklessly abandoning the script and making it all up as he went along. I have a videotape of it and it's a perfect example of how Anne could remain cool on stage under a heavy barrage of ad-libs. She obviously learned it from her days with the Crazy Gang.

In the shows at Winston's and then at Danny La Rue's own club, I used to play the hero to Danny's heroines. So I was Nureyev to his Fonteyn, for example, and Pinkerton to his Butterfly. So you had this big, tall glamorous, beautiful woman with me as this little busy bee of a hero buzzing round her.

So, naturally enough, my Shakespearean debut was as Othello to Danny La Rue's Desdemona, though it certainly was not a version that would be familiar to the two stately ladies who made me recite Shakespeare at the Glover Turner Robertson School in George Street, Edinburgh.

My friend the actor Robert Lang whom I had first met in the days I was working in the Buckstone Club had just taken over the role of Iago to Olivier's Othello and he gave tickets to Anne and me to see his performance.

After the play we went to supper with Robert at Chez Solange, a restaurant which a lot of actors went to, just round the corner from Wyndham's Theatre. Robert said Olivier might join us and sure enough he did. It was a spellbinding evening with wonderful conversation about acting and about memorable performances and then, to my horror, Robert turned to Olivier and said: "Shall we all go on to the club?" I thought "Oh God, please let him say no."

To my immense relief, Olivier said he was a bit too tired, but anyway, he and Robert Lang drove Anne and me to the club and dropped us off there. Little did they know what was going on inside and what disgraceful things Dan and I were doing to Shakespeare's play.

CHAPTER SEVEN

In which I have parts on two London musicals 'The Boys from Syracuse' and 'Twang!'. Other subjects also intrude, such as the story of the tightrope walker who persuades me to buy a house in New Cross where I find hidden treasure. I mention my agents. And my bank manager has a small walk-on part in this story.

In 1963 I was in a summer show at the Aquarium in Great Yarmouth with Jimmy Savile and Helen Shapiro. It was one of the worst shows I have ever been in. They actually decided to call in Cedric of the Monarchs – the harmonica-playing comedy trio – to nelly up my sketches. Cedric (whose real name was Les Henry) played the idiot of the group, the camp one, putting on a weird voice and lugubrious expression. He was a very nice chap, actually. We met again in a pantomime together in Newcastle a few years later and he was a very good Baron Hardup.

I had come to do the show with material which was really a bit too much like light revue, sophisticated sketch material, more suited to *Pieces of Eight* or to *The Lyric Revue,* where the audience had gin and tonic in the interval, rather than to Yarmouth where the audience came in to shelter from the wind.

The Monarchs were at the theatre across the road and someone from the management rang up Cedric and said: "I wonder if you could make these sketches a bit coarser than they are; you know, rough them up a bit." So Cedric came across the road and roughened up the material. I remember there was a sketch which was a parody of the "Beat the Clock" game on the television show *Sunday Night at the London Palladium*. It was a variety show with very high ratings and the "Beat the Clock" section was, I suppose, the beginning of the audience participation idea on TV. Members of the public came on stage to take part in the game and to be teased, cajoled and embarrassed by Bruce Forsyth – who has been doing it ever since.

I am a huge fan of Bruce Forsyth, actually. He is an amazingly energetic and spontaneous performer who can establish a wonderful rapport with the audience and he is a brilliant, piano player, dancer and singer. And he only needs the lightest excuse to perform. I used to say that when you ring him up, the answering machine message you hear is: "Please leave your name and number after my song."

I remember going to see Bruce once when he was playing Buttons in *Cinderella* and in the kitchen scene Cinderella was silly enough to say: "If only one of us could sing or dance or play the piano." The next time you saw her you had completely forgotten who she was.

While I was doing that summer season in Great Yarmouth in 1963 I was living in a flat in Caister and I got to know Brian and Julie Dewhurst who were very dear friends of Anne's from the days when she worked with Tommy Trinder. Brian was working in the circus at the Windmill theatre in Yarmouth and he and Julie were living in a caravan on the racecourse, on the seafront, and they had one of those glamorous low-slung Citroen cars to tow it.

Brian was a wire walker and his stage name was the "Boy Andro". He was very skilful and he did a comic, rather balletic wire act, juggling as he went along and doing little tricks, like rolling his hat down his forearm.

Julie was also in the circus business; she had a wonderful soprano singing voice and she used to do an act with her father, Max, who was a circus strong-man. Max would lie on his back and hold up one hand to balance Julie who was doing a one-handed hand-stand. (I hope you are getting the picture here. Try to hold on to it.) Then, very gradually, inch by tottering inch, Max would get up, still supporting Julie on his hand, until at last he was standing upright. And all the time this was going on, Julie, upside down and in her lovely soprano voice, was singing "Oh Mein Papa".

Brian and Julie had a son and a daughter who both became great acrobats. They live and work in Los Angeles where there is much more scope for circus work, and the son, Nicky, is with the Cirque Soleil. Brian is with them, but Julie sadly died of cancer.

The point of bringing Brian (or the Boy Andro) into the story is that, while were in Yarmouth together, he was the person whose advice led me to buying my first house. "Instead of living in a rented flat in Camden Town when you are in London you ought to borrow some money and buy a house," he told me. "Down our way, in New Cross, you can get a large semi-detached Victorian villa for about £4,000." So, really, he changed my way of thinking. For a wire walker, he had his feet on the ground.

It was while I was appearing in this summer show that I went to London to audition for *The Boys from Syracuse* which Christopher Hewett was directing at the Drury Lane Theatre. In fact I went to London several times for several auditions because they kept calling me back. The show was the Richard Rodgers musical based on Shakespeare's *Comedy of Errors*, with the two Antipholus twin brothers and their twin servants, both named Dromio.

Christopher Hewett had asked me to audition for the part because he had seen me do a bit in a charity show and had liked it. That was at a time when I was just making a start and performing on my own. At this charity show, I did a sketch that I had written myself – with some help from Roy Castle – about a conversation between the doves in a magician's pockets.

I was thinking about Channing Pollack, a wonderfully handsome performer who used to come on stage in his immaculate white tie and tails, didn't say a word and just produced about 32 doves from various parts of his suit. The act lasted about 12 minutes and he worked all over the world and was paid a fortune. When Channing Pollack decided to give up being a magician and go in for a career in films in Europe, he handed over his doves to his chauffeur who then appeared in variety as "Franklin and His Doves." I wonder if he went on wearing his chauffeur's cap and gloves for his act. Anyway, I think it was a nice gesture on Channing Pollack's part. Maybe the chauffeur didn't. Maybe, as he stood on the stage, plucking doves from about his person, he thought to himself: "Damn birds! If he'd left me the car I could have run my own taxi service."

In my solo spot, I simply imagined a conversation between these well travelled doves, crammed into Channing Pollack's suit:

"Dark, isn't it?"

"What sort of audience have we got in tonight?"

"Not up to much. Hardly worth getting out of these trousers for them."

"It's all right for you; I'm in the armpit again. It says in my contract, 'No armpit.' I'm telling my agent about this."

"Oh oh, I'm next one out. Are my feathers straight?"

"Lovely. Break a leg, darling."

"Byee. See you in the dovecote later."

"Ah, thank God, she's gone."

"Ghastly creature. Always boasting about her cousin who is supposed to be some champion racing pigeon."

"Hey, there's somebody in this inside pocket with me. I can't see in the dark. Who's there? Is that you Ambrose? Oh no, it's just the man's wallet."

"Right, it's time for me to go. Glad to be out of this waistcoat at last."

"Ciao, baby."

"God, I wish the man would get on with it. I'm *dying* to lay an egg."

"So much for the glamour of showbusiness."

Anyway, after the last audition when I learned that I had got the part of one of the Dromios and I was on the train back to Great Yarmouth and the summer show, I was really excited, because this was going to be my first proper part in the West End. I found myself sharing a compartment with a chap whose face I recognised and it turned out to be Anthony Fell, who was the MP for Yarmouth, on his way back to his constituency. He was very pleased to hear I had got the part at the Drury Lane theatre and we went along to the buffet car to celebrate.

As the journey went on and Mr Fell congratulated me a few more times on getting the part, and I congratulated him a few more times for getting elected, it suddenly dawned on me that I had had a few celebratory drinks too many. Let's face it, I was feeling seriously drunk, and, the problem was, I still had two shows to do when I got off the train. I had to wobble and lurch down the corridor to the end of the carriage, stand outside the loo and stick my head out of the window and hope that the fresh air would sober me up before I reached my destination.

Fortunately, fresh air is one of the regional specialities of East Anglia; I think they get it from Siberia. The treatment just about worked and I survived the evening performances.

It wasn't until years later that I learned Ronnie Barker had gone for the same Dromio part in *The Boys from Syracuse*. They were looking for pairs, so they would have cast Ronnie with a similar sized person. I think it was Peter Woodthorpe. My fellow Dromio was the Shakespearean actor, Henry Woolf and the two Antipholus parts were played by Bob Monkhouse and Denis Quilley.

It was a bit sad, because, during the rehearsal period poor old Henry Woolf got the push. I didn't think he was at all bad in the part actually, but maybe they thought he wasn't "vaudevillian" enough. Anyway, he just went one lunchtime. We all broke for lunch and when we came back there was a different Dromio there. He was Sonny Farrar.

Sonny was the same size as me, but much older. He was a vaudeville act, a concert party artiste. I always remember he would come to the theatre in the evening via Mooney's Irish House, a long narrow bar with a kind of shabby elegance about it, which used to be in the Strand, next to the Vaudeville Theatre, and he would arrive with a little touch of Guinness on his breath and his little felt hat on his head.

The Boys from Syracuse was a wonderful show, full of fabulous songs and Richard Rodgers was there for all the rehearsals. Before the opening, all the artistes had to go one by one into a theatre and sing their numbers just for him. I remember going into the Shaftesbury theatre and seeing him seated elegantly on a bentwood chair listening as I went through my songs. When the show was running, he was always supportive, turning up every night, coming backstage, talking to us all and saying "It's going really well. They audience are really loving it."

★

During the run of *The Boys from Syracuse* at the Drury Lane, the theatre held a special gala matinee in aid of the Royal Ballet. It was a dazzling occasion, the sort of occasion, where, if you turn your head too quickly to give a suave wave to a fellow millionaire, the flashing of all the diamonds makes you giddy and you fall into the lap of a marchioness.

Everybody showed up and there were a lot of tremendously grand items in the show, with pieces of ballet and excerpts from opera. I remember reading the programme and seeing that Rudolf Nureyev and Margot Fonteyn would be dancing the *pas de deux* from so-and-so and then later Mirella Freni and Tito Gobbi would be singing the duet from such-and-such; then between these two acts was: "Sonny Farrar – Five Foot of Fun and a Banjo."

Just before the opening of *The Boys from Syracuse* I remembered the advice of Brian, the wise wire walker, and made an appointment to go and see my bank manager at Barclays in Camden Town. When I entered his office he said: "Actually, there is another Mr R. Corbett who is a customer of this branch and when you rang up to make an appointment I thought you were him."

Anyway, he let me stay, so I explained to him that I had got a job at the Drury Lane theatre. "And, as you know," I said to him, "shows at Drury Lane last a good long time. You will recall, I am sure, that *My Fair Lady* ran for three years and *Plain and Fancy* went on for two years. So I would like to borrow some money to buy a house in New Cross for £4,500 and then I would rent out three bedsits in it for a total of £19 a week."

So, even though I was the wrong Mr Corbett, the manager agreed to lend me £4,000 and I walked out into Camden Town feeling quite cheerful – and *The Boys from Syracuse* closed after six weeks. I went ahead anyway and bought the house in Pepys

Road, New Cross, in South London, with the £4,000 loan from the bank and £500 from my dad. By this time, Max had retired as a circus strong-man and bought himself a furniture van and fitted it out with shelves so that he could sell fruit and veg in the New Cross area, and he helped me move my stuff from the flat in Camden Town in his van.

Anne came and helped me get the house organised and we found £130 in £1 notes under the linoleum on the stairs. An excellent moving-in present.

I kept that house until shortly after I got married in 1965 when I sold it for £13,000 and bought a huge, red-brick Victorian house in Upper Norwood for £7,300 – plus £1,000 for the work that needed doing to it. It was in an architectural style you might call grandiose-eerie and the Addams family would call cosy. We stayed there until 1971 when I bought my present house, next to the golf course, in Addington, in Surrey. Since then we have stayed put.

It was a great shame about *The Boys from Syracuse*, because it was a lovely show, with some wonderful songs by Richard Rodgers and Lorenz Hart. The trouble was that the Drury Lane theatre was too big for the show and the actual book, or libretto, by the legendary Broadway director George Abbott, was in my view tired and out of date.

My agent, at the very beginning of my career when I came to London in 1951, was Jimmy Grafton. He looked after a lot of performers like Spike Milligan, Tony Hancock, Harry Secombe and Peter Sellers after they came out of the forces at the end of the war. He was a witty, urbane sort of fellow who also wrote scripts for the comedian Dickie Henderson and for *The Billy Cotton Band Show* on television and on the wireless – in the days of *The Billy Cotton Band Show,* we called it the wireless, not the radio.

Jimmy ran a pub called the Grafton Arms, in Strutton Ground, near Victoria, and he conducted his business as an agent in an office at the top of the building. He was very good to me and sometimes when I was out of work he would give me a job in the office or serving behind the bar in the pub. There was another struggling actor who worked as office boy for Jimmy and lived for a while in a room above the pub. He sometimes played small parts on television and if it was live television he would dash back from the BBC at Shepherd's Bush as soon as he had done his bit so that he could get into the saloon bar at the Grafton Arms and be recognised and be bought a drink. I think he held the Shepherd's Bush to Victoria all-comers' record. This chap could be difficult at times and after one particularly famous episode, an understandably enraged Jimmy hurled a furry seal paperweight at him which embedded itself in the plasterboard partition.

After a while, in the period when I was working at Winston's in the early 60s, I thought it was time to move on. I had a meal with Jimmy at the Pickwick Club which was a theatrical supper club opened in Great Newport Street, near Leicester Square, by Wolf Mankowitz who wrote the book for the musical *Expresso Bongo*. I told him that I was leaving him because I didn't think he fully understood my potential. As far as I recall, it was all amicable and I always felt close to Jimmy, but my ambition then was still as clear and hard-headed as it had been when I was a teenager in Edinburgh going up the stairs for my first lessons in acting at the Glover Turner Robertson School, in George Street. I still had those high hopes.

My next agent was Norman Casey who told me "I think you could do quite well." At the time I was quite encouraged by this damn faint praise. Norman had been the accountant for Frank Barnard who, as an agent, shared responsibility for Harry Secombe with Jimmy Grafton.

Norman Casey decided to set up on his own and took me on. He was quite enterprising and imaginative and energetic, but our partnership came to an abrupt end over the matter of a chicken curry.

Norman used to act as an impresario and put on Sunday concerts as a showcase for his clients and he asked Anne and me to be in a show he was doing in Scarborough, with Lonnie Donegan at the top of the bill. He said he would put us up for the night, so we went back to his house after the show which had not done very good business.

"Right," he said. "I'll make you a nice bit of supper." This cheered us up until we saw what he was dishing up – a packet of Vesta chicken curry. Bateman, the cartoonist who specialised in depicting outrage at social solecisms, could have done a very good picture of that moment and called it "Man Offers Corbetts Vesta Chicken Curry." The Corbetts declined.

Anne and I returned to London the next day and soon after that Norman and I spoke on the phone.

"I'm very upset about the way you behaved at the weekend," he said.

"What do you mean?"

"I entertained you and offered you all that hospitality and you didn't even offer to pay for the laundry of the sheets."

"Excuse me, Norman," I said. "Would you mind repeating that?"

He repeated it.

"Right," I said, " will you please get all my papers, all the information you have about me, my CV and my photographs and send them all back to me straight away. That is the end of it." And I put the phone down. Quite hard. I think the memory of the packet of curry must have shortened my temper.

In the next week I got a telephone call from Joan Littlewood which changed my life and I often think Norman Casey must have been spitting about it, but after the laundry business and the curry I felt he got his dues.

My next agent was Sonny Zahl who also looked after Danny La Rue. Sonny was a very sweet man and the brother of Hymie Zahl, the legendary agent who had all the Scottish comics of the day sewn up. Sonny told me: "I could imagine that you might eventually be earning £8,000 or even £10,000 a year," which I found encouraging. He didn't say anything about laundry.

It was 1965 and I was working at Winston's at the time and I was at Anne's house in Streatham one afternoon when I got a message that Joan Littlewood, of the Theatre Workshop, in Stratford East, was trying to get in touch with me. Anyway, I got back to her and she said she was doing a show and she would love me to be in it. The music was by Lionel Bart, the design by Oliver Messel, and Paddy Stone was the choreographer.

The pedigree sounded very exciting and I was thrilled to be working with Joan Littlewood. Lionel Bart had already had great successes with *Fings Ain't Wot They Used t' Be* and with *Oliver!* This musical was *Twang!* It was a version of the Robin Hood story and it turned out to be one of the all-time disastrous musicals.

Robin Hood was played by Jimmy Booth, who had been the leading cockney spiv in *Fings,* Toni Eden was Maid Marian, Barbara Windsor was also in it, Bernard Bresslaw was Little John and I was Will Scarlett. As it turned out, I found that Joan Littlewood's way of working did not suit me so much, but perhaps she was finding it stressful because the material was not what she hoped it would be.

The opening in Manchester was a disaster and the critics said so – and so did a few members of the audience who shouted abuse from the stalls. Anne was there for the first night and was actually reduced to tears. We then came down to London, to the Shaftesbury theatre and tried to get it right. Poor old Lionel kept being asked to re-write sections and re-do songs.

It's an odd situation when you find yourself in a stinker, wondering if everybody is going to keep up a pretence of cheerfulness and optimism, not knowing if others are aware that it is a stinker. Some friends decide they are going to pretend they haven't read to the reviews; others treat you as if you have an enormous boil or your nose and they are not going to mention it.

Of course, if you have a really good part you may not see the stinky quality of the whole show. That is how it was with *Twang!* Those with good parts remained cheerful and optimistic.

And, of course Joan Littlewood did have a very loyal and trusting following – which she had earned with her achievements such as *Oh, What a Lovely War!* So she had this group of followers from Stratford East who she called her "nuts" and they followed her through fire and whatever. They believed in her methods of working and there was this feeling among them that she was bringing her team in to conquer the West End.

Bernard Bresslaw and I were not Joan's nuts and we didn't have particularly good parts in the show, so we were not such merry men, finding ourselves in the stinker, hanging around in the background, just hoping we were wrong about it. We were like peasants who had been called in to see the Sheriff of Nottingham on one of his bad days and still vaguely hoping things would turn out all right.

Perhaps when I said that Joan's methods did not really suit me, I should actually say my methods did not suit her. She probably thought me a bit facile, because I was able to turn on a performance quite comfortably and easily. This was the result of my training at Winston's. Joan may have thought things came to me too readily and without enough trouble and torment. I presented a facade which was presentable and watchable, but did it have enough depth?

Did I know where this character, Will Scarlett, had come from and where he was born? What motivated him? Did I know who his mother and father were? What did his nephew's chihuahua have for tea? Was he in a stable relationship with his longbow? What on earth did I think I was doing, just looking at the text and going out and trying to make something of it?

Joan wanted to see us at rehearsal groping for something. Groping for each other actually. We would be rehearsing at the Shaftesbury theatre and all the lights would be turned out and we would have to feel for each other in the dark, touch each other and see who it was. Sometimes the lights would be turned out and we would have to hide somewhere on the stage and someone would have to come and find us.

She wanted to get the company spirit going and make us feel we knew each other better than we really did. It was supposed to be a way of breaking down barriers.

People used to joke, in the early stages of rehearsal, that with Joan Littlewood you daren't go to the lavatory at the wrong time because when you got back you would find your part had disappeared. While you were away, some more talkative and imaginative actor, doing the improvisation, would say: "I know, why don't we put all these three roles together and I could play them?" Then you would come back and say "Hey, where's my part gone?"

I can remember one jolly moment from the rehearsals and that was when Paddy Stone, the choreographer, was trying to get the dancers and Robin Hood's merry men to hide behind trees in the forest. "For God's sake!" he suddenly shouted. "Hide where I can *see* you!"

129

Joan would sometimes take us by surprise saying something like "You are Adolf Hitler's tailor and you're coming to see him because you're making him three suits for a big parade. Now I want you to play the scene out." If somebody was talkative enough he would go on for absolutely ages about it, leaving the Lincoln green outfits of the Merry Men of Sherwood Forest miles behind.

On other occasions, Joan would have some thought that, for example, Robin Hood wanted to cook the breakfast in Sherwood Forest and we would all have to gather round and improvise a breakfast scene. Many people, like the director Mike Leigh, do this sort of thing very successfully, but with a musical there are so many things that you have got to get exactly right that I really don't believe that this way of working is appropriate.

Actually, it always rather alarms me when a lot of people gather round a written text and, in some way, set about trying to give it extra energy. The same sort of thing happened years later, in 1997, with the film *Fierce Creatures* which starred John Cleese, and in which I had a part as a zoo keeper. It was one of those films that are over-revised and it didn't really come off.

I like things to be more ordered. It always frightens me when people are trying to get more out of something than actually appears on paper. I know the actor's performance heightens what is written down, but sometimes people try to froth up a text beyond its actual capacity. It's like adding too much oil too quickly to a mayonnaise that can't take it.

Or, to change the metaphor, if a tailor, even Hitler's tailor, cuts the cloth for the jacket wrongly in the first place, there is hardly ever any chance, whatever you do, that you are going to get that jacket right. You just have to start all over again.

Before the London opening of *Twang!* Joan sort of half left the project. It was then that I saw what I thought was this strange contrast in her. She was running this great socialist people's theatre in the East End and at the same time traipsing around with Tom Driberg, the scandalous, gay Labour MP, and drinking pink champagne. I felt it was all a camp left wing sort of thing. I remember Tom Driberg one day had a birthday "wake" in Regents Park and we were all there at dawn, drinking pink champagne.

Anyway, there was some sort of row over *Twang!* And Joan apparently walked out in a huff. She did not return to the East End, but instead she set herself up in some style in a suite at the Savoy. She was later seen coming out of the hotel. Wearing her black beret looking a little like a belligerent barmaid who is on the point of throwing someone out of the pub, and carrying a beige folder under one arm. And on this folder, prominently scrawled in thick black felt-tip pen were the immortal words: "Lionel's final fuck-up". This must have been the re-worked script – and what she thought of it.

Bernard Delfont, the impresario, did all he could to rescue the show. He called in Burt Shevelove to re-direct it and pull the book together. He had come over from America where he had just had a big success with *A Funny Thing Happened to Me on the Way to the Forum* and it was a real treat to work with him and to see a great Broadway director operating. He would be on the telephone all night to writers in America and then he would arrive at the theatre in the morning with sheaves of Robin Hood jokes and great piles of Sherwood Forest gags. But he couldn't breathe life into *Twang!* It just would not work. It survived for about six weeks.

Before the rehearsals for *Twang!* had even started, David Frost took me to tea at the Ritz. This, by now, was David's sort of *milieu*; he liked a good *milieu* and a decent cucumber sandwich. He told me that he wanted me to join him in a new television series he was making. It sounded very exciting and I really wanted to do it, but I explained that there was a big problem: I had already been signed up by Robin Hood and I wouldn't be able to combine appearances in the musical with rehearsals and live broadcasts of the TV show. When *Twang!* went phut after six weeks it changed the whole picture. I was now free to become one of David Frost's merry men.

CHAPTER EIGHT

This is the one in which I first get to work with Ronnie Barker on 'The Frost Report' and John Cleese looms over me for the first time. After this, Ron and I move to 'Frost on Sunday' and we encounter the mysterious Gerald Wiley. A contretemps with Ronnie Barker is cleared up. We move back to the BBC and launch 'The Two Ronnies'.

When David Frost and I sat down to tea at the Ritz he explained that he was going to do a live show on BBC Television on Thursday nights and it would go out immediately after the News. It was a move away from the pure satire of *That Was the Week That Was* to something more general and it was going to be called *The Frost Report*.

As I have mentioned, at the time David was outlining his plans to me over the Earl Grey, I was committed to Joan Littlewood and *Twang!* and, although I loved his ideas, I knew I couldn't be part of them. It was like being shown a slice of delicious glistening fruit cake and then having the Ritz waiter whisk it away before you could reach for it. Now the musical had closed and I could have a second bite of the cherry cake, so to speak.

If *Twang!* had been a hit and had a long run my career might have gone in a different direction. It might have been even better. Who knows? Longfellow wrote:

> I shot an arrow in the air,
> It fell to earth, I know not where.

My arrow misfired, but it landed conveniently on David Frost's head.

None of the people from *TW3* was to be in *The Frost Report*, apart from David, of course, who would front it. The sketches were to be performed by three people. The first was a newcomer called John Cleese, who had very quickly made his name in the Cambridge Footlights and was at this time in Canada with a University show, *Second City Revue*. The second was Ronnie Barker, an actor I vaguely knew. And the third one was me. Julie Felix, the folk-singer, would play the guitar and do the songs.

This show turned out to be a very happy turning point for me and led to me working with a whole lot of new performers. This is when I met the people who were to go on to create *Monty Python's Flying Circus*. Graham Chapman, Michael Palin, Terry Jones and Eric Idle all wrote sketches for *The Frost Report*, as well as Barry Took, Barry Cryer, Marty Feldman and Tim Brooke-Taylor. Programmes like *Do Not Adjust Your Set* and *At Last the 1948 Show* also grew out of *The Frost Report*.

As a show business professional, I belonged to a different breed from the university revue types I was now working with, but I didn't feel uncomfortable or out of place. At Danny La Rue's night-club, Barry Cryer and I, who were kindred spirits, had already been doing a good deal of what you might call satirical material and I found this new programme a lot of fun and very refreshing.

This was the first time I worked with Ronnie Barker, although I had met him on a few occasions when he had come into the Buckstone Club and I was working behind the bar, so we were on nodding and smiling and "same again" terms.

When I first used to see him in the club he was already doing well as a character actor in the West End – among other parts he played one of the French gangsters, in the musical *Irma La Douce*. He was also doing a lot of radio shows, including *The Navy Lark*. His wife Joy was a busy stage manager.

Our early meetings, working on *The Frost Report,* were in a rehearsal room above a pub off the Earls Court Road. Soon after that, we moved and got the show ready in a church hall in Crawford Street. I have to say our first encounter in Earls Court was a low key occasion; the earth didn't actually move when we started to rehearse together. Neither of us felt that we had just met the Ron with whom we were going to spend a large part of the rest of our professional lives. Momentous occasions can pass unnoticed at the time – which can be tough for autobiographers. There was not even much fraternising in the pub afterwards, because Ron was a family man and keen to get home to his wife and children.

All the same, there was very soon a kind of bond between us, because our careers seemed to have run so much on parallel lines. We were both born in important university cities, but neither of us made it to the university; he was born in Oxford and I was born in Edinburgh. He started out working in a bank; I started out working in the civil service; both of us had been looking for a way to escape from these jobs. Ronnie went to Amersham rep; I went to perform in little concert parties.

By the time we arrived for our first script meeting for *The Frost Report,* Ronnie was 36 and I was 35, so we had both had a good deal of experience – Ronnie's in the theatre and radio and some television, and mine in summer seasons and night-clubs and also some television. It was the beginning of a long and easy friendship. Our wives, Joy and Anne, got on well together right away and still do, and we found that the whole shape of our lives has been very similar.

The difference between Ronnie and me is that he is not at all an outdoor or sporty type, whereas I am. We are both interested in food, but in different ways. Ron loves his grub, but he usually goes for the plainer stuff. In the days when we were working on *The Two Ronnies* I used to say that our partnership worked so well, because Ron would write the material and I would queue for the lunch.

When we were filming *The Two Ronnies* on location, we did it in some style; we had a caravan and we each had a dresser to help with our costumes. Ron's was called Derek and mine was called Denis. When Derek brought Ron his lunch it used to come in relays. There would be a series of deliveries. The salad delivery would be followed by the risotto with sauté potatoes delivery. After this came the apple crumble with custard and ice cream delivery.

Meanwhile my lunch would consist of salad, with a little bit of avocado perhaps and maybe a wee touch of mozzarella. And, oh all right, just a couple of tomatoes and, if pressed, a few cherries. Ron wolfed; I nibbled.

Geoff Lewis, the National Hunt jockey and a friend of ours, once said that Ronnie Barker's lunch looked like something Arkle couldn't jump. My lunch, I always like to think, looked more like a Hockney painting.

After that little gastronomic diversion, we can go back to St Mary's Church Hall, in Crawford Street, London in 1966 where we prepared *The Frost Report* every week.

Each programme would have a theme – like the Law, or

Public Schools, Leisure or Trends. Tony Jay (subsequently the creator of *Yes, Minister*) would write an essay on the theme which would be distributed to the writers who contributed to the show – as many as 16 of them. David's introductory monologue would follow Tony Jay's essay and the writers would then offer sketches on different aspects of the theme; the producer then chose about half of them for John Cleese, Ronnie Barker and myself to rehearse.

The combination of the three of us worked very well. John often played the manic, pop-eyed authority figure, while Ron, with all his experience as a character actor could do all the voices and the accents, and I was the cut-down version, doing some of the voices and some of the accents. I remember one sketch, written by John Cleese and Graham Chapman, was about the planning of D-Day, with me as the Field Marshal, Ronnie B as the Admiral and John as the Air Chief Marshal. I had chosen the invasion of France to take place on Sunday – because it was my birthday. The Admiral couldn't make it on Sunday because he had people coming over for dinner and he had put them off twice already. So we made it Friday. The Air Chief Marshal said that was OK because he was free on Friday afternoon . . . And so it went on. The Monty Python flavour was already discernible. John Cleese and Graham Chapman nearly always wrote as a team, Michael Palin and Terry Jones worked together, while Eric Idle tended to write on his own.

I suppose the sketch that most people remember from *The Frost Report* is the one on Class, written by John Law, where the three of us stand at attention in a row in descending order of height, from left to right, with John wearing a bowler hat and City suit and carrying a rolled umbrella, Ronnie B in a trilby, and then me in a cloth cap and muffler. We all speak our lines in slow, formal, explanatory voices, and when we need to indicate who we are talking about we give a sort of curt nod in his direction.

JC: I look down on him (*indicating RB*) because I am upper class.

RB: I look up to him (*indicating JC*) because he is upper class. But I look down on him (*indicating RC*) because he is lower class. I am middle class.

RC: I know my place. I look up to them both, but I don't look up to him (*indicating RB*) as much as I look up to him (*indicating JC*) 'cos he has got innate breeding.

JC: I have got innate breeding, but I have not got any money. So sometimes I look up to him. (*bending knees and indicating RB*)

RB: I still look up to him (*indicating JC*) because, although I have money, I am vulgar. But I am not as vulgar as him (*indicating RC*) so I still look down on him

RC: I know my place. I look up to them both. But, while I am poor, I am industrious, honest and trustworthy. Had I the inclination, I could look down on them. But I don't.

RB: We all know our place. But what do we get out of it?

JC: I get a feeling of superiority over them. (*indicating RB and RC*)

RB: I get a feeling of inferiority from him (*indicating JC*) but a feeling of superiority over him. (*indicating RC*)

RC: I get a pain in the back of my neck.

That sketch has survived amazingly well. Rather like the class system.

I still treasure a review of *The Frost Report* in the *Listener* magazine in 1967, written by the great author, Anthony Burgess, commenting on the different shapes and sizes of John, Ronnie B and myself. "Funny singly, the men are funnier still together, and part of the funniness derives from grotesque physical contrast – the very tall, the medium chubby, the very small," he wrote. "They are a kind of visual epigram made out of the intellectual fact of human variety. This epigram is also a paradigm for conjugating social statements – about class, chiefly – with great neatness." I don't know how the others felt, but I was tremendously chuffed about being a paradigm. I still often say to people: "Have you got any social statements you want conjugating?"

Ron and I, having been brought up in the theatre, were well aware of all the disciplines and unwritten rules of being professional. We understood about being in the theatre 35 minutes before the show starts and not sitting down in your costume so that it gets creased. If we went home with three sketches which we said we would learn for the morning, we knew them in the morning. And if we said we would come in at 9.40 to do something before the 10 o'clock start we would be there at 9.40.

John Cleese, coming from a quite different background, was usually a bit late and generally unshaven. He would arrive looking flustered in an expensive taxi from some strange address, while Ron and I had a more ordered and suburban existence; Ron lived out in Pinner and I came in to work from Crystal Palace. None of this caused any acrimony; it was just that Ron and I were aware that John was likely to be late.

At this time David was already pretty upwardly mobile and was doing very well, having made his mark with *That Was the Week that Was*. In fact he had become quite a fashionable soul, with all his energy and his drive – and that strange hairstyle of his. How did he get it to stand up at the front like that? And why? With that sort of reversed fringe he looked like a startled Roman emperor.

He attracted an enormous amount of attention whatever he did and many of the things he did were designed to attract attention. His parties then were famous – as they still are. At the end of the first series of *The Frost Report* in 1966 he took over

Battersea Funfair and the next year he invited 300 people to the White City stadium for sports and fun and games. It was the social event of the season, to rival Ascot. Everyone showed up, from Professor A.J. Ayer, the philosopher, to Vidal Sassoon, the hairdresser. Tommy Docherty, then manager of Chelsea football club, won the Sack Race in which Len Deighton, the author, ended up an also-hopped. The Wheelbarrow Race was won by John Cleese with Graham Chapman as wheelbarrow. Julie Felix supplied one and a half legs to the winning partnership in the so-called Patience Strong Three Legged Race and my wife Anne was a sensation in the Women's Egg and Spoon Race. The whole affair ended with a 2 a.m. football match with David Frost leading his team to victory over the show's writers and, in the words of one breathless newspaper report, with "Ronnie Corbett making a remarkable showing". I think they were referring to my perfectly judged through ball which many people have called a visual epigram.

This was all part of the general sense of fun and excitement associated with the programme. I liked the people I was working with, and I found their approach to life and the material they were writing refreshing and invigorating. And they were all well educated chaps. Graham Chapman was a qualified doctor, John Cleese had read Law at Cambridge, and most of them had been to university. Ronnie Barker and I would sometimes listen to their conversations in a sort of wonderment. They would say things like "My father naturally wants me to go and practise medicine, but I'm not really sure. I might poke about a bit in television for two or three more years and then go back to being a doctor. Or I might just do something entirely different." And our reaction would be: "Christ! We've been knocking our socks off here for 17 years to get on television and here you are, casually saying you might give it a go for a bit longer or, then again, you might not."

I suppose another example of a difference in attitudes, occurred over the business of Jimmy Gilbert's briefcase. A small group of us, including John Cleese, Ronnie B and myself, decided to give an end-of series present to Jimmy Gilbert, the producer of *The Frost Report*. We were each going to put in a small sum – I think it was £7 – and buy him a briefcase. We all paid our bit, except John, who didn't show any sign of coming forward with the money – he'd probably forgotten all about it. But I felt a bit stubborn and decided that I wouldn't let him forget. So, when we were both in the changing room on David Frost's great sports day at White City, I said: "By the way, John, you still owe us seven quid for the present."

"Oh," John replied. "How bourgeois!"

I thought: "It may be bourgeois to you, but it's seven quid to us, and we need the seven quid for this week's rent, if you don't mind." I stuck it out and got the money. Actually, that was another Class Sketch, in its way. And I ought to add that John is not a bit like that nowadays. He's a most generous person; the sort of chap who would willingly give you his last briefcase, if you were in need.

David Frost used to come to quite a few of the rehearsals in Crawford Street and when he did they always ended early. He and John Cleese were mad about football and we used to play a rather pathetic three-a-side game with a tennis ball, with David, in goal and a natty suit, diving spectacularly all over the place in this rather dirty church hall. Then he would get into a car and go off for lunch with somebody grand like Lord Snowdon or Norman St John Stevas or Princess Margaret, covered in dust from the floor.

Ron was not yet writing sketches when we worked on *The Frost Report*, but he was re-writing little bits of things. He would often go in for a bit of tinkering. I tended to take the script home, learn it and just put it away, but Ron has always been a bit more of a worrier and a harder worker than me.

Sometimes John, Ronnie and I would rehearse all week and would not see David until the day of the programme, then he would come in after lunch with a great armful of papers, with jokes written all over them in thick felt-tip pen. All this was material for David's C.D.M. These awe-inspiring initials stood for "continuing developing monologue" which was another way of describing his links between the sketches, following the chosen theme for the week. The programme would be put together in the afternoon and then broadcast live after the news from the Shepherd's Bush theatre. It was a bit alarming for all of us, assembling the show in the scramble of the last couple of hours and then going out live, but I think it was most alarming for John Cleese, who didn't have any experience of learning lines up to the last minute. Ron knew all about that from his time in rep and I had to get used to it at Winston's and Danny La Rue's.

In 1967, Graham Chapman teamed up with Barry Cryer and Eric Idle to write a sitcom called, *No, That's Me Over Here* for me and Rosemary Leach. I played the bowler-hatted bespectacled bank clerk, a sort of standard sitcom character of the times, but the whole thing was above-standard quality, and the executive producer was the extraordinary and funny man, Marty Feldman.

Graham had just recently come out as gay, was starting to drink heavily and behave wildly when we were working on this programme, but the script survived. After that, Graham and Barry wrote a comedy for me called *The Prince of Denmark* for the BBC. It was not very funny, rather mad and not a success. It lasted six shows. The Prince of Denmark in the title was a pub and I think Graham lured Barry into doing more on-the-spot research than was really necessary. More time was spent at the bar than at the typewriter. Even at his wildest, Graham somehow managed to be sweet and charming. My impression was that he was quite shy, and he had these violent comic outbursts because he somehow thought they were expected of him. The next day he would be pipe-smoking, contrite and quiet. He once dropped his trousers in the middle of a party at our house, and Danny La Rue stepped forward with a tea-towel to preserve his modesty. It was terrible that he died so young in 1989.

David Frost moved away from the BBC when the consortium of which he was a member made the successful bid for the ITV franchise for London at the weekends. So that was the end of *The Frost Report* and the beginning of *Frost on Friday,* and also *Frost on Saturday*, and not forgetting *Frost on Sunday*. Ron and I moved to ITV with him because we had by this time signed up to be managed by his company, Paradine Productions.

Paradine guaranteed that we would do 26 *Frost on Sunday* shows together, but also that we could do our own separate programmes. This was important for Ron and me because we didn't want to be utterly dependent on each other, so I got to do *The Corbett Follies* and Ron had *The Ronnie Barker Playhouse*.

I was still doing work outside television, topping the bill at various clubs and I also got an act together with my wife Anne. We did a dinner-time cabaret at the Savoy hotel in London. Anne sang numbers and I would interrupt, sashaying on as various people like an usherette, or the girl with the fishnet stockings and the ice cream tray. Then I would go up on stage and do a bit of patter or play the piano while Anne sang.

One number we did at the Savoy ended up unfortunately with me being served up as dish of the day. Anne sang the number from *Gypsy*, "All I Need is the Girl", but changed it to

"All I Need is the Boy" and I appeared in an absurd top hat, white tie and tails outfit, with short trousers and white socks. As we danced sublimely together bits of my costume would disintegrate and fall off. After a twirl, Anne would end up holding one of the sleeves of my jacket; a tail from the tail coat would be left lying on the floor; the shirt front would part company with the rest of the debonair ensemble. My whole outfit, which had been Velcroed together, came apart, bit by bit, and it made a very funny sketch.

As a final flourish to the dance, Anne whirled me round, gave me a heave and sent me skimming across the polished, slightly raised Savoy dance floor. I travelled with such velocity that I slid right off the floor and landed on the table of Lord Charles Spencer-Churchill who happened to be dining there that night. There was nothing I could do about it – except try and look as appetising as possible.

Afterwards I told Anne that this would be the last performance for that particular act. I decided I didn't want to be humiliated like this any more. Suppose Lord Charles Spencer-Churchill had stuck a fork in me? Or, worse still, sent me back to the kitchen with a complaint? In future, I decided, I would stick to solo performances in cabaret, with perhaps just a pianist or a trio for company.

Actually, Lord Charles Spencer-Churchill was present on another occasion when it was Anne's dignity, not mine, that was under threat. He invited us to a charity evening at which Princess Margaret was going to be present. It took place at Queens ice-skating rink, in London, and there was a mixture of skating and dancing. Anne, who has appeared in ice shows and is an excellent skater, got on the ice and thrilled and impressed everyone there.

Later on, Princess Margaret suggested we joined her in an Eightsome Reel – the sort of thing the Royal Family dance at Balmoral or at Sandringham at Christmas time. I knew a bit about how to do it from my days at the church youth club at St Catherine-in-the Grange, in Edinburgh, but Anne had never done it before, so I was trying to teach her as we went along.

The trouble was that the dance area was wet from people coming off the ice and we were into the second set of the Eightsome when poor Anne came a terrible purler. Her legs slipped from under her and she landed flat on her back.

Her Royal Highness did not take this amiss, and we carried on with the reel. Slightly fazed. Then it happened again. Anne slipped on the wet floor and down she went.

Princess Margaret paused. "I think, if you don't mind, we'll stop the reeling now," she said. "I don't want anyone measuring *my* length on the dance floor." So we all returned to our tables. Gratefully.

The idea behind the television series, *The Corbett Follies,* was that I would host the show looking very natty in a fancy dinner jacket or a wild silk suit and I would be fronting a lot of very tall, very beautiful girls, the sort of girls that used to appear at the Talk of the Town, and I would do a few sketches and introduce visiting American artists, like Henny Youngman or Peter Nero. The importance of that show to my career is that it eventually led to my collaboration with Spike Mullins, a former painter and decorator and a keeper of exotic lizards from Slough. The exotic lizards originally came from even more distant places actually; it was Spike who came from Slough.

But first, back to David Frost. The format of the trio of Frost programmes was that Friday was the big heavyweight current affairs interview, Saturday was a talk show, along the lines of

Aspel or Parkinson, and Sunday was a big variety show, replacing *Sunday Night at the London Palladium*. For this show, there were big guest stars, like Sammy Davis Jnr, Frank Sinatra and Bob Hope, and Ron and I would do little pieces throughout the show. John Cleese was no longer with us, but Josephine Tewson – who was co-starring with Ron in the West End production of Tom Stoppard's *The Real Inspector Hound* – joined us for many of the sketches.

On *Frost on Friday,* David caused a tremendous fuss in 1977 when he interviewed Dr Emil Savundra, owner of the Fire, Auto and Marine Insurance Company which collapsed after he had milked several hundred thousand pounds from it. When the Board of Trade decided to investigate the collapse of the company, Dr Savundra departed discreetly to Switzerland.

After six months he returned to London and made the silly mistake of agreeing to appear on *Frost on Friday*. Wielding his trusty clipboard of truth, David was at his most indignantly probing while Savundra was at his most infuriatingly insouciant. He was confronted by a woman widowed in a road accident who said the insurance company's cheque had bounced, but he said he had no legal or moral responsibility.

When members of the studio audience started to heckle him Dr Savundra responded: "I do not want to cross swords with peasants." This went down about as well as Marie Antoinette handing out cake recipes.

Although this encounter might almost be considered a polite exchange of views compared with some of today's studio audience uproars, it caused a great stir at the time. It led to the first appearance of the expression "trial by television" and it added greatly to David's reputation. And Dr Savundra eventually went to jail.

While doing all this and fronting the three programmes, David was also presenting two live shows a week in America, jetting there and back. Meanwhile, on *Frost on Sunday,* Ron was also leading a double life, appearing as Ronnie Barker and writing sketches secretly as Gerald Wiley.

One day, these excellent sketches started arriving, written by somebody called Wiley. Nobody knew who he was. His agent, Peter Eade, who sent them in to the programme, said that Mr Wiley had particular reasons for wishing to remain anonymous. Peter Eade was also Ron's agent, but Ron seemed to be as baffled as the rest of us.

All the time these brilliant sketches were coming in and we were getting more and more intrigued about who Gerald Wiley might be. Some of the sketches were rejected, but we performed most of them. There was one, I remember, about a ventriloquist, which just didn't work at all.

"Well, Gerald Wiley really let us down that time," Ron said to me afterwards, but I defended him. "Be fair," I said. "He's got a very good record; most of his stuff is excellent." Ron gave a grudging grunt.

The first sketch Gerald Wiley ever submitted to *Frost on Sunday* – which was accepted – had a very good part for me, and I am going to quote some of it here:

It is set in a waiting room in Harley Street, with about eight or nine rather smart patients sitting round, reading copies of *The Tatler* and *The Field* in that special, tense, waiting room silence. Then I bounce in looking very dapper and carrying a copy of the *Daily Telegraph.* I sit next to a smart military type (i.e. Ronnie B) and start trying to make conversation.

RC: Isn't it extraordinary how no-one ever talks to each other in a doctor's waiting room? *(No response from Barker.)* Odd, isn't it? *(No response.)* No, of course it's not odd. *(Answering himself.)* Oh, I thought it was. Well, it's not, so

147

keep quiet. Sorry. Don't mention it. *(A pause. RC picks up the newspaper.)*

RC: I see they are stopping all the tube trains tomorrow. *(There is a slight shuffling and a lowering of magazines from the patients.)*

RC: To let the people get on and off. *(He smiles encouragingly. The patients, without a flicker, return to their magazines.)*

After that, in the sketch, I recite "Simple Simon met a pieman", I sing "Night and Day, you are the one", I do a soft shoe shuffle and a tap dance, until finally I goad the military type into standing up and reciting A. A. Milne's "John has great big water-proof boots on". This is followed by a maiden lady standing up and singing "If you were the only boy in the world and I was the only girl" and everybody joins in. Then we all conga out of the room and into the street, leaving the waiting room empty. The punchline is that I am a rival doctor, luring all the private patients away to my own surgery.

It was a wonderful sketch for me, and Ron said: "I think it works so well you ought to get the rights for it so you can perform it when you do one of your summer shows." So I got Sonny Zahl, who was my agent at the time, to ring up Peter Eade and find out what the position was. The message came back that I could have the rights to the sketch for £3,000. You could get a pretty thorough Harley Street check-up for that kind of money in those days.

"Any news?" Ron asked me a couple of days later. I told him what the answer was, and he said: "That's absolutely ludicrous. Far too much."

Anyway, the next day I got another call from Sonny. Peter Eade had been in touch and told him that Gerald Wiley thought I performed the sketch so well that he would like to give me the rights to it, as a present, in perpetuity. Ron agreed that it was a very nice gesture when I told him about it.

Anne and I went to Asprey's and had six cut glass goblets engraved with the initials G.W. and I told Ron that I was going to get Peter Eade to send them on for me. Ron said there was no need to do that because, as it happened he had just heard that Gerald Wiley had agreed to come to see the show, as it was the last in the series. And was coming to join the cast and the crew for dinner afterwards, so I could give the goblets to him then.

By this time we were all running a book about who this Gerald Wiley actually was. Among the people bets were being taken on, were Noël Coward, Tom Stoppard, Frank Muir and Alan Bennett, so it was certainly a field of thoroughbreds.

In the afternoon when we were doing rehearsals in the studio at Wembley for the last *Frost on Sunday* of the series, there was a knock on my dressing room door and Ronnie B came in and said: "I just want to tell you, before I tell anyone else tonight, that I am, in fact, Gerald Wiley." I was absolutely stunned. And thrilled. The possibility had never occurred to me.

We were meeting for dinner that evening at a Chinese restaurant, at a table laid for 14 people, with one place empty. Gerald Wiley was late. Well, people said, that's not really so surprising; he must be coming on from somewhere else. He has been at a party at the Pinters, perhaps, or he dropped in on Peter Hall and is having difficulty in tearing himself away. Maybe his flight from the Caribbean has been delayed.

Then Ronnie Barker stood up and announced: "I just want to tell you that this chair will remain empty this evening, because I am, in fact, Gerald Wiley."

There was an extraordinary silence for a couple of seconds, a moment of shock, a mass gulp, as if 12 crispy wan tans had simultaneously gone down the wrong way. Then, at one end of the table, Barry Cryer was heard to say: "Nobody likes a smart-arse."

Ron's reason for sending in sketches under a pseudonym was so that they would be judged entirely on their merits. If the rest of us had known who had written them we might not have been totally honest about what we thought of them; we might have tried to spare his feelings. I am certain this is true, but I am sure he also enjoyed the mystery. There must be a bit of a conspirator in him. He even went out and bought a special typewriter for Gerald Wiley's use, so that the typeface of his own machine would not be recognised. I suspect that a few of the writers on the show could never truly forgive him for the subterfuge. Here was a performer beating them at their own game and, perhaps, laughing at them behind their back.

Some of the goblets I had engraved for Gerald Wiley still survive. But only a few. Under some pressure from me, Ronnie B has had to admit that a few of them got broken. You imagine something like that might be put away in a cupboard and that Ronnie would take them out on some occasion and say: "These are the famous Wiley goblets," but, in fact, he used them. Actually, I'm pleased about that. Pleased, but a little surprised, because he is usually a great hoarder.

In the 20 years I worked with Ron, on *The Frost Report,* on *Frost on Sunday* and on *The Two Ronnies* we only once had a falling out. This happened when we were coming to the end of a series of *Frost on Sunday* and halfway through the rehearsing, Ron, with the backing of the producer Phil Casson, suggested that we should swap roles in one particular sketch.

I was dead against it, because the part I had was obviously the right one for me. Whenever we performed together, the casting was always pretty obvious – we knew which types we played best – and we always stuck to the roles we had in the read-through.

On this occasion Ron was determined to swap so that he could have my part, and I didn't like it at all. For the first and only time in our career together, I got the hump. I walked out to the loo to cool down, then I walked back again, even more annoyed. The whole atmosphere was uneasy and when we left to go home that evening after rehearsals our goodbyes were abrupt.

When I got home I complained to Anne. "I'm being manipulated and I don't like it," I said. All the time I had worked with Ron I was content to be the placid one, to be non-confrontational. I knew how much emotional involvement he put into our work, more than me probably, so it suited me to be the easy-going one. But this time I said "Bugger it."

Anne said I should just let it go, forget about it. This was the end of a series and it was not worth making a big deal about it. So I went back the next day, in a curmudgeonly mood, and carried on rehearsing.

I was right. I *was* being manipulated. Ronnie Barker, the master of intrigue, and Phil Casson and Anne were all in a conspiracy to get me to be the subject (or victim) of *This is Your Life* which, at that time, was presented by Eamonn Andrews. Afterwards, people said it was one of the neatest "catches" that Eamonn ever had.

For some time, during the *Frost on Sunday* series, we had an unperformed sketch lying around the office, about a man who was paranoid about being featured on *This is Your Life*. If the milkman or the postman or anybody came to the door he was convinced that it was Eamonn Andrews with the big red book. The tag line of the whole thing was that Eamonn would then suddenly show up and the man wouldn't recognise him.

The sketch had been on the back burner for some time, partly because we were not absolutely sure of the quality of it, but mostly because we knew it would be difficult to get Eamonn to appear in it because he was so popular and busy.

Anyway, it was the last show of this particular series and they said they had managed to get Eamonn to do the sketch. All the time, their manipulation with the role in the other sketch was so that they could get me into the right part for this one, although, of course, I didn't know any of this at the time.

Eamonn rehearsed with us all day and, while he was there, a rumour went about that he was going to do a real *This is Your Life* on David Frost. This was probably a cunning diversionary tactic by Ronnie Barker. I think at one point I wondered if Eamonn might be doing Ronnie or me, but Ronnie said: "Oh, it can't be one of us or we would have told each other." Devious, but it convinced me.

So when, at the end of the sketch, Eamonn said: "Ronnie Corbett, this really *is* your life," I was truly gobsmacked. It was quite a memorable coup. The set for *This is Your Life* was actually hung up in the flies in the studio, above the set for *Frost on Sunday* so they could just lower it and do the show right there and then. I just hadn't looked up all day.

After I got over the shock, it was really quite sweet and moving. My Sunday school teacher was there, and my sister Margaret came from America looking amazing because she was pregnant with her second child and was dressed in a sort of Bluebell Girl's costume, because she had once been a dancer. And my brother Allan was there, just to remind me and everyone else about how, being the tall one, he was able to beat me up from a very early age.

This is a chance to say something about my sister and brother, Margaret and Allan, who were last seen, in this book, as children when we took our walks in the Braid Hills in our Sunday best. We have always been a close family. Margaret studied dancing at the Scottish Ballet School, in Edinburgh, then went on to be a dancer in Howard and Wyndham's pantomimes and summer shows. She was also in a series of early evening Highland shows on television. Then she met and fell in love with Erik Gorm Hanson, a dentist in the US Air Force, based at Kirkliston, outside Edinburgh, they married and she left showbusiness, except for the odd foray into cabaret in Florida where they now live. She has two children.

My brother Allan is a dear friend. He is a very good golfer, much better than me; in fact he has always been better than me at almost everything; better at games and cleverer at school. Allan is somebody I look up to in every sense. While Margaret departed for Florida and I pursued my career in London, Allan, apart from a spell in the army, has spent his life in Scotland. He went to Edinburgh University to study Law, but didn't complete the course which I think was a bit of a disappointment to our dad. Then he made a great success as a restaurateur; he and his wife Jennifer bought a house in Fife which they opened as a restaurant, then they took over a pub in Coupar, moved to another in Strathlithgow, and finally he owned Skippers, a highly successful fish restaurant in Leith, which he sold when he retired. Allan and Jenn have three children.

That was their lives. Now back to mine, to Teddington Studios, West London, and to the occasion when Eamonn Andrews confronted an astonished me with that big red book. David Frost was there, of course, and Danny La Rue. I remember Danny arrived wearing exactly the same tie as me. It was the time of Mr Fish and the kipper tie which matched the shirt. My mum and dad were there and my mum forgot what she was supposed to say, and, off camera, my dad was prompting her, as always, putting the words in her mouth.

David, who, as we have seen, has always been a great party

giver, had booked the ballroom of Quaglino's – it was still a
night-club then – for a party afterwards, so the celebrations
continued. Clive Dunn (who had given me one of my very first
jobs in that summer season at Cromer) was at the party and
found himself seated at the same table as Herbie Flowers who
played in the band at Danny La Rue's club. Herbie had just
written a song called "Grandad" and was looking for somebody
to sing it. It was all agreed between them at that table and soon
Clive was spending several weeks at the top of the hit parade
with that song. A little musical footnote there. Or, if you hated
the song, a chance to put the blame on me.

Actually, I knew Eamonn Andrews pretty well before the
This is Your Life ambush, because I had done three seasons of the
children's television programme *Crackerjack* when Eamonn was
the host and Pearl Carr and Teddy Johnson were the musical
guests each week. I played the resident comic, for three seasons,
with different feeds each year. The first one of these was Eddie
Leslie who worked for Norman Wisdom for much of his career.
Eddie was the straight character who was always twisting
Norman's ear or giving him a punch.

This was something I spent quite a lot of my early career
trying to avoid – that is, having my ear twisted and being
punched. Because I was little, the general idea among showbusiness agents was to turn me into a sort of Norman Wisdom
or a Charlie Drake type of performer who was always being put
upon and persecuted with flour and water and hit with rubber
hammers, and that sort of thing.

All the time, I felt that wasn't me at all. It didn't feel right to
be put upon. There was something about the way I worked
which meant I didn't actually *feel* small. It may sound odd, but
throughout my career, I have been the last person to realise that
I was diminutive.

★

The big turning point for Ronnie Barker and me came when we were doing the BAFTA awards programme which was being broadcast from the London Palladium. We were hosting the programme and also doing bits and pieces in it. That night there was a technical breakdown and it was left to Ron and me to keep on entertaining the audience in the theatre while they sorted things out.

So we did things off the cuff – or apparently off the cuff, because we resorted to bits we knew and had done together before, and we held the audience for eight or nine minutes until the programme was back on the air again. Eight or nine minutes can be a very long time when you are facing a specially invited audience from the film and television industries and you are standing on the stage without a script and with nothing prepared. Let's face it, one minute of that can be a bit hair-raising. Somehow we managed to keep going and it seemed to go down well.

Paul Fox, the Controller of BBC1, was sitting in the audience that night next to Bill Cotton, the head of Light Entertainment, and he turned to him and asked "What are the chances of getting these two for the BBC?"

There had been some sort of a falling out which affected the ongoing relationship between Stella Richman, who was Controller of Programmes at LWT, and David Frost's company Paradine Productions. So when Bill Cotton made his approach to Paradine, it looked to me like Ron and I were effectively on the point of getting the sack from ITV.

So the BBC put us together with Jimmy Gilbert, the producer, and Terry Hughes, the director, and they decided to call the show *The Two Ronnies*. Because that is, basically, what we were. Or were we? I sometimes hope than in 50 years time, some hot investigative reporter will come up with a terrific scoop, headlined "Was This the Third Ronnie?" He will claim to have uncovered a shadowy figure who, because of some scandal, was made to "disappear". Maybe he will be like the Fifth Beatle, who never got to share in the success. The Third Ronnie could become a matter of great historical dispute, along the lines of, "Was there a fourth Bronte sister?" Perhaps, as some scholars have argued there was a Fifth Horseman of the Apocalypse; as well as War, Fame, Pestilence and Death, there was Mishap – but he fell off his horse.

Very bravely, the BBC broadcast *The Two Ronnies* right at the forefront of the schedules, right in the front line of the ratings battle, at eight o'clock on Saturday nights. They don't do that sort of thing these days; programmes get tried out first in quieter nooks and crannies of the schedule until the people in charge are convinced they have a winner. They don't go in for acts of faith any more. Anyway, *The Two Ronnies* carried on from 1971 to 1987, getting an audience of around 17 million – and 19 million for the Christmas specials.

We sat down at the beginning and thought quite coolly about how the show would suit our varied and different talents and also fit in with our limitations. We knew that we were not, strictly speaking, a double act; we weren't joined at the hip in the way that Eric Morecambe and Ernie Wise were and this meant that we actually had no way of talking to each other in front of an audience. That kind of relationship did not exist for us; it only comes from being a double act from a very young age. If you try to create it, the effect is false and the audience recognises that there is something artificial about it.

So we knew that each one of us would have to address the audience separately. One of us would speak to camera and then hand over to the other one who would say his piece – again to camera. There was very little chat *between* us, because we knew it wouldn't work. This was the first rule we had to observe. And that is why the News Item format was created, with Ron and me seated side by side at the beginning of every show. And, of course, at the end of the programme, it was goodnight from me and goodnight from him. We were "me" and "him" but never "us".

We worked out the formula for the programme right from the start and it hardly changed for the next 16 years – except, perhaps, that it became more lavish as the BBC was prepared to put more money in it because it was a success.

Ron and I were also quite calculating about maintaining our separate professional lives. In the years *The Two Ronnies* was going on, Ron had his own television programmes, most famously *Porridge* and *Open All Hours,* and I started by hosting a mid-week BBC variety programme with star guests and a big band called (not all that surprisingly) *Startime Variety*. At the end of the show I would sit at a grand piano and talk to the audience, so this was a variation on my solo chair spot in *The Two Ronnies* – the piano stool spot. From 1981 onwards, I had the sitcom, *Sorry!* and, in all the years that Ronnie B and I were working together, I also had my own pantomime, summer season and cabaret work.

In all the years we did *The Two Ronnies*, Ron and I quite deliberately maintained our separate identities. We never did, for example, a *Parkinson* show together and when we were interviewed by newspapers it was always separately. We didn't want to be seen as a pair, although we were, of course, in many ways. At the same time, the success of our partnership was due to the fact that we were so different.

When we went on location for the filmed bits of *The Two Ronnies* we would usually stay at the same hotel, somewhere comfortable and quiet, away from everyone else. When people heard we were in the area we often received invitations to dinner at local houses. Sometimes people may have thought that we would provide a bit of entertainment for their dinner party, engaging in a bit of polished banter, bouncing jokes off each other and that sort of thing.

Some of these invitations were tempting, but we managed to resist them, partly because we were too hard at work with the filming and partly because we were aware that we could easily turn out to be a big disappointment at the dinner table. Or it would take an enormous amount of energy *not* to be a disappointment.

This is a problem with a lot of comics; when you meet them face to face they turn out to be rather serious. If you invite a couple of Pythons round for a spot of pan-fried lettuce on wilted sea-bass, or some wild rice with a frenzied *blanquette de veau*, you are not going to get a command performance of the dead parrot sketch. They'll probably talk about the ozone layer. Or lawns.

There are some comedians who can just turn it on and be funny nearly all the time, as Eric Morecambe was, and also Tommy Cooper, Jimmy Edwards and Ted Ray and Jimmy Tarbuck. Because Ron and I were not a natural double act, we were nervous of getting in each other's way conversationally; perhaps one Ronnie would hold forth at length and the other would sit in silence. It was different with Eric and Ernie, because Ernie knew his place; he was there to help Eric be as funny as he wanted to be. Mike and Bernie Winters have the same sort of relationship, and so did Jewel and Warriss. Ron and I were never so sure of our roles.

Perhaps because of his training in the theatre, Ron does not really know who he is supposed to "be" when he is addressing an audience on his own. He can't just go on and be himself. He has to create a character, so, in his monologues in *The Two Ronnies,* he had to be spokesman-ish, the man in the moustache, the figure of authority, the slightly stiff official, the expert delivering a lecture in front of the blackboard, the manager, or the bureaucrat with the clipboard and a hint of a mad stare. On the other hand, I knew that I could do my monologue sitting in the chair and really being myself – or what people thought of as me.

When we were doing our shows at the Palladium, Ronnie B and I noticed another strange thing about his performing style. His gestures were exactly the same every night. The hands would go to the pocket at precisely the same moment; the arm would be raised at the same point as it was in last night's performance; the finger would touch the face just when you expected it to.

This was because he had created a character and a performance for that character which never varied. There was never a moment when he went out on stage and took a chance, said something different, changed the lines a bit. He was perfectly capable of doing so, but he just didn't want to.

He sometimes worried that there was not a looseness or a freedom in his performance and worried about what would happen if he was doing a solo item and forgot his words. He just didn't have the confidence to improvise, although I knew he could have done it brilliantly. It's remarkable that someone with such a gift for words should have that uncertainty. I remember being told that once when Alan Bennett was performing in his own *Talking Heads* on stage he forgot his lines and had to go off stage and check the script. You might think: "Well, they're *his* lines, so why can't he make some more up?" Obviously it doesn't work like that.

I have never been that kind of animal. When I do stage plays, I'm sure I don't give the same performance every night. This is probably because I come from more of a vaudeville tradition and didn't have a strictly theatrical training.

I am not sure what Donald Sinden would say, but I don't think I did all the same gestures when we were in *Out of Order* together. When I was playing Dr Moulineaux in the Feydeau farce, *The Dressmaker*, in 1990, I used to look for new little things to do each night – not leaving the other actors stranded or hanging about waiting for their cues, but just to try and give my performance a bit of freshness, or to take a new look at things each night to give me a bit of sparkle.

Before a performance, somebody might ask me, how are you going to do this or that? Or, how many of those little kicks are you going to do? The answer would be, I don't know; it depends on what the audience want me to do. There is a kind of relationship, or an interplay, between the performer and the audience and you are judging it each night, giving them what they want. You hope.

There is also a bit of a difference between Ronnie B and me when we are not performing. Ronnie B would not be really comfortable opening his local fete in Oxfordshire, for example, because of the old question of who he was supposed to be; what character he was going to play.

I am not quite the same. To be really outgoing I prefer to have the right surroundings. It's easier when I am on a stage, when the curtain has been raised, or the lights have gone up, but I can, if necessary, switch on and go into performance mode.

As I have got older I have become more relaxed and it is easier. On the other hand, I don't find it necessary to *prove* myself to be a comedian every minute of the waking day. I might go and play a round of golf with three men and at the end they could come off and say, "He didn't even tell a joke."

CHAPTER NINE

*More about 'The Two Ronnies'. The ingredients, the
routines and rituals. The way the show was put together.
The reader learns about the brilliant Spike Mullins, the
man behind most of the monologues. There is an alarming
account of my appearance at a Royal Variety Performance and
the mystery of an outsize shirt is solved. Some lizards are
mentioned.*

"Traffic news: a juggernaut carrying treacle has overturned
on the M4. Drivers are asked to stick to the inside lane."

This was one of the News Items we used in 1978. Every
programme began with Ronnie B and me seated at a desk, two
pairs of spectacles, glinting at the camera, taking it in turns to
give out these news items. There were also some News Items at
the end of the programme.

"First, this afternoon's Tipperary Games. In the final of the
tug-of-war, both teams were disqualified for pushing."

That's another one. All sorts of people, very young writers

161

and those who wanted to get into the comedy business, used to bombard us with these jokes.

"In an interview shown tonight, Angela Rippon confessed to having a selfish streak – she did it at four o'clock in the morning when most of us were fast asleep."

Some of them were very good jokes. Some of them were examples of that peculiarly British thing, the good-bad joke – the sort of thing that makes you laugh, perhaps out of sheer relief that it wasn't even worse.

"News that the latest from the Japanese electronics industry is the surgical truss-cum-calculator, which means that you can count on your own support."

Young people living outside Gainsborough or Bootle, in bedsits in Swindon and basement flats in Colwyn Bay were penning these jokes. That's how they hoped to get started as comedy writers – and how some of them did. After all, that's how Woody Allen began – by writing jokes for Sid Caesar.

"Further developments tonight in the case of the Hyde Park flasher, the man who jumps out in front of lady joggers, stark naked. Eye-witnesses have helped police put together an Identikit picture of his face, but are still not sure of his whereabouts."

The first thing to be said about these News Items is that they were not particularly newsy. They were not topical jokes making a comment about something which had happened in the previous week. That is why they have survived in all the repeats and retrospectives of *The Two Ronnies*. They were really just a new way of telling a joke.

Well, nearly new. The News Items were based on an idea that was used in *Frost on Sunday*. The genre was created there. David would say something like "The Prime Minister had discussions this morning with the Cabinet," and then Ron or I would add: "He then spoke to the wardrobe, the sideboard and the chest of drawers."

Actually, these sort of News Item jokes were once the cause of a situation on *Frost on Sunday* in which there was just a suggestion of an industrial dispute. There were masses of jokes every week and they were just being handed out indiscriminately. This meant that Ronnie and I were being asked to say things which we thought were not really funny enough.

We formed a two-Ron deputation and marched into David's room. "We've got to tell you something," we announced, standing to attention, "we're sorry, but these jokes are not funny. We'd like better ones or we'd rather not say them at all."

It was a difficult thing to do. David is one of those people, like Danny La Rue, who is so upbeat and positive, that it's extremely hard to tell them when something is not quite right. Any little criticism of the style or the content seems to rock the whole boat. Any reluctance to join in the general enthusiasm is considered frightfully bad form. Our complaint to David did not, in fact, lead to anything like a major fall-out, but we realised at the time that we both had to go in and see him together.

On *The Two Ronnies,* we had a particular ceremony when we selected the News Item jokes. Ian Davidson and Peter Vincent, the script editors, would have about 400 sent in every week from the ever-hopeful writers all round the country while the series was being made. They would sort them out and distil them and on the Tuesday afternoon they would bring in about 310 of them all typed out and numbered. Ron would start at the top of the first page, then we would read them out alternately.

The following week, I would start the proceedings off, by reading out the first one. As we read through the jokes we would tick them off or mark them.

We had one strict rule: we didn't allow ourselves to laugh at any of these jokes as we were delivering them, because we felt that this would give a particular joke an unfair advantage over the others. We did not want our judgment to be swayed by one of us giggling. So we had this weird ritual in which we two grown men (or one and a half grown men) would take it turns solemnly to read out 300-odd jokes with perfectly straight faces. Of course, when we came to do it on the screen we also tried to look serious and news reader-ish, but quite often a smile would fight its way out.

The essential ingredients of *The Two Ronnies* were worked out pretty well from the start. We knew ourselves and each other so well by the time we started that we knew what we could do. There would be the News Items, Ron's monologues, often involving some tormented wordplay or mispronunciation, and there would always be some sketches we did together.

In some of these two-handers we were tramps or yokels, but, over the years, there were also a good many party sketches; some variation on the theme of two chaps meeting for the first time at a drinks party.

I remember one in which we were two perfect strangers wearing identical ghastly check jackets and uttering identical social chit-chat simultaneously. It's a difficult thing to do, but we got into a certain rhythm and it worked and we remained synchronised. Out of sight of the camera, Ronnie B placed his left foot just next to my right foot and, at one point in the sketch, we did a long take with an extended pause in the middle of the dialogue, then he touched my foot with his and we started again, absolutely together. And, at the end of the sketch, we walked away from each other, both muttering, in unison: "Frightful bore."

There was always a dash of sauciness in the show – a few bottom and bosom gags and a generous dollop of *double entendre*, in the tradition of the postcards bought on the pier at the seaside. I don't think we ever got into any trouble over this, and the BBC never tried to censor anything – I think this was because Ron and I understood our audience. We had been in the theatre for a long time before we went on television, and if you have spent that amount of time entertaining live audiences throughout the provinces, or wherever, you have a pretty good idea of what the general public finds palatable and acceptable. If you don't have this sort of experience of entertaining people, in the flesh and round the country, all you can do is *imagine* what they like and how far they would like you to go.

I have a feeling that Ronnie B was a little saucier than I was in the show. He probably has just a little more Benny Hill in his comical make-up than I have.

My spot in the chair, getting round to telling a joke, was also a basic ingredient in the recipe – as was the 12-minute section involving a pretty lavish bit of filming, often a spoof of a popular television series. We did Poirot meets Miss Marple (with Ron as the moustachioed Belgian and me as Miss M) and we also did our version of *Doctor Finlay's Casebook*, our own travesty of *Upstairs Downstairs* and caricatures of *Jason King* and *The Professionals* and *Escape from Colditz*. And there was also one about vets which we called *All Creatures Grunt and Smell*. A retrospective of *The Two Ronnies* would give you a pretty comprehensive history of popular television programmes of the period.

In the later series we also had a serial, like *The Worm That Turned*, about a world in which women had total power – and in which our dreaded adversary was played by Diana Dors. We had the adventures of the super sleuths, Charley Farley and Piggy Malone investigating baffling mysteries like the serial killing of yokels in which all the victims had their trouser legs tied up with string.

And there was always a big musical number. Before the first series of *The Two Ronnies* went out, the BBC gave both Ronnie and me our own "special" – a one-off show in which we starred – to give the audience a taster, and a warning perhaps, of what was to come. Mine was called *Ronnie Corbett in Bed* and it included a musical number written by Dick Vosburgh. Dick had the inspired idea of setting *Romeo and Juliet* to Souza marches. It was such a success that we decided there must always be a musical item in *The Two Ronnies*. They were often written by Dick, although Ronnie B did a lot as well. They involved the two of us performing with a brass band or a ladies choir or a pipe band, or being an Irish folk band, or appearing as Nana Moussaka, as Charles Azenough, or Chloe Loon and Danny Jonkworth. I remember we also appeared as Rockers, singing "Hake, haddock and skate", instead of "Shake, rattle and roll".

Jimmy Gilbert was the executive producer of *The Two Ronnies* when we started, and Terry Hughes was the director. It was these two who were so important in helping us to establish the pattern and the tradition of the show.

Terry Hughes was one of the best ever judges of a sketch. If he said "You'll like this" or "That one's not much good" he was nearly always spot on. He was also very, very handsome and totally charming. Anne used to take different guests with her to the recording of the show every week and, when Terry Hughes came forward at the beginning to address the studio audience and say a few words of welcome to them, she would start counting silently to herself and, before she got to ten, her guests would turn to her and whisper "Who's that lovely man?"

Terry went off to America and produced *The Golden Girls* and they all adored him. Then he moved on to *Third Rock from the Sun* and he is still in America, being a tremendous success. And still charming everybody.

After Jimmy Gilbert and Terry Hughes, the next producer-director was Michael Hurll who kept up the same tradition. The succession then moved smoothly and sweetly on to Marcus Plantin, now controller of programmes at London Weekend Television, to Paul Jackson, now head of BBC entertainment, to Marcus Mortimer who is still a producer for the BBC. So the boys have all done well, I'm glad to say.

There was never a drama, never a walk-out – which makes it tough when one gets round to writing one's autobiography, but was a great blessing in every other way. For 16 years, it was smooth, professional and happy. When the scripts are right in the first place, they are a pleasure to do, and easy to learn, and there is no trouble.

If you are given rubbish to say each week, that is when it starts getting difficult. Everybody blames everybody else and they begin to fall out.

Ron and I had a great deal of autonomy in making the show. This was largely due to the fact that it was so successful. The programme had huge viewing figures, second only to Eric and Ernie, so the BBC was inclined to let us have our way.

When performers are well known and are having a good run it is difficult to stop them being autonomous. This particularly applies to those of us who are comics because we are so much more in control of our own destiny than actors are. We come as a complete package or "turn", I suppose. We know what works with us. At the same time we need somebody around who is strong enough to guide us and tell us when we are doing too much of one thing, for example, or being rude in the same way too often.

★

I have mentioned the ceremony of selecting the New Items, and this was just one of our eccentric ways of doing things. Over the years, we developed our own pattern of working and our own collection of habits and fads.

I think that is true of all performers. We all have our little ways. I have known people who worked with Charlie Drake and they said that they never actually rehearsed with Charlie. The supporting artistes were kept in a separate room while he rehearsed and they were called in when it was time to do their scene with him, rather like being summoned to see a specialist.

We were not like that, but we certainly had our rules. The first and most important one was that we picked our material early on. Weeks or even months before a show was due to be recorded we would read scripts at home of possible sketches to be done in the studio, and then we would come together to discuss them and to give them marks.

We would hold script meetings in a quiet corner of a rehearsal room or we would often get together to do this when we were away filming on location. Filming usually took four or five weeks and happened about two and a half months before we started rehearsing the sketches in the studio. If we were staying in some rather nice country house hotel we would work all day on the filming and then in the evening, or at the weekend, we'd take a little sitting room in the hotel to hold our script conference. We read all the sketches and decided exactly which ones we would do and which ones needed changing.

If something needed, say, a new last page, Ron would say "I'll take this away and have a wee think about it tonight." Or one of us might say: "This sketch is funny, but I think it is more Dick Emery than us." So that would go in a different pile. Sketches have a kind of feeling of fitting you – or not. And if they don't fit you it's sometimes possible to see them fitting someone else very well. It's not unknown for writers to re-type a sketch and re-cast it. If it has been slung out by Dick Emery it says "Ronnie Corbett comes into the room" where it used to say "Dick Emery comes into the room." They push stuff around a bit.

Anyway, the words for all the sketches in the series were all pretty well settled and all right before we even stood up for our first rehearsal. Neither Ron nor I was a great rehearser. We didn't want to do something over and over again if it was right. We spent less time rehearsing and more time meeting and discussing the script. We both had the same view that a good joke, or something that is well written, is very easily learned. What is difficult to learn is something that is not well written or something you don't have any confidence in.

Eric Morecambe and Ernie Wise had a different approach. They got to their feet to rehearse straight away, even if the material wasn't quite right, or was just a collection of bits and pieces, and then they would work on it from there. Eric and Ernie spent three weeks rehearsing a single show, while Ron and I took just one week. They devoted their three weeks to knocking the show into shape until they both felt more comfortable with it. This actually meant that they went on working on it until Eric felt comfortable and felt that he had exploited every single opportunity for an extra joke.

When we were making the series we made up our minds on the Monday about the contents of the show we were going to record the following Sunday and it was usually not until then that we would actually cast the other parts in the sketches. Somebody would ring up the actors – normally people Ron or I had worked with in the past – on Monday and they would come in on the Tuesday. So they didn't have much time to rehearse.

We spent from Tuesday to Friday in the BBC rehearsal rooms

in Acton, in West London, in what was known in the business as the Acton Hilton. It was a proper rehearsal complex with a canteen and all the facilities, so you might find Eric and Ernie on the fifth floor and Ron and me on the third.

I would drive myself to Acton from home in Addington while, cunningly, Ron had only a short journey from Harrow. I'd leave home after 9.15 to avoid the traffic and we tried to get away from rehearsals by about 3.30 in the afternoon. We were quick at learning our lines, so this made it easier for the director. We said "We'll learn these four sketches for tomorrow," and we did.

On Saturdays and Sundays we were in the studio at the BBC Television Centre, rehearsing and recording the show. We recorded our big musical number (the brass band, or "Hello Sailor" with the singing Wrens, or the rousing songs of the Army Catering Corps) on Saturday without an audience because it was all so complicated to set up.

We also had a set pattern for the Sunday recordings. Ronnie B always came in with a cool box – or an "Esky" as the Australians call it – with ice and beer and wines and gin and tonics and salted nuts and we set up our own private little hospitality room in a large dressing room in between our two dressing rooms. Wives, guests, directors and some of the writers could come in for rather a nice little party after the recording and Ron Waverley (the lovely man from Kelso who I first met in pantomime in Bristol) would dispense the drinks.

After that, it was the custom for just Ronnie and Joy and Anne and me to go out together for a curry at an Indian restaurant in Westbourne Grove. It was a happy coincidence that, at this time, Indian restaurants in London were starting to get really good and managing to escape from the stereotype of flock wallpaper, dim lighting and unexciting chicken Madras.

We tried to plan the Sunday recordings to keep the hold-ups to a minimum, so the studio audience didn't get restless or uncomfortable. So this was another list. The running order, with the changes in make-up and costume, was organised to make the show as seamless as possible. Our warm-up man was usually Felix Bowness, who played the jockey in *Hi de Hi,* the holiday camp sitcom. He was very good with the audiences and his style of comedy didn't cross with ours. Felix also did a lot of the warming up for me in *Sorry!* and also with *Small Talk.* He lives in a house called "Strugglin". I just thought I'd mention that.

Joy and Anne always sat together in the middle of the audience at the studio recordings and their presence was a great reassurance to Ronnie and me. We always had a worry about the sound, wanting to be sure that the studio audience could hear comfortably and easily, so that the jokes would be laughed at.

So we would always call out to the audience "How is the sound?" And sometimes these two ladies, in the middle of the audience, who nobody knew, would call back: "Can't hear. We can't hear you. Not loud enough." And everyone else at the audience would turn and look at them, tut and think "Good heavens! Who do they think they are?" But every week Ronnie and I knew we could be sure of getting an honest answer about the sound level, when other members of the studio audience might be too shy or inhibited to say anything about it.

Ron and I were very cunning because we did not allow any of the shows to be transmitted until we had recorded the whole series – usually of eight programmes. When we had finished recording them all we divided them up into their component parts and then re-built them. This was another of our rituals. We had all these coloured index cards – lemon, pale green, pale blue, white, and so on, and each of these colours represented a different type of sketch. My solo spot in the chair might be yellow, for example; the pale blue would be the filmed item, the pink would be the musical finale, the white would be Ronnie's single. We then put all the pieces together like a jigsaw.

We'd say things like "Now, let's think what would be the best musical item to go here, remembering that we already have a sketch where you are playing a Red Indian . . . ."

"You've got two really cockney sketches in this one, so you really want a posh or middle class character here . . . ."

"And if one of the cockney ones comes out, you've still got an American and quite a posh one . . . "

"And then we could put the Scotsman in there."

"That means we'll have to shift the dyslexic tattoo artist."

In a way, it was rather like putting a magazine together, getting the right mix of the contents. So members of the studio audience who went one Sunday to see a show being recorded, would not see that actual show being transmitted. There would be bits of it, combined with parts of shows we had recorded on other Sundays.

Having constructed all the shows for the series we would then have to decide the order in which they would go out. We had a rule that the show we considered to be the best one went out first in the series. Then there was always a bit of a debate about whether the second best should go last or second. We always recorded more material for the series than we needed, so that we could leave out pieces that had not worked. Then anything that we thought was still a bit duff could be hidden away in show six or show seven in the series.

The costumes for *The Two Ronnies* were all designed by Mary Husband, a wonderful Welsh lady, who also did the clothes for the recent Millennium version of the Class sketch and she was involved in all the sitcoms than Ronnie Barker did at the BBC, like *Porridge* and *Open All Hours*. She didn't do the costumes for *Sorry!* but she nearly always does the clothes for anything I do nowadays, including the TV commercials, because she is so expert and so good to have around.

Mary paid enormous attention to detail working on the *Two Ronnies* and operated at high speed from week to week. In one show we would be the country singers Big Jim Jehosaphat and Fat Belly Jones, the next week would be all in pink satin for the ladies choir singing "Nymphs and Shepherds", and the next week the Japanese Noh Theatre, followed perhaps by a Russian choir, Pearly Kings and Drum Majorettes. We were a particular success as the long-haired country and western singers, Jehosaphat and Jones and we even made a record. I can give you a bit of the good ol' chorus here, written by Ronnie B:

> Don't come around here asking me out
> I ain't going out just to muck about
> You'll have to muck about on your own, my dear,
> 'Cos I'm gonna muck about here.

We appeared a good deal in drag; it was not something I particularly adored doing, but I didn't mind it. I suppose that working all those years with Danny La Rue gave me a good deal of confidence. I did get a certain *je ne sais quoi* from Dan. It was a very glamorous time at his club; no money was spared on the look of the show and our clothes were looked after beautifully. We all cared about what we looked like. It was not just the female costumes; the men all had splendid suits made by a tailor called Paul, in Berwick Street, in Soho. I felt at ease in drag in *The Two Ronnies* mostly just because I was used to being in stage clothes; it was something I had to learn over the years, so I am quite good at swishing about in dresses.

Ronnie Barker always says he hated appearing in drag,

although I think, if you counted up, you might find he had actually done so more often than me in *The Two Ronnies*. His wife Joy absolutely loathed seeing him in a frock, but Anne didn't mind at all seeing me in frocks. She was used to it and it didn't surprise her, having worked with Max Wall, who often played in drag, and having performed with the Crazy Gang who were always dressing up as women. Rather grotesquely. Anne often tells the story of going to Marks & Spencer in Glasgow, when I was playing one of the Ugly Sisters in pantomime there, and Emma or Sophie was misbehaving and she told them off sharply, "Will you please try to behave yourself? I'm trying to buy some tights for your father." The very sensible Glasgow lady assistant looked aghast.

Having these regular lavish musical numbers in *The Two Ronnies* meant that Ron and I had to learn a new song every week. We couldn't absolutely rely on our memories so we would read the words off autocue. Of course we both needed to wear our glasses to be able to see the thing, but if we did every number in our specs it would get boring. We tried contact lenses, but neither of us could keep them in for long without getting sore and weepy. We did use contact lenses a couple of times, but for most of the musical spectaculars we were bespectacled, even when we appeared as singing Mounties. Great efforts were made to have a variety of frames.

One name which always appeared on the credits for *The Two Ronnies* – and still does for a huge number of BBC shows – was Bobby Warans. Bobby is the buyer and anything you want, Bobby can get for the next day – if not the same day. If you want a bowler hat made out of plain chocolate, Bobby will know where to get hold of such a thing. Actually, we did once want a chocolate bowler, but I can't remember now why we did.

Bobby is brilliant at the art of what is called "dressing the set".

Ronnie B wrote a musical item about Oxford in which we were both undergraduates and Bobby Warans supplied everything for the dining hall scene – an enormous cheese, ancient portraits, a decanter, all the silverware and candelabras. Everything looked absolutely authentic and just right. I still get in touch with Bobby if I need advice on how to get hold of something a bit out of the ordinary for my own use – like a stuffed okapi, for example, or a two-bedroom furnished igloo. As one does from time to time.

Bobby's contribution was so important, because I've always believed that everything that is funny is even funnier if it is properly set. The doctor's waiting room sketch works so much better if you actually feel you are in a doctor's waiting room. If there is a wobbly door and the set is painted badly it spoils the joke. The one thing that has to be serious is the attention to detail.

Ronnie wrote a great many of the pieces we performed; Bryan Blackburn also did some, as well as David Newman and Peter Osborne whose work had been spotted by our director Terry Hughes when they were writing for an amateur pantomime. We had masses of material to sift through and select from. Our rule was always that if one of us was not happy with a sketch, or even had the slightest doubt about it, we would leave it out. There was never an argument.

When I was presenting *The Corbett Follies,* the writer Spike Mullins telephoned me one day and said: "I've noticed that when you do your introductions you waffle a bit. I think I could waffle a bit better for you." So Spike started writing for me and he created my monologue in the chair for *The Two Ronnies.*

Spike was a wonderful writer. He started out by writing jokes for Vic Oliver, the radio comic, and for a variety of variety performers. He would just send in the jokes and hope the performers would be decent enough to pay for them. Vic Oliver paid him half a guinea a gag – but only if the audience laughed.

Spike also supported himself and his family as a labourer, a barman, a porter in a block of flats, deckhand on a dredger and a painter and decorator. In 1963 he started writing for Max Bygraves and from there he began supplying material for *The Frost Report.*

Spike wrote me a monologue to go in my solo spot in my first ever Royal Variety Performance in 1969 – which was a particularly frightening and uncomfortable time for me. It was one of his exotic rambling stories – about a fictitious cousin of mine who had been thrown out of the Royal Army Medical Corps – and I think it was just a bit ahead of its time. It was certainly ahead of the time of the people running the show at the Palladium. After rehearsals, at about 10 o'clock at night, I was summoned to the Royal Box to be interviewed by Bernard Delfont, the impresario, Dick Hurran, the director of the show, Billy Marsh of the Entertainment Artistes' Benevolent Fund, and Robert Nesbitt, another director. I could tell at once that something was wrong. They said: "We're sorry, but we don't understand what these jokes are about." We then had a meeting with this formidable quartet going through Spike Mullins's script very slowly and saying things like: "Can you explain this one to us?" and "What's funny about this?" So I had the impossible task of explaining to them the point of each of Spike's eccentric whimsies.

It was a depressing business and they didn't look at all convinced. Then Billy Marsh said: "Why don't you do something else instead? Why don't you just go on stage now and do everything you did when you stood in for Cilla Black at the

Coventry Hippodrome?" That was a whole hour of material and they wanted me to do it there and then so that they could select something appropriate from it.

It was all very dispiriting, but somehow I still had enough fight in me to clamber up on to my high horse and say: "I'm sorry, but I'm not prepared to do that hour for you now, so that you can pick over it for bits you like." So I stuck with Spike's original material.

I arrived for my first Royal Command Performance with my confidence at nearly rock bottom, but I think my bit went pretty well. At least the Queen didn't summon me to the Royal Box to explain the jokes. And it wasn't long afterwards that everybody acknowledged how brilliant Spike's scripts were.

Actually, there was another unsettling thing about that night. I was sharing a dressing room with Buddy Rich, the great American jazz drummer, and his band, and before the show, Buddy needed some quite extensive dental treatment. The management sent for a fashionable dentist who used to do the teeth of all the great showbusiness visitors to London and he arrived and did Buddy's fillings right there in the dressing room. Watching someone else being drilled is just as bad as having it done to yourself. I was a nervous wreck when I arrived on stage.

Since then, I have done a good half dozen Royal Performances without mishap. Although there was one frightening incident after the 1973 show. When I got home afterwards and unpacked my bag, I thought "My God! I've shrunk!" I held up my dress shirt and it looked enormous. More like a medium-sized marquee. It was relief when I remembered I had been sharing a dressing room with Les Dawson and I had brought home his shirt by mistake.

When Spike Mullins wrote my monologues for *The Two*

Ronnies, his script – typed out by his wife Mary – used to arrive by BBC car from Slough. I would read it and I would laugh straight away. I would never alter it, although I might occasionally cut a tiny bit and then I would read it and read it throughout the week until I was completely familiar with the shape of it.

The scripts were masterpieces in the art of digression, jokes getting lost on the way to the punchline, side-tracks getting side-tracked, then out of the undergrowth there would pop up an old favourite gag – like "We were so poor that on a cold night my father used to suck a peppermint and we all sat round his tongue." Or: "We were so poor my brother was made in Hong Kong."

I can still recite many of these monologues by heart. A typical Spike preamble would go like this: "I actually found this joke in an old *Reader's Digest* in between an article called 'Having Fun with a Hernia' and a story about a woman who brought up a family of four with one hand, while waiting for Directory Enquiries . . ."

These monologues were a refinement of some of the work that I had been doing before and Spike was observant enough to see how it could be improved. He gave me a sort of coolness and a gentleness that I came to see suited me perfectly. There was no frenzy or panic, no going for a quick early laugh, no crash, bang wallop. There was a gentle, rather oblique introduction, which was a way of coaxing people into listening to the words.

Spike was a very funny man with a marvellously eccentric turn of phrase and was extremely highly regarded in the business. I think it is a great shame that he never got down to writing a play. In these monologues, he always managed to create a wonderful rolling picture, piling wild images on top of each other, as in his description of a church fete, which was supposed to be in aid of the Send the Old Folks Up the Amazon Fund – "The crowd at its peak was estimated to be somewhere in the region of 16. The beauty queen from the tyre factory – Miss Re-Tread of 1969 – sold kisses at 5p a time and old Fred at the butchers had a quid's worth and got a bit over-involved. However, disaster was averted thanks to the local fire brigade, four policemen and a chap with a humane killer. Then we had the Unusual Pets competition, which, owing to lack of support, was won by my wife's brother with a tin of salmon."

There were two main recurring themes in Spike's pieces and they were Catholic priests – because he was a Catholic – and really awful boring parties, presumably because had endured a few in his time. Here's his description of a party given (allegedly) by the producer: "My God it was quiet. It wasn't so much a party, it was more like waiting to take part in an ambush."

In conversation Spike's humour tended to be gloomy and this led to Dick Vosburgh nicknaming him the Despond of Slough. He lived in a very small house on a council estate, but he created a small kingdom for himself in the garden, with just a couple of tomato plants, a water feature and his exotic lizards.

I am happy that Spike's skills really reached their peak in the chair monologues he wrote for me – and I think he felt that his material had never been performed better. It was a terrific comedy marriage. He always wanted me to be even more laid back in my performances and he used to come and see me and say "You're still rushing it. You've got to slow down." And it was true; I had so much to say, so much material, such an outpouring of words and funny jokes that I would tend to take a terrific rush at it.

It is only nowadays, after all these years, that I feel I'm walking on to a stage and talking in the way Spike always wanted me to. I can just come on, walk up and down a bit and let the people sort of take me in. "Oh my goodness, he's smaller than I realised," they might say. Or: "He's a bit taller than I thought." Or: "The suit's nice."

Then I can just let them hear my voice and get used to it. I don't want to go out and hammer them straight away; I want to draw them in, not expect too much of them too quickly. It's like tickling trout – or guddling, as we say in the Borders.

Eventually Spike decided to give up writing the monologues because he felt he could not do any more, so they were taken over by David Renwick. David was one of the people who graduated in comedy writing after first offering us News Item jokes. He was trying to break into television and he was soon contributing sketches to the show and made a great success of the chair spot. David Renwick managed to capture the flavour and also followed Spike's tradition of abusing the producer – "Before we go any further, I must blow a kiss to our producer – the man who makes Boy George look like Charles Bronson . . ." After his stint with *The Two Ronnies* he went on to even greater success writing the sitcom *One Foot in the Grave* and also *Jonathan Creek*.

Spike Mullins died in 1994 and his funeral took place at a crematorium somewhere behind some gravel pits near Slough. A suitably eccentric location. As befitted such a brilliantly funny writer, it was an occasion for laughter as well as sadness. Dick Vosburgh made a very funny speech and he recalled that Spike was a non-driver who refused to go to any conference or meeting or to deliver a script unless a car was sent to pick him up. It was important to him, maybe the most important part of any deal he did. It may have been partly a matter of status, but it was also a foible. So, at the funeral, Dick was able to remark: "I am pleased to say that today they have sent a very special car for Spike."

CHAPTER TEN

*Concerns the filmed items in 'The Two Ronnies'. An account
of life on location and a discussion about the identity of the
Phantom Raspberry Blower. Also an account of my sitcom
'Sorry!' and the character of Timothy Lumsden and how we
made the show. An apple charlotte is mentioned. Finally, a
Viking imparts some surprising news.*

Of all the pieces for *The Two Ronnies* which we filmed on
location, I have fondest memories of our spoof of *The Admirable
Crichton*, J.M. Barrie's 1902 play about the grand London family
who are shipwrecked and survive on their desert island thanks
only to the resourcefulness of their butler. I was Lord Loam, the
head of the family, and Ronnie B was the butler. Susannah York
was Lady Loam and Koo Stark (who owed some of her fame to
being the girlfriend of Prince Andrew for a while) had a small
part as the housemaid Lord Loam runs off with.

Everything about the film looked wonderful. There were
brilliant props, including an animated rubber crocodile that
Ronnie B had to wrestle with in a terrific mock heroic scene.
We filmed in the New Forest, in Hampshire, at a time when the
countryside was truly looking its best and the set designer had

enhanced the woodland scenery with bits of rustic furniture and rough-hewn doors and windows, apparently made out of branches and tree trunks.

For the scenes shot in London we had elegant, open-topped vintage Bentleys and we filmed outside houses in Eaton Square. We were dressed in plus-fours, argyle socks, two-tone shoes and jaunty eight-piece caps. It was all very swish and lovely.

The great joy of *The Two Ronnies* was that it gave us the chance to play unlikely roles. I could play the Earl of So-and-So and Ronnie would be the butler. In other circumstances, even the most imaginative film or television director would be highly unlikely to cast me as the Earl of So-and-So or Lord Somebody. There is a tendency in casting to see an earl or a public schoolboy as being a certain sort of person who certainly doesn't look anything like me.

Let's face it, nobody is going to consider me for the role of Young Churchill; they'd be more likely to make me the bookie's clerk. If they put me in a film like *The Shooting Party* they would not make me one of the guns, along with Edward Fox and co; I'd be the gamekeeper's assistant, or a beater, or the man who brought the tea. There is an in-built sizeism here; a sort of snobbery about the shape a person is and the shape he is expected to be.

In *The Two Ronnies* I had a chance to break away from this. In sketches and films in the show I tended to be the one who played the aristocratic figure while Ron was often the truculent underling. I was the exasperated, pin-striped, posh gent in the restaurant while Ron was the surly waiter; I was His Lordship dining with Her Ladyship, seated at opposite ends of the long table in the country mansion, and Ron was the retainer who served the meal with a sort of offhand menace ("Your nuts, my lord").

Because he had years of experience as a character actor,

Ronnie B tended to go for the richer character role. If anything, I was more likely to play quite a bit of "me". I would play the sort of Jack Buchanan type with the easy charm. In a way, this was how I had imagined myself when I was a boy in Edinburgh, going to the Glover Turner Robertson school and picturing myself as an actor in light comedy, but it had not turned out in the way I had dreamed it.

If a part required a "voice" – a Yorkshire accent or a bit of American, for example – Ron, because of his experience, could do it without allowing it to ruin the actual performance. I could do the accents, but I always had to take extra care that they did not overload the character.

The important thing was that, for these 16 years, we were in the happy position of being our own casting directors.

As well as the one-off spoofs, like our version of *The Admirable Crichton* and *All Creatures Grunt and Smell*, we also had the serials, the baffling cases solved by the intrepid sleuths Charley Farley and Piggy Malone, and *The Worm That Turned*, the ultimate triumph of women over men.

And, of course, there was also the Victorian crime melo-drama, *The Phantom Raspberry Blower of Old London Town* – a sort of Jack-the-Ripper-meets-the-Keystone-Kops. This was full of thunder and lightning and portentously dramatic music – and over-acting.

It was written by Spike Milligan and, as it said on the credits "A Gentleman". This gentleman, not surprisingly, was Gerald Wiley. Ron and I played a multitude of roles in this melodrama, but my main part was that of the mutton chop whiskered Scotland Yard detective – known as Corner of the Yard – who had the impossible task of tracking down the blower of the phantom raspberries. There wasn't much of a plot – just a weekly headlong rush from pun to pun.

I believe that Spike Milligan said that we could have the rights to this surreal serial free of charge on condition that he was allowed to blow all the raspberries for the sound-track. They turned out to be notably loud, full-blown and squelchy raspberries, but I am not altogether certain that they were the work of Spike Milligan. I have an idea that, in the end, Ronnie B got somebody else to blow them. I don't know who that person might be. As far as I am concerned, that raspberry blower remains a phantom. His (or her) identity remains a mystery to me. This is one of the unsung makers of rude noises of history.

The Phantom Raspberry Blower was filmed partly on location and partly in the studio. The other serials and spoofs were done purely on location. The New Forest was not only the setting for *The Admirable Crichton,* but also for other films such as a jerky black and white silent and sub-titled Western about the goldrush. We also went to Chagford, in Devon, for Charley Farley and Piggy Malone.

In fact, Ron and I became experts on country house hotels all over the country, sometimes staying in the same place for three or four weeks while we were filming. We did our own research into hotels and made our own decisions as to where to stay. Sometimes we ended up in the same hotel, but not always. I liked to stay in a place that was near to a golf course, or even had a golf course of its own, so that I could have a solitary walk over the course in the evening, enjoy the soothing smell of newly cut grass, and unwind after a day's filming.

When you are staying in the same hotel for three weeks or so you get very well looked after as they get to know your preferences and your little ways. I have happy memories of staying in places such as the Green Man, at Shurdington, near Cheltenham, and the comfortable routine I got into – leaving my shoes outside the room to be cleaned, a bath and a change at the end of the day, sitting outside on the lawn with a tincture and applying myself to the serious study of the menu.

Ron got up earlier in the morning than I did. He was always interested in what order we would do the filming, what the weather was going to do, which scenes should be shot before the rain started and what the light would be like. He was always concerned with this sort of detail and all the practicalities and that's why the years of *The Two Ronnies* took much more out of him than of me.

The only time we went abroad for filming was when we sailed on the cruise liner *Canberra* for some episodes of Charley Farley and Piggy Malone. We got on the ship at Southampton, filmed on board, then also filmed during stopovers in Marseille and Madeira. There were separate quarters for Ron and me and the crew (I mean the BBC crew, not the lot running the ship) and we had our own bit of deck set aside for us, but by that time Ron and I were well known faces and we were in constant danger of being added to the list of interesting features and landmarks which could be sighted by passengers during the cruise. On a ship you are trapped and it's hard to preserve your privacy. I found myself becoming as furtive as a stowaway, opening my cabin door a tiny crack to see if the coast was clear, scurrying down passageways, ducking behind corners and doing a great deal of lurking.

The other occasion Ron and I travelled abroad together was when we flew to Montreux, in Switzerland, to collect an award at the television festival in 1976. This was not for *The Two Ronnies*, but for a 45-minute silent film called *The Picnic*, written by Gerald Wiley. It wasn't *actually* a silent film; there were sound effects, but the dialogue was a rhubarb-ish series of grunts and mutters. It was a farcical but idyllic short story, an account of a sort of grand Edwardian family, with servants, going for a day out in the country. Ronnie B wrote two others like it, *Futtock's End* and *By the Sea*.

On this trip to Montreux, we must have given some people a misleading impression of what we were like together. We always thought that off-screen we were disappointingly more serious than people would imagine comedians to be. Many people expect comedians to be japing every minute of the day and find it difficult to think of us as serious human beings.

This occasion at the airport before our departure for Montreux must have convinced onlookers that we were a sort of permanent comedy turn. They must have thought "My God, they're so funny *all the time!*" Little did they know.

Passengers were being taken to the aircraft by coach. We walked from the terminal with our hand baggage to the coach and it happened to be pretty well full by the time we got there. Ron boarded the coach and, just as I was about to follow, the automatic doors closed leaving me shut out. So there was one Ronnie inside and the other Ronnie stuck outside, peering through the window, quite taken aback. What clever timing! What hilarity! So it was *bon voyage* from me and *bon voyage* from him.

Of course, everyone on the bus thought it was hysterical. And I've always thought those people must have gone home and said: "I saw them once and they were so funny; everywhere they went they were doing something funny. There was this time when Ronnie Barker got into the airport coach and then the other one . . ."

While we made *The Two Ronnies,* Ron and I took care – as I have said – to keep our separate identities and have our separate careers with our own programmes. For me, the most important one was the sitcom *Sorry!*

A family portrait, with Anne and the girls. Emma is on the left and Sophie on the right. The dog is Cindy.

A golfing lesson from Henry Cotton in Penina 1969.

Golf at Penina. Jimmy Tarbuck is on the back of Pacifico
the donkey who can't bear to look as I take my shot.

It's a big smile from me and it's a big smile from him.

Two ladies on the pier.

© BBC

© BBC

Piggy Malone and Charley Farley in one of the filmed serials
we did in *The Two Ronnies*.

The Mounties – a musical number from *The Two Ronnies*.

Another *Two Ronnies* musical number, this time two characters loosely based on Kid Creole and Boy George.

My appearance as one of the Dromios in the muscial
The Boys from Syracuse. With Maggie Fitzgibbon.

Cinderella at the Palladium in 1972.

With Diana Dors and Ronnie B in *The Worm That Turned*,
another *Two Ronnies* production

Here are the News Items – an important ingredient of *The Two Ronnies*.

A scene from the sitcom *Sorry* with me as Timothy Lumsden, Barbara Lott as my overpowering mother and William Moore as my father. It looks as if she is blaming me for the two microphones which can be seen at the top of the picture.

In the script of *Sorry* by Ian Davidson and Peter Vincent, there was something heroic about the way Timothy endured the stifling presence of his mother.

Ronnie B and I were awarded the OBE (one each) in 1978.

Sean Connery and I grew up in Edinburgh at the same time. Here he is
appearing at a golf charity day I gave in aid of the Lord's Taverners.

My father, a brilliant golfer, at the Prestonfield
course, in Edinburgh. This was the course on
which he died in 1975.

With John Cleese and Michael Palin in the film *Fierce Creatures*.

In a rubber sea lion outfit for *Fierce Creatures*.
Only slightly better than being an ape.

In the chair. And on the way to the punchline.

I first saw a script of *Sorry!* written by Ian Davidson and Peter Vincent, when I was making the pilot of a different sitcom for the BBC. The pilot was for the usual sort of sitcom of the period, about a married couple living together in a complicated sort of way, just divorced, or just about to get divorced, or thinking of getting back together again, with a difficult teenage daughter somewhere in the picture, probably, and no doubt a half-crazy cleaning lady and an interfering next door neighbour. And they probably lived in the suburbs, and I expect there was a mother-in-law somewhere on the horizon. I can't remember it in detail, but that's how they usually were.

The pilot went fairly well, but, while I was doing it, I was carrying round this script which had been sent to me by my ex-agent Jimmy Grafton who acted for Peter Vincent. I hadn't looked at the script because I didn't want to be distracted from the pilot I was doing; a BBC executive happened to see me with it and said: "I don't think you need bother to read that."

All the same, I read it and I liked it immediately. I thought it was a very good idea with a strong plot. I showed it to Ronnie Barker and he agreed with me. "This is the best possible script for you," he said.

It was clear to me straight away that there was something special about this conflict between the domineering, control freak, suffocating mother and her grown up son, who was 41, but treated by her as if he was four. He always seemed to be desperately trying to make a life of his own, but when he got the opportunity he funked it.

He was a lovely and funny character to play – a kind of Walter Mitty. He thought his motor scooter was a Ferrari; he wanted to have a flat of his own and invite girls round, but it was all a fantasy; he pretended to be bold and worldly but he was really just a timid mother's boy.

The first series went out in 1981. I played the part of Timothy Lumsden, and I had a little curly hairpiece fitted at the front, just to give myself a different, sillier appearance. Barbara Lott was my nightmare mother and my father was played by William Moore, the husband of Mollie Sugden. David Askey was the director for every series.

The father in *Sorry!* was also appallingly bullied by his wife and always trying to smoke a secret cheroot and being driven out to his compost heap or the garden shed. Sometimes he would make an unconvincing attempt at putting his foot down with his regular cry of "*Language,* Timothy!" He and Timothy were actually in a sort of timid conspiracy together against the tyranny of Mrs Lumsden.

Timothy was a sad and pathetic character and also a very true one. I got many letters from viewers saying: "We have a boy in the office where I work and he actually *lives* Timothy's life." As the character worked in a library I also received a lot of letters from librarians saying: "We are trying to improve the image of librarians and we're not sure that Timothy Lumsden is a step in the right direction."

The theme of the all-powerful mother and the crushed grown-up son has been taken up quite recently by Caroline Aherne and Craig Cash as Mrs Merton and Malcolm, but in a much darker way, I think. What redeemed Timothy from being a total wimp was his humour. He was cheeky and positive and, above all, in his ghastly family circumstances, he was resilient. There was actually something heroic about the way he endured the stifling presence of his mother.

He could be quite sarky with his mother. Every time he walked back into the house there would be a cry of "Is that you, Timothy?" followed by "Have you wiped your feet?" He would come up with some cheeky reply and crack good jokes about her cooking and the way she kept the house – because she was quite terrible at these things.

"How sweet!" he said once, staring at something awful on a plate. "You've been all the way to Foulness to bring me back an oil slick."

The mother's recipes were surreally inventive. "You *like* marzipan and piccalilli," she informed Timothy in one episode. "Separately, yes," he replied. "Together, I like them as much as coconut matting and a sick headache."

She also cooked ghastly stews which re-appeared day after day, even for breakfast, and she specialised in the long-life tea-bag. And she was funny, too, following Timothy on his doomed escapades, hiding behind trees and trying to spy on him with girls.

Of course the character was not a bit like Barbara Lott the actress who played her. As well as being a lovely person, she was actually a splendid cook. I remember that before we went to film on location, Barbara would always take care to prepare a whole lot of meals to leave behind for her husband who was not such a great one for looking after himself.

There was a good bit of physical comedy in *Sorry!* – mostly inspired bits of clumsiness by Timothy. I've always rather prided myself in my ability to stumble – and mainly stumble intentionally over words. I'm quite good at . . . er, pretending to forget the words, or lose my place in the . . . you know. And then . . .

Where was I? Actually Ronnie Barker wrote a brilliant two-hander sketch on this theme for *The Two Ronnies*. It was a dialogue between two old blokes in a pub.

RB: How are you then?
RC: Mustn't grumble. I've just been up the . . .
RB: Club?
RC: No, up the . . .

RB: Dogs?

RC: No . . .

RB: Fish shop?

RC: No . . . .

RB: Doctors?

RC: Doctors, yes. Up the doctors. I've just been up the doctors. I've been having a bit of trouble with my, er . . .

RB: Chest?

RC: No, with my . . . .

RB: Back?

RC: No . . .

RB: Side?

RC: No . . . .

RB: Backside?

RC: No, my wife.

And so on and on. It was a very successful sketch and one of the things I liked about it was the way that the character I played never once got angry, or even a tiny bit put out, at all the Ronnie Barker character's attempts to finish his sentences for him.

The excellent thing about *Sorry!* was that the episodes were always very good stories – even Kinglsey Amis mentioned this in some article he wrote for a magazine, which really delighted Ian and Peter. Not only were they very good stories, they were also very eventful. A lot happened and there were plenty of twists.

There was a very well-plotted episode about Timothy playing Bottom in an amateur dramatic society production of *A Midsummer Night's Dream*; it had a touching ending when his girlfriend told him it was all over between them and he just sat there wearing the ass's head. There was another in which he had a heart scare while playing tennis and he thought he was about to die; he daydreamed his funeral which was a magnificent Walter Mitty affair, complete with full military honours and the appearance of a glamorous central European aristocratic lady who turned out to have been his secret lover.

In another story, the mobile library van broke down on a blasted heath and he met three witch-like old crones who convinced him he was about to be promoted in the library service. I remember there was also a very good episode about Timothy going on a self-assertiveness course. The boys were very good about that sort of storyline – and also about plots involving, mysticism, faith healing and herbal medicine.

The first episode was actually top of the ratings in London – I think many people were curious to see me in a sitcom – and after that it always had high audience figures. The programme also had a very important admirer in Bahrain – but I'll come to that later.

We did about three weeks of filming for every series of *Sorry!* This took place in Wallingford, in Oxfordshire, where we could shoot people going in and out of the Lumsden house, scenes in the street and the car park, and so on. It was good to go back to the same place all the time, because the natives got used to us and we were able to fit into the community in a way. We usually stayed in a pub hotel in the high street and it was a very happy arrangement.

Rehearsals for the studio recording took place in a church hall just off Kensington Church, in West London. It was rather a smart sort of place, much nicer than the Acton Hilton, and in an area of antique shops and sandwich bars which used nice multigrain bread. There was also a wonderful cake shop, halfway down Church Street on the right. The comedian Dave Allen has lived most of his life in the area and, on the first day of rehearsals, he very sweetly left me a little present in the cake shop. It was an apple charlotte, tied up with a bow and with a message on it, saying: "Welcome to the district, happy rehearsals – Dave Allen."

The church hall was grand and stylish, as church halls go, and had rooms on various levels. We would rehearse upstairs and downstairs there would be a ladies' sale of work, or the blood transfusion service, or something like that. We rehearsed there from Tuesday to Friday, working very hard all the time and hardly stopping for a sandwich with that multi-grain bread. I always learned my lines very early in the week, so that I was able to relax and concentrate on enjoying playing the part of Timothy. On Saturdays we had a camera rehearsal in a studio at the Television Centre and on Sundays we recorded the programme with a studio audience.

Felix Bowness did the warm-ups, but I also did quite a lot of them myself, and I found I could quite easily slip in and out of the role of Timothy. So if there was a hold-up I could entertain them as Ronnie Corbett, then go back to playing my part. It helped to reduce the tension and create a relaxed atmosphere. In a way, they were getting two shows for one, and it helped the performers if the audience was kept bubbling. A studio audience ought to go away at the end feeling entertained, not wearied. Sometimes they are not very well looked after, or they are taken for granted.

On a few occasions when we were making *The Two Ronnies,* Ron and I would get things a bit wrong on purpose, just to help the audience relax a bit and to stop them feeling overwhelmed by all the technical mystique of the studio – and, anyway, things sometimes go better a second or third time.

Ronnie Barker and I were both dressed as hairy and disgusting Vikings with big horned helmets when he first told me that he was going to retire. It was in 1986 and we had just finished breakfast in our caravan on the coast, near Corfe Castle, in

Dorset. "I thought you ought to know that I have decided that next year's Christmas Special will be my last," he said. It was a secret between us. The head of Light Entertainment at the BBC was told a little later, but no-one else was told until the actual recording of the 1987 Christmas Special. After the recording, he and Joy and Anne and I went out for our usual Indian meal in Westbourne Grove, and that was that. Ron then went home and changed his telephone number, leaving a recorded message on the old number which simply said: "Ronnie Barker has ceased performing and is no longer at this number." So that was absolutely that – and rather typical of Ron.

Because he had taken the trouble to warn me, it did not come as an awful shock. I didn't think "Christ! What am I going to do now?" *The Two Ronnies* was still getting huge audience figures, but we had begun to find it increasingly difficult to get material that was new and not just like something we had done before. After all the series we had done, we seemed to have performed sketches on just about every subject.

From time to time, we even talked about giving the show a rest for a while and perhaps doing a sitcom together, something on the lines of *The Odd Couple,* but then Ronnie decided to stop altogether and retire to Oxfordshire and his antiques.

He was also concerned about his health, particularly his blood pressure and he wanted to make a complete break from writing and performing. He had, after all, been doing the work of two men – Gerald Wiley and Ronnie Barker. Good old Gerald had been at it since the days of *Frost on Sunday* in 1968. As I have mentioned, in all the time we worked together, Ron was the worrier. He was the one who tweaked the script and fretted over the details. He involved himself in the editing, too, because he enjoyed it, but this also put a greater burden on him.

As we had always made sure that we preserved our own independent professional lives, the end of our partnership was not like an amputation. I think, in a way, I was prepared for it from the first day we starting working on the first programme of the first series, back in 1971. Our partnership began in a steady, practical and thoughtful way – and that was how it ended.

At the time *The Two Ronnies* stopped I had been doing the sitcom *Sorry!* but then the head of BBC1 changed and Jonathan Powell came in and he decided he didn't like it, or he thought it had come to the end of its natural span, so that came off at the same time. I was disappointed about that; I thought there was scope for one more series, but there it was.

Changes of senior staff at the BBC inevitably affect the careers of performers; I think they have certainly affected me. We are all creatures of fashion; you go out of fashion and then you come back into fashion, and you've just got to hang around long enough – like clothes – until you are back in style.

I think Jonathan Powell's television background was in drama, and I didn't feel he was especially interested in the light entertainment side of things. I've always had the suspicion that light entertainment people were considered lightweight, although amusing people is a seriously difficult thing to do. I think that perhaps some of the more cerebral controllers and commissioners of series and dramas regard those of us in light entertainment as trivial.

Anyway, it meant that in a very short space of time, I lost my sitcom and I lost the programme that put me near the top of the ratings every week it was on. I was left feeling a bit solitary for a while. But I had been hankering for some time to do more solo stand-up work, so this was a new opportunity. It was time to start again.

CHAPTER ELEVEN

The art of pantomime is discussed and the secrets of Dames, "slosh" and the Kirby wire, are revealed. I describe my experiences as an Ugly Sister and as Buttons. Cary Grant puts in an unexpected appearance. The scene suddenly switches to Australia where Ronnie B and I, with our families, spend a year. The window cleaners of Hong Kong get a look in. We return to the London Palladium where I am struck down with a frightening illness.

The Palladium has always been an important place for me, ever since I took my girlfriend, the RAF nursing sister, to see Danny Kaye perform there and I sat in a box from where I could watch him going off for his first break and see his dresser waiting for him in the wings. That was, in a way, the beginning of my love affair with the Palladium – and, as it turned out, the beginning of the end of my love affair with the nursing sister.

Ever since my appearance as the wicked aunt in *Babes in the Wood* at the St Catherine-in-the-Grange church youth club, pantomime has always been special to me. Recently, panto-mimes have been rather mocked by the posh press, probably because people have taken less trouble over them than they should. Stars from television soaps and sitcoms have been put into them, even though they have had no particular skills as pantomime artistes and they have been there to earn a nice lump of money rather than to do justice to the show.

Proper pantomimes were always performed by the real vaudeville artistes – people like Norman Evans and the outrageous Dougie Byng. Evans was a great northern comedian, born in Rochdale in 1901 and discovered by Gracie Fields, making his first appearance in London in 1934. In variety, he was most famous for his "Over the Garden Wall" sketch in which he played the hideous Lancashire housewife Fanny Fairbottom, leaning over her wall exchanging gossip with her (unseen) next door neighbour. It was an earlier version of Les Dawson's female creation who was always manoeuvring her dentures and hitching up her bosom.

Douglas Byng was tremendously camp and saucy and hugely popular in cabaret in London in the 1930s. Helena Pickard, or Pixie, who was such a support to me in my early days in London, was a friend of Dougie Byng and she arranged for me to go and see him for advice and encouragement. I went to visit him in his dressing room at a theatre in Glasgow. The thing I remember most vividly about meeting him was the discovery that, offstage and in everyday conversation, he had the most violent and obvious nervous twitch in his chin and his neck. Amazingly, this completely disappeared when he went on stage to perform. On this occasion I first met the director, Freddie Carpenter, never guessing that many years later he would become a great friend and would actually direct me in *Cinderella* in the same city.

There were other famous dames in Scotland, like Harry Gordon and Dave Willis who were big names purely and simply for the pantomimes they did, and the summer seasons of revue. Harry Gordon, who died in 1959, appeared as a Dame at the Glasgow Alhambra for 16 consecutive seasons.

And there were legendary Ugly Sisters in the old days, like Ford and Sheen, the oldest established double drag act, and then Bartlett and Ross; Terry Bartlett was the over-the-top Dame with the outlandish costumes, while Colin Ross was the stylish and elegant one. Dames like these had wonderful costumes which they spent most of the year making. In fact there were some Dames whose entire lives were devoted to the pantomime season.

In 1971, Louis Benjamin, the impresario who ran the Palladium and Albert Knight, the director, asked Ronnie Barker and me to play the Ugly Sisters in a new production of *Cinderella*. This was at the time when our long run with *The Two Ronnies* on television was just beginning. Ron was not really keen on doing that sort of work, because he wasn't interested in the vaudeville side of things, so I said I would play Buttons instead. Clodagh Rodgers, the singer, was Cinderella, the Ugly Sisters were played by Julian Orchard and Terry Scott and David Kossoff was the Baron.

It helped that it was a pantomime I knew very well as a performer. I had already played an Ugly Sister – with Stanley Baxter as the other one – in a spectacular production in Glasgow in 1966 which had gone on the following year to Edinburgh.

This was at the time my face was first becoming known to the public because of *The Frost Report*. Before I played the Ugly Sister in Glasgow, Danny La Rue very generously gave me a master-class in make-up. He invited me into his dressing room, gave me all his make-up materials and showed me how to put them on. Unfortunately, he was really too good at it and I came away looking like a lovely little china doll. Not quite the thing for an Ugly Sister and I had to wipe a lot of it off, so that there was less glamour and more of my own face shining through.

The Glasgow *Cinderella* was directed by Freddie Carpenter

who was really the king of pantomime; the designer was Berkeley Sutcliffe and Anthony Holland did the Sisters' costumes. The whole thing was as sumptuous as an opera. Lonnie Donegan, the maestro of skiffle, was Buttons, Paula Hendrix was Cinderella and Lynn Kennington (who was later in *The Boys from Syracuse* with me) was the Principal Boy. In the following year, in Edinburgh, David Kernon was Buttons.

The thing about pantomime is that the story has to be told but you also need a lot of "bits" that are really funny. Stanley and I did an enormous number of bits. We did the "slosh" routine, where you re-decorate the room and get whitewash all over you, and we did the two musical sisters, with me playing the saxophone and Stanley at the piano. We were dressed as 1920s flappers, with the band round the forehead and the feather in the middle. And then we came away and did a flappers' routine, dancing the Charleston and swinging the beads round our necks.

This was a scene at Prince Charming's ball, but Stanley and I also did lots of other little extra bits in the show, like the Haunted Bedroom routine and an exquisite cod ballet.

I am told that there are records of the great pantomime "decorating the parlour" or "slosh" slapstick routine going back 200 years. More recently, the great practitioner of the slosh art was Charlie Cairoli, one of Britain's best-known clowns who died in 1980. The secret is to start very slowly, even gracefully, and build up to totally messy climax, a whitewash Armageddon. The whole thing is choreographed in detail, like a ballet. You have the mishaps with the stepladder, the paste table, and the pasting of the strip of wallpaper, with the ends suddenly and unhelpfully rolling up, the attempts to press the paper to the wall, where each decorator needs five pairs of hands, and that appalling moment when one of the decorators climbs the ladder, trampling the roll of paper which has been carefully laid out on the steps.

Then the two performers whitewash each other with their huge distemper brushes in a ritualised fight which might be regarded as vaudeville's answer to Japanese kabuki theatre, before the final glorious moment when one of them pours the paint into the other's hat and jams it so hard on to the other's head that the paint spurts out like a fountain through a hole in the top of the hat.

There is a special recipe for making the traditional slosh. You grate sticks of shaving soap and whisk them in a certain temperature of water in a plastic bucket. After that you can get different colours by adding cochineal or various cooking dyes. When Stanley Baxter and I did it we had pink, blue and white slosh. The assistant stage manager responsible for getting it ready was John K. Cooper and it was quite a headache for him. Still, it was probably good training for the job he had later as head of light entertainment at London Weekend Television.

Sometimes people cheat and use aerosol foam instead of the old-fashioned slosh made of shaving sticks. The audience don't respond to this in the same way. They know that shaving foam is not a *real* mess and that you can just brush it off, so it's not funny.

Of course, the real thing is not such a joke for the performers. The slosh gets in your eyes and makes them pretty sore. During the run of a pantomime you are getting sloshed twice daily and every time it happens you have to go off in the interval and have a complete shower, make up all over again and get dressed again, so it is a messy way of getting laughs.

Stanley and I and Peter Darrell, who was director of the Scottish Ballet at the time, also created this very funny ballet for the two of us, and afterwards I developed a version of it for myself. It's an elaborate travesty of *Swan Lake*, with me as the cygnet on my teetering points and in white tulle at the end of the line, getting little things wrong at first, then gradually getting into a worse and worse muddle, then panic, then chaos. It is a huge success with the mums and dads and the children.

I did the ballet routine in the Palladium *Cinderella* and I did it again when we did a couple of seasons of *The Two Ronnies* at the same theatre. So, I'm quite experienced at it. If you want an *entrechat* I can do you one at the drop of a hat.

I don't think I would be able to count the number of *Cinderella* pantomimes I have been in, and I have been Buttons all over the place (sounds like the aftermath of a too-tight pair of trousers) from Bromley to Newcastle.

I was all set for the part at the Palladium in 1971 because I had done it the year before for Derek Salberg's production in Birmingham. Derek used to put on a very good family panto-mime and so I felt I had really got the hang of the *Cinderella* book and the storyline in Birmingham and this was the ideal preparation for London.

I was thrilled that my dad could come and see me when I starred in the London Palladium *Cinderella*. He came to the first night and afterwards he and my mum and Anne and I went to the Talk of the Town where the management made a fuss of us -which I think he privately enjoyed. Before the first night, Anne took him to buy a new suit. He really didn't think it was right for a woman to be there when he was getting a suit, but, because it was Anne, he was prepared to make an exception. "This is probably the last new suit I'll ever have," he said, and he was right.

The Patton Brothers and Charlie Stewart were with me in the show in Birmingham and they also joined the cast in London, at my request. Charlie Stewart was the Scottish comedian I had written to for advice 20 years ago, in 1951, shortly after I arrived in London and when I was trying to get started and he was in the *Fol-de-Rols*. So it was really good to be working alongside my early mentor.

The Patton Brothers are a wonderfully funny double act and they come from a long line of theatrical people, so they tap dance well, they sing well, they "feed" you well and they can also do their own act and fit in with all the little bits of shtick – i.e. the routines, or the set pieces. So if you say to the Patton Brothers "Can we do 'Busy Bee' here?" or "Shall we do the 5p con trick bit?" they know exactly what you mean. If you are ever short of a "front cloth" act, while the scene is being changed behind, you know that the Pattons will do it.

They are still doing very well – and so are their younger brothers who are called the Chuckle Brothers and they do a thing on afternoon television for children called Chucklevision.

After Birmingham in 1970, every time I have done a pantomime I have tried to get Charlie Stewart and the Patton Brothers in it as well, because we've had so many bits worked out together. It's a godsend for the management when you can come along to *Mother Goose* or *Jack and the Beanstalk* with these prepared routines and all the props for them. Each time I've done a pantomime I've had my ballet bit and my trapeze bit and also these strong visual things which can be slotted into the show.

The Pattons and I had this wonderful balancing act routine. We all came on like circus performers, in leopardskin leotards, and they started lifting me and throwing me to each other. I was on a wire, so they could balance me on one finger or toss me through the air, right across the stage. The whole thing ended with me flying across the stage and being supposed to land, sitting on the platform they were holding up for me. Of course, in all the excitement, they accidentally on purpose, got the thing upside down, so I came to land on my backside on the wrong end of the pole which was the handle. Then blackout.

You have to be quite courageous to go on the wire and you

have to trust the person on the other end, in the wings, because your fate and your dignity are in his hands. It's called a Kirby Wire and is operated by a specialist firm called Kirby's Flying Ballets which has supervised just about all the flying in all the productions of *Peter Pan* there have ever been. The Kirby people come in and set you up in the harness, then probably stay for about 10 days of rehearsals before handing you over to the most intelligent stagehand.

And the most sober stagehand, you hope. When you come from the dressing room to do your flying act it's a good idea to take a close look at the chap who is going to be holding on to the other end of the wire, say "Hello, Dave" in a specially friendly voice and hope he hasn't been to the pub yet.

Rehearsing with the wire can really be a humiliating business. You show up on stage at about 11 o'clock in the morning and you are wearing this harness thing, like some kind of torture instrument, over your trousers. So you are all wired up and you're ready for take-off.

"Now, take it gently, please. Oops, not so fast."

You dangle a few feet above the stage, swinging gently to a fro.

"OK. Up a bit."

You rocket towards the lighting in the roof. Then you stop suddenly. Don't look down or you might discover that your groin is on fire. Now you are slowly beginning to spin on the end of your wire.

"OK. That's fine."

Whatever you do, don't say anything to upset Dave.

"Now lower me down a bit. Gently. GENTLY."

Your descent stops at once. Oh God, Dave's feelings are hurt. He's going to let go of the end of the wire and storm out to the pub. The harness is gripping you a bit tighter.

★

"Maybe down just a tiny bit more, Dave, if you wouldn't mind. And perhaps just a wee bit slower if that's all right with you."

Why is your voice so high-pitched? Nothing happens. Perhaps Dave didn't hear you that time. If you shout you might give him a fright which could lead to him letting go and to you plummeting.

"Would someone ask Dave nicely to lower me a bit?"

You are now, horizontal, doing the breast stroke in mid-air.

"Actually, I think that might be a bit too low. Could we rise, just a bit, ever so slowly?"

Now you are hanging upside down and swinging.

"That's excellent. Shall we hold it there for a bit?"

They say Peter Pan never grew up, but while he was rehearsing on the wire he must have aged about 30 years.

At one performance of *Cinderella* at the Palladium I was putting on the harness while the Patton Brothers were marching up and down on the stage to circus music before our big balancing act when suddenly a strap broke. The webbing had just rotted. It was amazingly lucky that the thing had come apart then and not while I was actually flying through the air.

There were the Pattons parading up to that pom-tiddle-om-pom music suggesting something tremendously exciting was about to happen and I was in the wings, miming like anything to them that I couldn't go on. I often wonder what the audience must have thought, seeing all this build-up and then nothing at all happening and the Pattons just marching off again.

After that performance, the actual Dave who was in charge of hauling on the wire that day came round to my dressing room in a high state of exasperation. "Would you believe it?" he said. "Of all the afternoons that could happen it had to happen when my mum and dad were in." His proud parents had come in

203

specially to admire his expertise in operating the wire and their day was ruined because of the rotten harness. Things didn't often go wrong like that – although once there was a power failure at the Palladium and we had to do the whole show by candlelight.

It was a long and strenuous run – 16 weeks, twice daily, every day. I used to go to the theatre at 11.30 in the morning and not get home till after eleven o'clock at night. I never used to leave the theatre between performances; I would just have tea, watch television and have a little sleep. The run started at Christmas and when it was all over the crocuses were coming up at home.

The following year I was asked to be Buttons again in a follow-up production of the Palladium *Cinderella* and I could choose if I wanted to do it in Bristol or in Manchester. I couldn't make up my mind and in the end I just said to Anne: "Oh, I might as well go to Bristol; you never know, Cary Grant might visit his mother at Christmas and pop in and see the show." Cary Grant, who was born Archie Leach, came from Bristol and I had heard that his mother still lived there.

In Bristol the production was re-directed by Dick Hurran, a wonderful showman who added all sorts of extravagant touches and lavish tableaux. The Ugly Sisters were played by John Inman and Barry Howard and it was during the run that John Inman went off to audition for *Are You Being Served?* so it was an important turning point in his life. And not long afterward Barry Howard got the part of the ballroom dancing instructor in *Hi de Hi*.

One day, after the matinee, I was sitting in my dressing room resting when the theatre manager came round and said he had just had a telephone call from Cary Grant's secretary; Cary Grant had booked seats for tonight's performance and would it be all right if he came round afterwards for a drink?

That's the sort of storyline you normally only get in panto-mimes; some fairy godmother, with not much to do and generally mooching around, had overheard my idle remark to Anne, decided to treat it as a wish, and had magicked Cary Grant.

That night he arrived in my dressing room in his tortoiseshell glasses and his suit made of black and white checked Glen Urquhart tweed, looking exactly just like you would expect Cary Grant to look if someone had waved a magic wand to make him appear, gleaming and immaculate. I could hardly believe it was true. Anyway he was real enough to accept a gin and tonic and he told me he had enjoyed the show. He also told me that there had once been plans for him and Fred Astaire to play the Ugly Sisters with Mickey Rooney as Buttons. That would have been really something.

It was while I was in Bristol that I first met Ron Waverley. He was the man from Kelso I mentioned earlier who used to refer to people as "fresh in frae' fair oot". Ron was a member of the chorus in the pantomime and he was trying to make up his mind whether to give up the business or stick with it. Finally he decided to give it up and came to work for Anne and me, mainly helping with the driving, but doing all sorts of other things for us. He became a dear friend and he died, far too young, of cancer. Ron was very sweet and, like a lot of country boys, he was a bit of a Tory. His mum had been a nanny for the Duke of Roxburghe and he was very proud of the fact that he had sung in the choir for the Duke's son's christening.

He was Ronnie Barker's dresser for one of the seasons we did at the London Palladium, but most of the time he drove me around and was my dresser. He was so unassuming. He couldn't come into a room without first giving a very diffident knock and murmuring "It's all right; it's only me." His real name was Ron Elms, but professionally he called himself Waverley after the Walter Scott novels – another little reminder of the Borders.

In 1973, after *Cinderella* in Bristol, I decided I was successful enough to have a golden coach of my own – a new Rolls Royce. With *The Two Ronnies* going into its fourth year, I suppose I was beginning to feel prosperous enough. I had had a second-hand Rolls before, which I bought when I was doing pantomime in Birmingham, but this was going to be the real thing. Anne and I went to the Rolls Royce headquarters in Crewe where they made a fuss of us, gave us lunch and invited us to choose the colour. We went for Le Mans blue, with pale cream for the roof, actually.

The car was due to be delivered to me in Eastbourne where I was appearing in a summer show. I remember it was supposed to arrive at 2.30 in the afternoon and the family gathered for the big moment. Nothing happened. After a while, I started pacing up and down and looking at my watch in the manner of a person who is wondering what can have happened to his brand new Rolls Royce. This is rather like a man pacing up and down and looking at his watch and wondering what can have happened to the No. 31 bus, but there is a bit more shoulder movement involved. Anne and Emma and Sophie started giving me the sort of looks you give a person who thinks he is about to get a new Rolls Royce, but is sadly deluded.

Then the telephone rang. "Mr Corbett, it's about your Rolls Royce . . . ."

"Which one?" I replied.

No I didn't, but I would have if I had thought quickly enough.

It turned out that the chauffeur bringing the car to Eastbourne for me had decided to pull into a lay-by as he approached the town so that he could straighten his cap. The trouble was, it wasn't a lay-by. It was one of those pits of gravel that lorries can turn into if their brakes fail. The poor man found himself sitting in my magnificent new car sedately sinking, until the thing was up to its hub-caps in gravel. It had to be hauled out, put on a lorry and taken back to Crewe, leaving me in Eastbourne wondering if fate had decided that I wasn't really meant to be the owner of a brand new Rolls Royce.

A week later my new Le Mans blue and pale cream status symbol was back in Eastbourne and I set off with Anne and Emma and Sophie to drive it to London. On the way we tested all the features. As one does. "Ah this is the button that makes the windows go down," I observed expertly. Unfortunately, because of some minor electrical fault, the windows would not go up again. So, with all the windows open, we continued our stylish journey to London. And then it started to rain. At 90 miles per hour the only sound you could hear was of the raindrops dripping off our ears.

Looking back on it now, buying a new Rolls Royce seems a strange thing for me to be doing, but in those days it was somehow more appropriate. Anne and I have never regarded ourselves as being flash, and I didn't really feel that I had become a wealthy man; I suppose that buying a Rolls Royce didn't seem quite such an outrageous extravagance at that time – I think mine cost about £13,000.

It was in the summer season at Eastbourne that Emma and Sophie, who were seven and six years old, were allowed to come and see the first house of the show on their own. Anne was actually standing at the back of the theatre and the girls were in the stalls about 11 rows back. All through the show I was looking out for them to watch for their reactions. Then it came to be the time for my 18-minute solo spot towards the end. As

I walked onstage, said "Good evening ladies and gentlemen," and started telling my jokes, Emma took Sophie's hand, they got up off their seats and solemnly walked up the centre aisle and out of the theatre. Most encouraging.

Ron and I did two seasons of *The Two Ronnies* at the London Palladium in 1978 and 1983. They were at the time when we were at the height of our success and we packed the theatre for these two 12-week seasons, although the second season wasn't such a happy one for me, as I'll explain later.

The shows contained the sketches from our television series which we felt worked best on stage and also some new material specially written for us. Dick Clement and Ian La Frenais wrote a special episode of *Porridge* for Ron and I put on my tutu and did my ballet performance. There were also supporting acts – like Omar Pasha the illusionist who somehow manages to take the heads off people and throw them in the air. There was also an acrobatic act from Poland, called The Koziaks. And in the 1978 season there was this very exotic act with eight very tall glamorous black girls in white kid thigh boots who were called the Love Machine. And I should jolly well think so.

In 1979, after our first season at the Palladium, Ron and I took the show to Australia, to do six weeks in Sydney and six weeks in Melbourne. In fact it was a year-long exile in which we cut ourselves off completely from Britain. Ron had got the idea from Dick Clement and Ian La Frenais, who wrote *Porridge* for him, that the Inland Revenue would very sweetly let us off income tax on one year's earnings if we spent 12 months abroad. We wanted to be certain that this was all true and legal, so we went to see a QC called Andrew Park who was an expert on taxation. I remember that while sitting in the car on the way to his chambers, Ron and I were wondering what a QC who was an expert on taxation would look like. We imagined a character who might be played by Alastair Sim, or perhaps by John Le Mesurier, who, apart from being Sergeant Wilson in *Dad's Army,* specialised in subtly portraying monochrome officialdom in scores of British films. Perhaps this QC would be like one of those unnerving characters played by Ronnie Barker, seated behind a desk being president of the loyal society for the relief of sufferers from pismonunciation or perhaps chairman of the annual meeting of the Society for People Who Use a Lot of Words and Say Very Little.

As it turned out we were surprised to find he was more like a younger version of Alan Bennett, with the same slightly flat accent. His expert opinion was refreshingly straightforward – "All I can say, gentlemen, is that I'd like to be coming with you." It came as no surprise to Ron and me that shortly after this, Andrew Park was given a knighthood.

For the year before we went away, Ron and I took on every money-earning job there was going. We did a television commercial for Hertz cars, which was very well made, and we also did commercials for wallpaper, some kind of glue and lots of those ads for odd household goods that only get shown in the Norwich region of ITV.

We were taking our families with us, of course, and renting flats close to each other in Sydney. Ron was just going to do *The Two Ronnies* Palladium show while we were there, but I was also going to do a TV series, hosting a variety show.

Ron went on ahead with his family, but I took the scenic route with Anne, Sophie and Emma, and Debbie who was helping us with the girls at the time, going via India and the Taj Mahal, Malaysia, Phuket, Pattaya and Bangkok. Debbie had never been abroad before, not even on a day trip to Boulogne, but she was very brave, stayed the whole year and enjoyed every minute of it. She turned out to be a brilliant traveller – the sort who has only one suitcase, but has brought everything you don't have in your eight. If we didn't have a piece of Elastoplast or a pair of funny shaped scissors or a thimble, we knew we could count on Debbie.

It was while we were staying at the Oriental hotel in Bangkok that I realised I was not feeling at all well. I went to see the hotel doctor who took some blood tests and announced that I had hepatitis. He said that I would have to lie down in an air conditioned room doing nothing for at least a month, preferably six weeks. This was terrible news, because, on the next stage of our journey, I was supposed to go on to Hong Kong and do a six-week cabaret in the Pink Giraffe Club at the Hong Kong Sheraton.

We contacted the general manager of the South East Asia Sheratons and he made this extraordinarily generous offer: we could spend a month at the Hong Kong Sheraton if I would agree to do the cabaret afterwards when I had recovered from my hepatitis. He has my gratitude for life for allowing me to be ill in such style.

It was a very hard time for Anne and Debbie who had to keep the girls entertained, taking them out on trips while I lay in the hotel room, reading and watching Chinese TV all day. I watched horse-racing from Sha Tin and Happy Valley about three times a week, thousands of cartoons, hundreds of puzzling Chinese documentary programmes with English-subtitles. Lim, the houseboy, brought me clear soup, Lucozade, and rather tasty individual sponge cakes which were specially ordered for me. Lim was tremendously attentive and he pampered me like his own pet silkworm and he was also very sweet to Anne and the girls.

It was a very long six weeks. Apart from the reading and the TV cartoons, the other diversions were having a blood test once a week, watching the bed-linen being changed twice a day, as it is in the best Far Eastern hotels. Then the highlight of the available entertainment, and the most exciting event of the week, was watching the window-cleaners at work.

The window-cleaning in these high-rise Hong Kong hotels used to be a thrilling death-defying display as the scaffolding they put up to do it from was made of lengths of bamboo cane roped together at the junctions. These immense bamboo structures would sway in the wind and the men cleaning the windows wafted alarmingly to and fro. It was far more thrilling than the cartoons.

Our jockey friend Geoff Lewis was there at the same time to ride in various races and he was so disappointed that I was laid up and we could not go out together that, to make up for it, he got his tailor to make me a dinner suit. The tailor, Richard Ha, came to my room and measured me for the suit as I lay there on the bed. It was rather like being measured for a coffin. Anyway, Mr Ha delivered the suit and I wore it at the first night of my cabaret at the Pink Giraffe Club when he was our special guest. When I did my weeks of cabaret at the Pink Giraffe Club I still hadn't got all my energy back, but it was a comfortable show to do; our room was on the 10th floor of the Sheraton hotel and the club was on the 18th, so I just caught the lift and walked along the corridor to get to work. The club was a lovely jewel of a room and the upholstery of the banquettes was made of pink fake giraffe skin. My act went down well in the club, because there were lots of ex-pats in the audience who were starved of this kind of entertainment.

When it was time to leave Hong Kong, Lim gave Anne and me and both the girls a watch each as a present, which was a lovely thing to do. Unfortunately, three days later, the backs and the faces fell off.

When we finally got to Sydney, Ronnie Barker and his wife

Joy came round to welcome us on our first evening and tell us some of the things they had discovered about living in Sydney. Back in London I had done a lot of research about the best districts to live in and I had found an apartment in Wunulla Road, which estate agents would call "much sought after," meaning extremely posh. It looked right out over Sydney Harbour and we had a roof garden and we could admire the view of the harbour as we bobbed about in our private swimming pool.

While I was planning our year in Australia I wrote to Rowena Danziger, the headmistress of this wonderful girls' school called Ascham and this is where Emma and Sophie went while we were there. It was their happiest time at school anywhere. Emma hadn't really enjoyed school in England and the place she went to in Croydon was old-fashioned compared with Ascham, which was just down the road from our apartment, so they just got on the bus to go there.

I found that Rowena Danziger was very modern in her attitude to her pupils and they were encouraged in every department of their lives. She made Ascham very comfortable and secure for the girls. There was a high percentage of boarders at the school — that's quite a requirement in Australia where so many of the schoolchildren come from distant outlying areas, maybe thousands of miles away. The large number of boarders made it such an excellent all-round place. Obviously it was an expensive and prestigious school, but it didn't have the same kind of old-fashioned upper class atmosphere of public school in this country. Kerry Packer, the great Australian media tycoon sent his children to Ascham, because he lived nearby, and he also very generously donated a theatre to the school, an absolutely proper theatre, with all the equipment, revolving stage — everything.

I already knew Kerry Packer from a visit I made to Australia six or seven years previously when I did a show in the Concert Hall of the Sydney Opera House and I managed to fill it for three nights on the trot. As I was top of the bill, I was given the big dressing room which was a wonderful and immense suite. It was almost the size of a concert hall itself and there was a seven foot Bosendorfer grand piano in the lounge area in case a concert pianist wanted to warm up there. David Frost brought a party to see one of my shows and among the party were Kerry Packer and his wife Ros. David took us all out to supper, so that was the beginning of my acquaintance with Kerry Packer.

Ronnie Barker's two older children had already left school by the time we all got to Australia, so they spent the year doing odd jobs. Adam, the youngest went to a school called Cranbrook, which was a bit more traditional. The boys used to parade in tartans and they had pipe bands, so that was a little taste of the old country. My old country, not Ron's.

The eastern suburb of Sydney, where we lived, stretches from Double Bay to Rose Bay and is full of very expensive houses and extremely expensive shops. Both Double Bay and Rose Bay have the same mixture of chic fashion boutiques for women and men, and extremely good butchers, greengrocers, fishmongers, Italian fruit merchants, and dry cleaners. As so many Europeans have been there for years, you find old-established French bakers, Hungarian goulash shops, Greek grocers, cosmopolitan bars etc. There is a fascinating mixture; you can buy an expensive lady's gown and then go round the corner and get a delicious home-made pizza. I used to love wandering round the area, pausing to look into the fishmongers, then pausing a little longer to look into the patisserie . . . .

During our time in Australia, Ronnie B and I saw a lot more of each other than we ever did in England and got to know one another even better. It was partly because we were in exile together – although it was an extremely comfortable exile – but mainly because we were living so close to each other, so we could easily have a meal or pop round to each other's flats. Our children saw a great deal of one another too, which gave us all a feeling of belonging together.

Ronnie B went on a terrific weight-losing campaign while we were there, and so did Harry Secombe who paid one of his many visits to Australia at the same time. We all went out to dinner together and we did a few calculations as we sat at the table and worked out that, between them, Ron and Harry had lost *me*. In weight. It gave me an uneasy feeling. I kept looking over my shoulder, wondering where I had gone.

Anne, the two girls and I took a trip, driving round the coast from Sydney to Melbourne during that year. I think the journey took about three days and it was quite eventful. We stopped at a little village called Narooma which is famous for its cheese and also for its golf course, which is right on the coast, so that on one hole, you actually have to hit the ball from the clifftop across the bay.

We stayed in a nearby motel and the headmaster of the village school was my host for a round on this course. He gave the school a half holiday so that he could play with me, and all the children came out and cheered us on. Afterwards there was a ceremony at which I was presented with a cheese – which I absent-mindedly and rather ungraciously left behind in the motel bedroom. I hope it's not still there.

After that, we stayed the night at a place called Gypsy Point at a strange hotel where you slept in timbered huts. The restaurant had no windows, had Chinese patterned wallpaper and was, for some reason, called the English Dining Room. There was a grandfather kangaroo who stood in the corner of the bar in the evening and was fed with the odd Polo mint and the occasional half pint of beer.

I went back to our room after Anne and the girls, went the wrong way and found myself being chased by a gaggle of geese. I just got to our door in time before I was pecked or beaten to death – or whatever geese do. Everybody had a good laugh about it and I believe that now I am nearly coming round to seeing the funny side of it myself.

Just outside Melbourne and feeling rather weary, we stopped at a McDonald's – which is rather a dangerous sort of thing for me to do because I get recognised and can be a bit pestered. Anyway, I agreed to go into the kitchens to meet the staff and I signed autographs for everybody and I kept my patience and good humour – which I don't always manage to do. In this case, it was very lucky that I did, because when we were ready to take our leave I discovered we had locked ourselves out of the car and I had to go back and ask the manager to pick the lock for me.

At the end of our year in Australia, Anne and I gave a rather grand outdoor party at our apartment in Sydney. Rowena, the girls' headmistress, came with her husband and Kerry Packer and his wife Ros and all the television people and all the people who had been so kind to us while we were there. It was the first time in our lives that we had ever asked an outside caterer to do all the food and the wine and the flowers and everything, and a nice young woman came along and organised it all.

It was wonderful, but it left Anne a little stranded. She didn't feel she had enough to do, as everything was being taken care of so briskly, and it made her feel a bit out of touch and nervous – much more nervous than if she had been organising the whole thing herself. So she started sipping champagne rather early, before the guests arrived, and by the time Rowena got there, she was in such a state of nerves and excitement that she collapsed into the rose bed – that's Anne in the rose bed, not Rowena – and the poor thing had to be carried indoors. Luckily she recovered in time to come back and enjoy the party, and it was a great finale to a wonderful year.

Anne and I have always loved Australia. The people are lovely, the food is wonderful and it is fabulous for outdoor activity. Sydney is tremendous – and so is Melbourne. And what's more, they are packed with great golf courses – with lovely weather to play in. I've worked it out that Anne and I have made no fewer than 17 trips to Australia. And I've played on no fewer than 37 golf courses in Australia. I also worked that out – I ticked them all off in a book once. I am planning to make some more calculations along these lines. If I added up all the minutes I have spent searching for a ball in the rough on Australian golf courses, how many hours would that come to? I imagine it might be about the equivalent duration of four long-haul flights from London to Sydney. And if all the divots I have replaced on Australian fairways were piled on top of each other they would reach the height of a London bus parked on top of the Sydney Opera House. And if all the grains of sand that have trickled into my golf shoes in Australian bunkers were tipped out on to Bondi Beach . . . Oh, never mind.

I've done many cabaret tours of the marvellously equipped clubs they have out in Australia, and it was on one of these tours that I had an idea and contacted Ron about it. I rang him in England and said: "Would you like me to talk to Kerry Packer about the possibility of our doing some of *The Two Ronnies* shows, with our extra material purely for Australian television audiences?" Ron said yes, so I rang Kerry at home on a Sunday night – which is something you couldn't really do in this country with a big tycoon. Anyway, Kerry said: "Yes, I'd be very interested and thank you for calling. Can you come round and see me tomorrow morning?" Now, how many media moguls in this country could you get to see the very next morning?

I went to his office and at once he said: "I'll have as many shows as you are prepared to do." And he told me to go and see a man in his organisation called Lynton Taylor who organised everything in no time at all – the fees, the *per diem* expenses, the accommodation, everything. Ronnie B and I would go back the following year and do six shows for Channel 9.

Actually, for most of that meeting with Kerry Packer we talked about golf which is one of his passions. He's a great friend of all the star golf players and perhaps closest of all to Jack Nicklaus. He told me that he had telephoned Nicklaus and said he felt his golf wasn't in very good shape and he asked him if he could suggest somebody he could hire for a week of intensive instruction, morning and night. Jack Nicklaus had suggested the American professional Phil Rodgers as the ideal coach. So Phil Rodgers was flown over from the United States to Sydney, Australia, and put up in an hotel, so that he could help Kerry Packer polish up his putting and get his swing right.

When I went for my meeting with Kerry Packer he had just finished his week of intensive instruction with Phil Rodgers. He passed on some of his secrets to me, there in his large office, demonstrating with his chipping iron and his putter.

It was on another visit, when I was doing a cabaret in the St George's League Club in Sydney, that I lost my trousers. In fact, more than my trousers. We went to supper afterwards with a friend and came out to discover that the car had been broken into and my dinner suit – but not my patent leather shoes, fortunately – had been stolen. It must have been one of the most baffling cases the Sydney police ever had to deal with. Who would want my dinner suit? Was there a Mr Big behind this crime? The only thing to do was put all smart social events in Sydney under surveillance and keep a lookout for a man with a fed up expression and knee-length dinner suit trousers.

Anyway, the loss of my suit left me in trouble with another appearance due a night later and nothing to wear. How could I get a dinner suit my size? *The Sydney Morning Herald* printed a photograph of me standing outside our house, just in my shirt tails and a black bow tie and making an appeal for help. British Airways came to my rescue, flying out my spare suit, which I had at home in Surrey, and delivering it to me in Sydney within 24 hours.

On another visit, I went to do a week of cabaret at a casino called Wrest Point, in Hobart, Tasmania. Anne and I arrived a couple of days early to recover from our jet lag, so we got a chance to see the last night of a show in the casino called *Voila.* We were both stunned by this one girl in the show who seemed to be about 8ft tall, wore her clothes magnificently and was just outstanding. When we spoke to her and the cast afterwards we assumed that she must have been trained in Las Vegas, at least, or Lake Tahoe or Paris, but it turned out that she had just been to ballet school in Perth. Her name was Lisa Murphy.

Shortly after that, we were in Paris, visiting a night-club called *Paradis Latin,* which had a wonderful floor-show where a lot of the performers were actually British, and we talked to the owner who told us that, very sadly, the leading lady was leaving in a month. We don't normally do this, but Anne and I said: "We know the very girl for you – and you could not do better if you searched the whole world." And we told him about Lisa Murphy, this fabulous girl from Tasmania.

★

The owner of the Paris night-club tried to get in touch with her, in Hobart, but she had already moved on and was appearing in some very big glamorous show in Seoul, in Korea. After that, we forgot all about it until, out of the blue, we received a picture postcard from Paris. "How sweet of you to think of me and mention me," it said. "Here I am, the leading lady at the *Paradis Latin*. Love and best wishes, Lisa Murphy."

It was in the second season of *The Two Ronnies* at the London Palladium in 1983 that I had a confidence-shattering experience which was really to scar me for years afterwards. It occurred during one afternoon performance when we were doing "Hello Sailor", the big musical number which closed the first half. Ron and I were dressed as Wrens and we were accompanied by a troupe of naval ratings as we sang and marched about the stage.

We sang Ronnie's words to the tune of "A Life on the Ocean Wave" and "Hearts of Oak" and "Drunken Sailor" and "Bobby Shafto" and "Rule Britannia".

I realised quite soon after the beginning of the number, that something was badly wrong. The brightness and the heat of the lights were affecting me and I was feeling quite giddy when I got to my bit of the chorus:

> Heigh ho, and up she rises
> She's got knees of different sizes
> One's very small, but the other wins prizes
> Early in the morning.

It wasn't helping me that I was wearing my Wren's high-heeled shoes. As I got more wobbly I became more alarmed. Somehow, I managed to get to:

Bobby Shafto's gone to sea,
He'll be back in time for tea,
He's in charge of the W.C.
On the channel ferry.

After that I felt I was going to fall into the orchestra pit and I don't know how I got to the end of the number. I tried to recover during the interval and I came on and did the second half of the show, but, by then, it was just a matter of survival. The stage was spinning, the auditorium was a swaying blur, the lights seemed to lurch towards me then suddenly pull back. I felt more panicky all the time and my hands were running with sweat. Harold Fielding, the producer, called in a doctor, named Martin Scurr, to see me after the matinee and Martin Scurr put me on a drug called Ativan. Half an Ativan – and then another half if the first half didn't work.

It just got steadily worse, so I was sent to see a neurologist called Nigel Legg who told Harold he would have to close the whole show for a fortnight to allow me to rest and unwind. It turned out that I had labyrinthitis, an infection of the inner ear which affects the balance. I came back to my home in Addington and rested, and I continued with my medication, but I was behaving most oddly. I just sat in a chair for hours and stared out of the window at the garden. I was probably going through something like a breakdown although I didn't realise it at the time. Anne was really concerned.

During my second week at home Martin Scurr came to see me and told me to forget about the show and just relax. "Then go out on Saturday night," he said, "have a lovely dinner and a nice glass of wine, enjoy yourself, then spend a quiet Sunday at home and start again refreshed at the Palladium on Monday."

So, on the Saturday night, Anne and I went to this place

called The Lodge, in Limpsfield. I had more than one glass of wine and I started to talk to Anne about Martin Scurr, actually describing him as "the Messiah" for the way he saved my life. Anne thought this was a bit extraordinary and extreme and became more concerned. Martin Scurr was (and still is) a marvellous doctor but being the Messiah was not one of his qualifications.

I must have been deranged in some sort of way. In fact, I got so carried away at that dinner that I actually had *four* puddings. Now, I hardly ever have any pudding at all, let alone four. I don't think I finished them all, but still, it was a warning to Anne and a sign that I was still rather odd.

I went back to finish the season at the Palladium but it was really too soon and I was struggling all the way through the last three weeks. I couldn't walk down the steep steps on to stage for the big opening number, but had to make my entrance from the side. I felt that at any moment the stage would tilt sharply and tip me into the orchestra pit.

The memory of these attacks, and the fear of them recurring, haunted my life for up to 10 years afterwards. Every time I did something in the theatre I would get halfway through the run and become a bit tired and the balance problem would return. The odd thing was that it only happened in the theatre. It got so bad that it even affected me when I was in the audience. I would sit in the stalls look at the actor on the stage and think "Gosh, I couldn't do that, standing up there with nothing to lean on." Most people have heard of stage fright, but this was a case of the much more rare affliction, audience fright.

Every time I went to the theatre to get ready to perform, the awful fear came back. I used to have to time it carefully so that I would arrive at the theatre, and be able to go straight to the dressing room and then straight out on to the stage, so that I just didn't give myself a chance even to think about it. And then when I was on the stage I needed things to touch or to lean on, for reassurance.

Some years later, when I thought I had got over the problem, I went back to Australia to do a cabaret tour. Anne and I were staying in a flat in Sydney and we were sitting by the swimming pool and it suddenly hit me that I had 27 cabarets to do and I just couldn't face them. I said to Anne: "I can't do these concerts. It's no good." She said I should just keep calm and we decided to contact a psychiatrist we knew in Sydney called Ken Dyball. We had met him when Ronnie Barker and his wife Joy, Anne and I and our families were spending our year in Australia doing the *Two Ronnies* tour. Ken's daughters had been at school, at Ascham, with Emma and Sophie.

We rang up Ken, but he wasn't at home. He was on the tennis court at the Royal Sydney Golf and Tennis Club. His wife said if it was really urgent we could go and see him at the club. So we got in the car and drove round there straight away. It was rather like a scene from some Woody Allen film; the psychiatrist was playing tennis and Anne and I were outside the wire cage, waving to him and trying to attract his attention. By this time, I was in a bad way, quite distressed about what I was going to do about these 27 cabaret engagements.

Anne was mouthing to Ken Dyball: "Ron would like to see you and ask you something," and he said: "All right, but just let me finish this set." So there he was in his sweatband and his knee bandages – because he was always strapped up all over the place as he played too much tennis and suffered from injuries and torn muscles and pulled hamstrings all the time – and there was I, outside the court, praying: "Please God, don't let it go to deuce *again*."

At last he came off the court and we went off and had a consultation sitting on the grass behind some bushes at the club.

I told him about my balance problem and how I was panicking about the cabarets. He said: "Have you got any Ativan?" And I said yes, and he said: "Go back home and take one and a half milligrams." I did that and an hour later the fear left me.

So I did the tour, taking this Ativan discreetly when I needed it, and somehow it got me through it. But it was still a battle. When I did my act I always had a chair beside me, just in case. It quite suited me, because people expected me to speak from a chair, so if I felt my balance going and needed to sit down, it was quite natural for me to do so.

Ken Jeacle, who was my tour manager, was always in the wings and, whenever I got a bit anxious that the trouble was coming back, I would just casually mention, as part of my act, "It's a little hot, Ken," and he would know that the spotlights were too bright and he would take them down a bit. Ken was my tour manager on all my visits to Australia to do cabaret and he organised everything, treated me like a sultan and somehow managed to make things always go smoothly.

So I made it through the 27 cabarets, but the labyrinthitis had become a shadow over my working life. While performing my act, going through my lines, gently trying to draw the audience in, I always had this fear that, at any moment, I could turn into a falling-down comedian.

It still troubled me three or four years later in 1992 when I went to Australia again, this time with Donald Sinden in Ray Cooney's farce *Out of Order*. I was really more affected by the fear of it, but when I got tired it would raise its head again. The first act opened with Donald on stage and me on the other side of the door, waiting for the cue to make my entrance. All the time I was standing there I was wondering if I would be able to go on and where I could move to on stage so that I would be standing close to something.

Even though I had the constant worry about my balance, I

loved doing *Out of Order*. There were two very good parts in it
and Donald and I were just right together. It was a success in
Melbourne, even though the critics were rather sniffy about it –
I think it was a time when they were tiring of jokes about silly-
ass Englishmen. It was certainly one of the funniest plays I've
seen – or been in. Before I left for Australia I went to watch it
at the Shaftesbury Theatre in London, with Michael Williams in
the part I was to play. It was a hilarious evening. I heard terrific
laughter at the Palladium when we did *The Two Ronnies* there,
but this audience reaction was even more amazing, particularly
in the second half. And it was the same in Australia. So, in spite
of feeling tired and a bit frail, I got the maximum amount of
pleasure out of it.

It was the fear of it that tired me out, thinking about it all day
and wondering if I would be all right. It didn't exactly turn into
stage fright, but it was an ever-present anxiety, chipping away at
me all the time. At the end of the tour when we were in
Tasmania and I was even more tired, it got so bad during the day
that I couldn't bend down in a bookshop to look at a book on
a lower shelf for fear of toppling over. When I got home the
thing had built up so badly that I could not even stand over a
putt on the golf course.

The labyrinthitis seems to have gone for good now, touch
wood, but has diminished the thrill of the theatre for me. I don't
think I could manage eight performances a week any more. But
cabaret is still fine and, oddly enough, I can still go on at the
Palladium, stand on that huge expanse of stage, hold on to the
mike and not be bothered at all. There must be something
special about the place.

CHAPTER TWELVE

In which I write about golf and its importance to me from my early days. My meetings with great players like Henry Cotton and Peter Thompson are described. I also get slightly side-tracked and give accounts of summer seasons in which I have appeared, including my first ever solo spot in Yarmouth. A golden retriever and a donkey also put in an appearance. And Sean Connery is mentioned again.

Because my father was a baker and worked through most of the night, he was able to play golf during the day. He was a brilliant golfer and played off a handicap of three or four. He must have been just naturally gifted, and, being a baker, kneading all that dough, he also had very strong hands and forearms. He had only one lesson in his whole life.

I am nowhere near as good a player as my father, and my handicap is 16. My brother Allan, who is bigger than me and can hit the ball a really long way, is an excellent player and has probably inherited our dad's gift.

I was about 12 years old when dad first took me up to one of the courses in the Braid Hills, in Edinburgh, and started me swinging with a set of cut down clubs. Since then, golf has been a hugely important part of my life and it was a great bond between my father and me.

Edinburgh has a fabulous selection of golf courses run by the Corporation and in those days you paid just sixpence to play. It is part of the tradition in Scotland that you can get started very cheaply and a huge number of working people are able to play golf. At school I joined the Golf Society and that meant that on Saturday mornings we were allowed to be guests on many of the courses in the city – and there are something like 16 or 17 of them in the area to choose from.

My best friend at school was Tom Fell whose father was a master baker in Penicuik – I suppose it was because we had baking in common that we became friends in the first place – and he was also mad about golf.

In 1948 Tom's father gave him a wonderful brand new black Triumph 500 motorbike for his 17th birthday and he took me on it to Muirfield to watch the Open Championship. We followed Henry Cotton round the course. Cotton won it that year, with his scores getting better every round, if I remember correctly. It was his third Open victory and a tremendous occasion. King George VI came down to watch him. Henry Cotton was a great national hero.

I will always remember it. Henry was looking quite divine in various shades of grey – dark flannel trousers, paler grey cashmere cardigan, an even paler grey sports shirt and white buckskin shoes. Of course, he always did look a picture; he was a most stylish dresser.

I had no idea in 1948, as a wee schoolboy wandering that course, that one day I would get to know Henry Cotton quite well and that I would actually become a member of Muirfield and even have a house there. These were dreams that it wasn't worth even dreaming. Riding home on the back of Tom Fell's Triumph 500 I had no idea that I had just been at the start of a would-be golfer's fairy tale which was eventually going to come true.

In the RAF I played a little golf, but then, in the early days after I arrived in London and was living in bedsits, there was no time or money for it and my career – or lack of it – was occupying too much of my time. When I started working at Winston's night-club and was getting a regular wage at last, I was able to get my clubs out again.

In 1961 I was appearing at the Palladium with Harry Secombe. To be honest, I wasn't appearing there quite as much as Harry Secombe was, because he was top of the bill and my name was on the posters in much smaller type. I had a modest part in a big bill which included Eddie Calvert, "the Man with the Golden Trumpet", the singer Marion Ryan, the King Brothers, and Roy Castle. I played little roles in some of the sketches; all I can remember of them now is that I was an Indian bearer in a big game hunting sketch. Another member of the cast was Jeremy Hawk who was Harry's straight man until I took over from him when he went off to television to present *Criss Cross Quiz*.

It was Jeremy Hawk who introduced me to that admirable organisation, the Stage Golfing Society. This is a wonderful society because it is not too expensive for actors to join and it is affiliated to half a dozen clubs around London. Golf is a great boon for touring actors, as I learned when I was young in Edinburgh and I walked Harold Warrender, carrying his clubs, all the way down the Lothian Road, back to the Caledonian hotel. If you are visiting Liverpool or Sheffield with a show you can always ring up the local club and arrange to have a round.

The Stage Golfing Society is also very good for the morale of actors. It's a terrible thing to be waiting at home for a job, willing the telephone to ring and getting on everybody's nerves, so it's much better to go off and have a good game of golf – then just sneak to the clubhouse phone and ring up and check if there are any messages.

The other nice thing about the Society is that it has a tremendous number of trophies with theatrical connections, like the Ronald Squire Trophy, the Ben Travers Salver, the Harold Warrender Cup and the A.E. Matthews Trophy. It is great to see all the great actors' names engraved on the silverware for posterity.

Actually, the business of checking for messages has always been an important part of theatrical life. "Any word from my agent?" is the most repeated line, spoken usually in a tone of what you could call casual desperation. Let's face it, messages are an important part of most people's lives. There's always the hope of a big offer or a big opportunity, the thought when we return home that there might be a scrawled note on the kitchen table saying "pse ring Steven Spielberg." Or: "A man called Bill Gates phoned – twice." However many times it doesn't happen, there is still the faintest tingle of expectation. Nowadays, people carry their hopes around with them in the form of mobile phones.

A man I met in a summer season at the Manchester Palace (when Jimmy Young was top of the bill) was a master of great expectations. His name was Humphrey Kent and I think he was a member of the family which manufactured Kent hairbrushes. He and his wife Jean both had modest parts in the show.

Humphrey used to do the football pools every week and when he checked his coupon on Saturdays, he used to cover up the results with a sheet of paper and then expose them slowly, one by one, just to prolong the agony of anticipation and the sense of excitement before his Saturday hopes were dashed.

In London, to support himself while waiting for parts, he worked as a publisher's reader and travelled from his home in Crystal Palace to somewhere like Wigmore Street, in the West

End, to collect the manuscripts to take home and read. He was considered a very good publisher's reader, although there was a whisper that he had given the thumbs-down to the huge best-seller *No Orchids for Miss Blandish*.

After visiting the publisher's office, Humphrey would travel back home on the 187 bus. When he got off the bus and turned the corner into his road, he could just see his lavatory window, from a distance. He and his wife Jean had this arrangement that if she was flying the Abyssinian flag outside that window, there were no messages. But if the Union Jack was flying it meant he had a message. Or even several messages – from his agent, or from some publisher. So it gave him the whole walk down the road to build up the excitement – if the Union Jack was flying. He could wonder all the way what the message might be. Could it be an exciting offer? The big break? An urgent message from Littlewood's pools? If it was the Abyssinian flag he could just relax and saunter.

Humphrey once told me about his first appearance in the theatre. He started late in life, when he was in his forties, and he was in his dressing room when the usual backstage tannoy announcement was made – "Overture and beginners on stage please."

So Humphrey dutifully trooped along and stood on the stage. The stage manager then came along and said: "Excuse me, Humphrey, you're not on until the second act, are you?"

"No," said Humphrey, "but I am a beginner."

My golfing life has progressed in parallel with my show business career and I always used to take my clubs with me when I was in summer shows. In 1962 I was appearing with Harry Secombe again, this time in Yarmouth and the King Brothers were going to be in a different show in the same town. The King Brothers were a hugely successful vocal and instrumental trio who had a big hit in 1960 with "Standing on the Corner Watching All the Girls Go By" and, as we got on very well, we decided to share a house in the area and spend our days playing golf. The whole arrangement didn't start off all that splendidly for me. We agreed that I would finish my show at Winston's nightclub, then drive down to the brothers' family house, at Buckhurst Hill, in Essex, at about one in the morning, stay the night and then we would go off together to Yarmouth and look for suitable properties.

After a foggy drive from London I arrived at the house in the early hours. Everybody was asleep and they had left the key for me under the mat. I opened the door very quietly and started to go in. The family's golden retriever, Sherry, was lying in the hall right in front of me. She knew me pretty well, but she wasn't so sure of me now, as she saw me furtively slipping through the door in the middle of the night. She gave one of those long, rumbling, tentative growls, so I decided to go out again, shut the door behind me and walk around with my hands in my pockets and look at the fog for a bit, hoping the dog would nod off again. After a while, and a few deep breaths, I opened the door again. Sherry did not get up, but she growled again and this time I could see her upper lip wobble and I got a definite sighting of a fang. I'm not sure what was happening to my own upper lip at this time, but I decided to leave. I think if I had taken two more paces forward, Sherry might have stood up and wagged her tail, but I was not in the mood to take the chance. I left the key and a note for Mike, Tony and Denis King and then got in my car and drove back to London and to my flat in Camden Town. When I showed up in Buckhurst Hill again later in the morning they were amazed to hear that I had been frightened off by their placid old golden retriever. Sherry just looked enigmatic.

★

We managed to find a bungalow at Caister, near Yarmouth, which was conveniently close to the golf course. We all had a room each and shared the shopping duties and expenses. Tony, who was the most financially astute one of the King brothers, was in charge of the book-keeping and I do remember that there was a bit of trouble because somebody in the household was eating too many of the Victoria plain chocolate fingers and Tony wanted to know who it was. I am saying nothing, but I remember that accusing glances were exchanged. We were on constant alert for the faintest rustle of the packet.

It was a pretty idyllic summer season and we played golf just about every day. We used to leave our order at the fish and chip shop on the way to the course, then pick it up on the way back at lunchtime and then we would have a quiet afternoon, with perhaps a discreet plain chocolate finger or two, before going on to do our shows.

My mum and dad came for a week's holiday in Yarmouth and also to see the show. One evening they came to our bungalow and dad made us a steak and kidney pie – with a puff pastry top which he was specially good at – and then he and my mum went back to their hotel. When the King Brothers and Harry Secombe and I returned from doing our shows, this wonderful pie was waiting for us in the oven.

Harry Secombe used to play golf with us sometimes. There was one alarming occasion when he had quite a nasty accident, getting his foot caught in a rabbit hole and twisting his ankle. He actually wondered if he would be able to carry on with the show. I had to drive his car to take him back to his hotel for treatment; actually, that was a bit of a treat for me, because he had a very sporty Daimler Dart.

It was in that season at great Yarmouth that I did my first ever stand-up act on my own. It happened because Wilson, Keppel and Betty decided to retire. Wilson, Keppel and Betty (actually there was a succession of about four or five Bettys) were a classic comedy act of eccentric dancers. Jack Wilson and Joe Keppel, each wearing a white night-shirt and a fez, would do a sort of Egyptian number on sand they scattered on the stage, while Betty would be the glamorous, exotic and veiled Cleopatra. As often seems to happen in showbusiness partnerships, one (Keppel) was very careful with his money and ended up amassing quite a fortune, while the other (Wilson) was reckless and finally broke. The comics Jewel and Warriss were the same. Jimmy Jewel was very canny with his pennies, while Ben Warriss, the straight man, was quite the opposite.

Anyway, Wilson, Keppel and Betty decided to hang up their fezzes in the middle of this Yarmouth season, so the producers were stuck for about four or five minutes in the first half of the show. Harry Secombe said to me: "Why don't you do a spot?" It was short notice, but I sat down with Don Arroll, who had been a compere at the Palladium, and he helped me put together about five minutes of jokes and patter which I tried to learn.

In those days Harry Secombe used to take pills to help him get over his nerves. He used to call them his "nadger" pills. I never asked what was in them. Anyway, he gave me one of his pills and I went on to do my five minutes. Unfortunately, thanks to the nadger, I don't remember anything about that night. This important milestone in my career, my first solo spot, passed in a blur.

I actually did the spot for only three or four nights, because the management wanted a bigger name and they brought in Donald B. Stuart who was six feet seven inches tall. He was also an excellent comic conjuror, a sort of forerunner of Tommy Cooper.

He had a way of balancing a tennis ball on a parasol, apparently very cleverly, then folding the parasol so that the audience discovered that the ball was actually attached by a piece of string. So, on this occasion in Yarmouth, the short stand-up man was replaced by the very tall conjuror.

I returned to Yarmouth a couple of years later to do a pre-season show when the town was full of old age pensioners who were getting a cheap deal. They used to say in those days that they had the OAPs there at the seaside in May and early June just to air the beds, but they also arranged these pre-season shows to keep the poor souls entertained. I was there to try out my first proper solo act. Danny La Rue was going to do his show in Margate and I had agreed to go with him if I could have a solo spot of about eight minutes in the second half of the show. I had some material written for me by Neil Shand and Barry Cryer and I was running it in, so to speak, in Yarmouth.

Jimmy Tarbuck was in town at the same time rehearsing for a full summer season at a different theatre and he came over one night to watch me perform. He must have thought that I was pretty gauche for a stand-up because I was in my very early days and he had been doing his routine in the Liverpool clubs since he was about 16 or 17. Anyway he came round to my dressing room afterwards and was kind about my act.

"It all works very well," he said, "but I can't understand why you don't wear your glasses." Until that moment, it had never occurred to me that the glasses were part of my image. In my television sitcom, *No, That's Me Over Here*, I appeared in black-rimmed glasses and a bowler hat and in *The Frost Report* I always wore my specs, but on stage in Yarmouth I didn't. After that simple bit of advice from Jimmy Tarbuck I kept them on wherever I appeared. It also meant I could find my way round the stage more easily and stop mistaking the microphone for a very thin member of the chorus.

It was while I was in Edinburgh, performing in *Cinderella* with

Stanley Baxter, that a chance meeting in a shop led to one of the most exciting bits of good fortune for me in my life as a golfer.

Anne and I had a flat in Edinburgh quite near the King's Theatre and, at the time our daughter Emma was quite young and Sophie was on the way. Anne was in the grocer's shop one day – it was called Reid and Brown, by the way; I don't know why I can remember the names of these food shops all the time, but I just can. Anyway, in this grocer's shop, a lady came up to the heavily pregnant Anne and said: "Excuse me, are you Anne Hart?" It turned out that she was Sarah Laird who had been the PR girl for Simpson's, in Piccadilly, when they fitted out the entire cast of the Crazy Gang – including the singers, showgirls and dancers – with top hats, white ties and tails for a big production number of the Bud Flanagan and Chesney Allen song "Strolling".

Now she lived just across the road and was married to a chap called Barry Laird. So I got to meet Barry and although I was just a bit of a hacker in those days, he was extremely kind to me and invited me to play golf with him at Muirfield, the grandest of courses. We would play at Muirfield on one Sunday and at the Royal Burgess the next Sunday – and in between these times I was an Ugly Sister at the King's Theatre.

In those days, to take someone of my standard of golf onto the hallowed turf of Muirfield was really quite brave. And Muirfield probably wasn't used to show business faces, so, by taking me there, Barry was being brave twice over. Of course, Muirfield probably didn't mind certain show business faces like Bing Crosby and Bob Hope coming to play, but they wouldn't be so sure about a rather overawed Ronnie Corbett.

Over the years I played a lot of golf with Barry at Muirfield and on other courses, and then one day in 1980 he telephoned me out of the blue and said that he had been talking with Mike

Kennedy (an Edinburgh stockbroker and a past captain at Muirfield) and they wondered if I would like to be put down for membership of the club. My first thought was of my father and how thrilled he would have been if he had known that someone was actually offering to put me down for membership of the greatest golf club in the world.

Sadly, I couldn't tell him. One day in 1975 he set out to play his third round of golf of the week on the Preston Field golf course, in Edinburgh, and he was on the fairway, playing the 15th hole when he collapsed and died of a heart attack. He was 75 years old. He had always been a very healthy man – apart from the diabetes – and nobody knew, at the time, that he was at risk. It was a wonderful way for him to go, but, of course, it was awful for my mum, waiting at home with the tea ready, looking at the clock.

I was at home in London on the day it happened. I was just about to go out and do a job, to perform at some function in Hornchurch, when the telephone rang. Anne went and answered it and it was my brother Allan to say that our father had died. Anne came back into the room and said nothing about it and she let me go out and do the job.

When I got back at about midnight Anne was waiting up for me and she broke the news to me. "Willie's dead," she said.

It was a terrible shock. He had had a few angina attacks before, but nobody had ever associated them with a heart condition. I felt an awful bleakness; he had always been so important to me and it was his example that had given me the determination to make something of my life.

My mother always told me that the man playing golf with my father that day never came round to see her afterwards. There may have been a perfectly understandable explanation for why he didn't, but my Mum always felt that after the funeral he might have sent a little note or rung up and asked if he could come round. But she said she never heard a word from him until the day she died in 1991.

Anyway, thinking how thrilled my father would have been to know about it, I told Barry I was ecstatic at the very idea of being put down for membership of the Honourable Company of Edinburgh Golfers at Muirfield. Then I telephoned Brian Huggett, the professional golfer, to break the news to him, because he has always been a great help to me with my game and a good companion on the course. And then I waited. And I waited . . . Actually I waited about 12 years, because it takes quite a while to get in once you have been put down.

My dad was also a great fan of Henry Cotton. He admired everything about him – his swing, his look and his tremendous style. The only golf lesson he ever had in his life was from Henry and that was when I was very young, shortly after Henry won his first British Open in 1934. Right to the end of his days, Henry was always keen to earn a few extra quid, even though his wife Toots was extremely wealthy, so he used to do these coaching sessions for members of the public.

It was in 1936, I guess, when he happened to be up in Scotland and he was giving 20-minute lessons for ten shillings a time. My dad went along for his ten bob's worth, proudly wearing the Lotus Anglespike golf shoes which were endorsed by Henry at the time. Dad was absolutely thrilled when the great man told him that there was nothing he needed to change about his swing and he shouldn't tamper with it.

Because of my dad and this famous lesson, and because of that visit to Muirfield on the motorbike in 1948, it was specially lovely for me that I eventually became a friend of Henry Cotton. It was in 1969, on my first holiday in the Algarve, in

Portugal, with Anne and our two girls Emma and Sophie who were then aged two and one. We had rented a villa for £9 a week from Michael Medwin, who was a star in the television series, *The Army Game*, and used to be in just about every British film they ever made, playing some dodgy cockney character.

Henry Cotton was the pro at the nearby golf course at Penina which he had designed himself – in fact he was a pioneer in making Portugal a great golfers' resort. While we were in our villa, Jimmy Tarbuck was on holiday in an hotel in the area and together we decided to ring up Henry and ask if we could play his course. He was very welcoming and invited us for drinks and then to dinner at an hotel.

So we went for drinks at Henry's house which was as elegant as he was. It was beautifully furnished and there was a particular reason for this. In his younger days, when he was at the height of his golfing powers, Henry used to play very serious gambling golf matches with some of the most swish Bond Street dealers. Instead of playing for money, he would play for a pair of Louis XIV chairs, or a Georgian side table or an oil painting. He once confessed to me that he found he was practising harder for the furniture than he was for the serious competitions. I suppose it concentrates the mind when there's a Hepplewhite cabinet hanging on the last 14ft putt.

At dinner with Henry that night at the hotel, there were Anne and myself, Jimmy Tarbuck and his wife Pauline and an Irish couple, a successful banker and his wife who we hadn't met before. Henry showed up on his own for the drinks beforehand while Toots stayed in her room. She didn't join us for dinner either, and we discovered later that she and Henry had had a major row. Their relationship was always pretty fiery.

That evening, Henry was wearing a wild silk Nehru-collared jacket and a cravat, really looking the business and he entertained us in style. Afterwards he started telling a few racy stories – which was something he tended to do. You would never imagine that this rather *distingué* looking Englishman could tell stories like that, and they were certainly too indiscreet for the Irishman and his wife who left very promptly. Jimmy remembers me saying "Now the floodgates have opened," because I knew if Henry started telling stories like that, Jimmy would almost certainly want to follow on with a few even heavier ones.

We survived the night, and the next day Jimmy and I arrived at the course for our game of golf. Henry met us there and told us "As a special favour, I am going to give you the services of my caddie, Pacifico." The unusual thing about this particular caddie was that he was a donkey. Henry had rescued him from some cruel farmer and now looked after him and spoiled him like a favourite poodle, feeding him on Polo mints and all sort of other treats. Pacifico always carried his clubs and knew that he wasn't allowed to walk on the greens or the tees. This time he was carrying our golf bags, like panniers, Jimmy's on one side and mine on the other.

"All right, I'll leave you in the hands of Pacifico," Henry said, going off back home. Probably going to admire his golfing trophies. Including most of his furniture. Jimmy and I were tremendously pleased with ourselves as we made our way to the first tee, with the donkey following behind. "Would you ever believe it?" we said. "Here we are playing the great Henry Cotton's very own course, having dined with him last night, after having drinks in his very own house, and now he has given us his very own donkey, this wonderful Pacifico, to carry our clubs. Who'd have thought that two working class boys like us . . ."

We would have continued with our eulogy, but we were interrupted by a powerful gushing noise. We turned round and saw Pacifico peeing copiously on the edge of the first tee. That seemed to be his opening comment on our presence. It went on for a very long time while we stood and waited in awe and humility.

When he had finished, we found a dry area of the tee and prepared to play our first shots. Pacifico gazed into the distance, adopting a detached attitude, as Jimmy and I twitched and fidgeted and shifted our weight from one foot to another in preparation. My shot skimmed off to the right and Jimmy's went in the opposite direction. Pacifico ambled off and stood by the first ball, and then he made his way to he second ball. There was something about that amble – a touch of hauteur. Like a waiter in a smart restaurant returning to the kitchen, letting you know that your choice of wine has failed to impress him.

We went to play our second shots, determined that this time we would impress our caddie. We did a lot of that business of shading our eyes and looking towards the horizon as if we were about to discover new lands – or at least send the ball a pretty considerable distance. I was doing some graceful, Henry Cotton-ish practice swings when Jimmy suddenly said: "Where's Pacifico?"

I stopped in mid-swing and looked about. Our caddie was no longer with us. "There he is," said Jimmy pointing. And there he was, trotting off into the woods in the distance with our golf bags wobbling about on his back. We ran after him, shouting things like "Come back, you silly ass," but it was no good. Pacifico made it quite clear that he did not want to keep company with us, so we had to do without a caddie after that.

Val Doonican and I used to play golf together almost every day when I was starring in a summer show in Paignton with Kenneth McKellar in 1975 and Val was starring in Torquay. The show I was in was a pretty good one and it had been a success the previous year in Eastbourne, but it wasn't going down particularly well in Paignton. Val's show, in the meantime, was doing brilliantly. We played golf at Newton Abbot which meant that in the morning we had to drive past the theatre where Val's show was on and every time we did so I had to cover my eyes or look the other way because the queues were already forming at the box office, whereas at my theatre the only queues would be of people trying to get out. It was a sight to put me off my putting.

It was in Paignton, one hot day in that summer of 1975, that I got the dreadful news that my agent Sonny Zahl had committed suicide. He had thrown himself out of the window in the office of George Brightwell who handled my career with Paradine Productions. There was no warning that it was going to happen. He had been having a perfectly ordinary meeting with George and Joan Grimwade, George's secretary. At the end of the meeting George stood up went to fetch his coat and said: "I've got to go now." Sonny stood up as well and said: "I've got to go, too," then he walked quickly to the window and jumped out.

George Brightwell was devastated. He telephoned Anne, my wife and said: "Something awful has happened; Sonny has just thrown himself out of my window." While George was telling her about it, Anne could hear, over the telephone, the siren of the ambulance arriving. Sonny was a very dear man; we knew he had been having treatment for mental troubles, but nobody realised how serious they were.

I have been lucky that my work has taken me all over the country and all over the world and everywhere I have gone I have taken my golf clubs. I have played a great deal of golf in Australia. Ranald McDonald, a dear friend of mine, adopted me golf-wise when I was in Australia and he saw to it that I was allowed to play in all the best places, like the Royal Melbourne club. And my brother-in-law Iain Gray to the Royal Sydney, which made me a temporary member for a year.

Through Ranald, I got to meet and play with the great Peter Thompson, who won the British Open five times. I remember Anne and I went to stay at the Sheraton Mirage, at Port Douglas, north of Cairns, where Peter Thompson had designed the golf course and where he has a holiday flat. We had just arrived in our hotel suite when the telephone rang. I answered it and a voice said: "I was wondering if you would like some company for your golf?" It was Peter Thomson. I'll never forget it – that diffident invitation from this great champion.

Later I played a memorable foursome at the Royal Melbourne with Ranald and with Peter Thompson and Kel Nagle, the two giants of Australian golf.

I also had the opportunity to play with Arnold Palmer and Gary Player when the BBC did its *Pro-Celebrity Golf* series on television. The idea was that an American show business person would partner a British professional and a British showbusiness person would play with an American professional. We would play over nine holes with Peter Alliss following us round with his microphone, chatting to us and trying not to put us off.

The one thing about golf is that even the busiest person will drop everything to show up if there is a chance of playing with someone like Arnold Palmer. So we had people like George C. Scott, Jack Lemmon, Bing Crosby, Sean Connery, Christopher Lee, Albert Finney, Val Doonican, Jimmy Tarbuck and myself all getting together.

The added attraction was that we played one year at Turnberry and the next at Gleneagles, staying at their magnificent hotels. And you just signed all the bills. Actually, everybody was generally restrained and well-behaved about that, although I do remember a couple of the Americans getting carried away and ordering Chateau Lafite.

One person who was not in the least restrained or well behaved was the American film actor, George C. Scott who got appallingly drunk, started pulling telephones off the wall and generally carrying on in a disgraceful way. In the end, they had to discreetly ship him out and back to America. Jack Lemmon was very sweet – though not averse to a vodka and orange juice at breakfast time – and his standard of golf was about the same as mine.

We played with Lee Trevino and Sevy Ballesteros and anybody who had seen us in the little coach which took us to the ninth tee for the start of our match would have thought that Trevino was both the pro *and* the entertainer. There was just this constant outpouring of funny stories. Jack Lemmon sat there, struck dumb and pale with fear. The thought of being filmed playing golf with such great golfing pros just made him so nervous. Well, it made us all nervous.

Many of us "celebrities" were doing summer seasons while the pro–celebrity golf was being filmed, so we would fly up from Blackpool, or wherever, to take part. When Val Doonican came up, the poor chap had an experience which was the sort of opposite of an epiphany. He was put off golf for just about the rest of his life.

Val was due to play with Sevy Ballesteros and Greg Norman and Glen Campbell, but when he got to the tee on the Sunday morning the organisers told him that the plans had changed.

"Glen Campbell can't make it."

"Oh dear."

"But, never mind, we've got a wonderful replacement to play with you."

"Oh, good. Who is it?"

"Bing Crosby."

Val is a beautiful golfer and plays off a handicap of six or seven, but the thought of playing with the legendary Bing Crosby frightened the life out of him. He went out on the course in a terrible nervous state and played really badly in front of his hero Bing.

Since then he has never really wanted to play again. He has said he might come and play nine holes with me some time, but if I tried to make it more of an occasion and invited two other people he just wouldn't come.

In 1992, the long 12-year wait was over at last and I got the letter telling me that I had been elected a member of Muirfield. The news arrived on the day before I was due to leave for Australia for six months to appear with Donald Sinden in *Out of Order*, so there was no time to go up there and enjoy my membership before I went away. Barry Laird and Mike Kennedy posted the red, blue and gold club tie to me in Melbourne and I wore it for the first time at the first night party for the play.

Afterwards Peter Thomson took me to the Royal Melbourne Golf Club and signed me in, so, in the book, it said: Guest: R. Corbett. Home club: Muirfield. Signed in by: Peter Thompson. Not a bad treble. In fact, it is about the best billing I have ever had.

Anne and I bought a house in Scotland in 1982, in the village of Gullane, and it is right next to the Muirfield course. So both my homes are next to golf courses which is very handy for me. After I bought the Scottish house, I was also made a member of the Gullane Golf Club. It is a wonderful area to live in, with fantastic views and the only problem about it is how to pronounce it. If you live in the village and are working folk you pronounce it "Gullan", but if you are from the swish Charlotte

Square area of Edinburgh and are part of the stockbroking or private banking mafia or you just commute to play golf there, you say "Gillan". Anne and I call it Gullan in front of people who call it Gullan and say Gillan to people who say Gillan. It's a tricky business, and you don't always get it right.

Actually, someone once told me that, because of the Grand Alliance, the historic link between France and Scotland, Gullane could possibly be named after the French name for a seabird – possibly gwelan which is the Breton word for a gull – so the posh pronunciation may not be such an affectation after all.

Henry Cotton's last visit to Muirfield was in 1987, the year of his death at the age of 80. Even when he was so old and distinguished he still had an eye for the extra little earners and, on this occasion, he was helping to launch the new train service from Waverley station, in Edinburgh, to Drem, next to the Muirfield course. He was engaged to ride on the footplate, dressed in a train driver's outfit – which, of course, he wore very elegantly.

He telephoned us a couple of days before he arrived and said that he would like to come and see us. "And," he added, "I'll want some of Ron's home-baked brown bread with some smoked salmon." We were all ready for him on the day and we had some Australian golfing friends staying who were longing to meet him, and, of course, I had baked the bread. He walked in and said: "I tell you what I fancy – some Drambuie."

We had everything in the drinks cupboard, except Drambuie, but Anne rushed next door and, thank goodness, she was able to borrow a bottle. Our friends, David Mercer, who was a pro in Sydney, and his wife Barbara just sat at Henry's feet – as people did, because he was such a legend. Then, for their benefit, he just "talked" the last 18 holes he had played in that 1948 Open, not boringly, but with tremendous charm and a fantastic memory. "I was just nestled in there at the 14th," he said, "and

I thought, shall I play a spoon or a brassie?" He remembered every shot. And, as he spoke, he brought it all back to me, and I remembered being there, the schoolboy who had come to watch his hero, riding on the back of Tom Fell's brand new Triumph 500 motorbike.

CHAPTER THIRTEEN

After my early experience as an ape, I get the chance to play a
sea lion in Fierce Creatures. *I mention my appearance on the*
Edinburgh Fringe and some of the younger comedians with whom
I have worked. I describe how I have become accustomed to public
speaking and how I function at corporate functions. There is a
meeting with an important sheikh in Bahrain.

When I returned from Australia in 1993 after touring with
Donald Sinden in *Out of Order* my next big job was presenting
the television show *Small Talk* for the BBC. This was the
programme in which young children were asked factual
questions such as "What is a harmonium?" or "Where would
you expect to find a courgette?" and various adult contestants
had to guess if a particular child would get the answer right.

I then asked the children philosophical questions, like "Is
homework necessary?" or "Is it important to be rich?" or "Why
does God allow Jeremy Beadle to happen?" Well, obviously, not
the last question; I made that up. That would be one for *The
Moral Maze* on Radio 4. Anyway, the adult contestants then had
to pick one of the boys or girls and guess what their attitude
would be.

It was a simple idea and it worked very well. When the BBC decided to do a pilot of the programme I was chosen to present it. I believe Janet Street-Porter, who was Head of Something Quite Important at the BBC at the time, was the person who suggested my name, and I'm grateful to her because I hugely enjoyed doing it.

The programme was cleverly made, because the audience imagined that I had the children with me, but, in fact, they had all been filmed in advance and all their answers recorded. The good thing was that I was able to create a sense of a rapport with the boys and girls even though they were just faces on a screen.

I knew what their answers would be if they were picked by the contestants, and I had a few little jokes and remarks up my sleeve, but it was really just a lottery and I had to be ready for any of them, so it kept me on my toes and I found it stimulating. Sometimes we could record three shows in a day and I would appear in a different jacket or pullover or suit to give the impression they were all separate occasions.

The *Small Talk* formula was irresistible and I was surprised when it came to an end in 1996 because I got a huge amount of mail about it and hundreds of people kept asking me why I wasn't doing it any more. I think it was actually due to another re-shuffle of senior positions at the BBC and the appointment of Peter Salmon as controller of BBC1.

At the time I was recording *Small Talk,* I was also taking part in the filming of *Fierce Creatures* which was supposed to be a sequel to the very successful comedy *A Fish Called Wanda* and starred John Cleese, Jamie Lee Curtis, Kevin Kline and Michael Palin.

When I first heard that John Cleese was writing the screen-play I dropped him a note and asked him if there might be a part in it for me. We have always kept in touch since our days on *The Frost Report* and, being a kindly sweet soul, he arranged for me to have the role of the keeper of the penguins in the zoo. Then, there was a change in casting and I was made keeper of the sea lions. The makers of the film discovered that penguins can pass on a very nasty skin condition to human beings, so they thought I'd be happier with sea lions. The trouble was that, in the plot, as part of all the PR for the zoo I was supposed to dress up in an embarrassing sea lion costume made of Sorbo rubber.

This wasn't much progress from my days wearing a Barbary ape outfit in *Operation Snatch,* the film about Gibraltar.

Filming *Fierce Creatures* was a struggle from the start. There is always a sort of gloom and a feeling of unease on a film set when the words are not quite right, and, in this case, there were too many good people in the film with not enough for them to do. It was difficult for the director Robert Young because everyone was coming up with new ideas all the time and trying to give him guidance. It was really a mammoth task – actually, mammoths were about the only animals which were not in the film – and when it was first edited they realised that it was just not right at all.

After previews in 1995, they knew that they needed to make a lot of changes and they also decided that they did not want the zoo owner's son (the character played by Kevin Kline) to die. This meant they had to get the cast together again – which took a long time – and shoot a whole lot of new scenes with a new director, Fred Schepisi. He was full of confidence and imagination, but even then it didn't really turn out right – which confirmed my theory that there is a limit to the amount of tweaking you can do on these occasions. It must have been a great strain for John Cleese, who wrote the screenplay with Ian Johnstone. He was extremely brave and kept his spirits up throughout – and did his best to keep our spirits up as well. But the film was not well received by the critics and did not do much for me. I don't think the seal lions were very happy either.

★

After *Small Talk* was cut off almost in mid-sentence and *Fierce Creatures* ended up a rather tame affair, what I needed was another tea at the Ritz to get my career moving again.

This time the invitation came from Ben Elton. It was in 1997 – more than 30 years after my first visit to the place with David Frost when David approached me about being in *The Frost Report*. Things had moved on for me, but I was glad to see that tea at the Ritz had not changed. I suppose I was a bit surprised to be asked to go to this place with Ben Elton – I thought he might disapprove of it – but the reason he wanted to see me was even more of a surprise. He asked me if I would revive my monologue-in-the-armchair from *The Two Ronnies* and do it on the coming series of *The Ben Elton Show* on television.

I was flattered and delighted about this, not just to get back in the armchair, but to be quite honest, because being with Ben Elton made me seem trendy again. And for all his on-screen ferocity, I found him quiet, sweet, warm and affectionate. He has a wonderfully fertile mind and is a compulsive writer. He actually wrote three of my monologues for the series and I thought he was very clever at making me a bit naughtier, without ever going further than an audience would expect me to go. I developed a real admiration for him.

Harry Hill is another modern comedian I have come to admire and I was very pleased when he asked me to be on his radio show with him. I find him very quirky and funny and I like the way he has created a character for himself which is not really like him at all.

At this stage in my career, it means a lot to me that I am able to perform with people like Ben and Harry and some of the other younger comedians and to know that we enjoy each other's work. I have already mentioned the famous Class sketch which

John Cleese, Ronnie Barker and I performed for *The Frost Report* back in the 1960s. Stephen Fry told me he was eight years old when he first saw that sketch and then in 1999 we recorded a new version of it for a millennium programme, *The Nearly Complete and Utter History of Everything* for BBC Television on January 2nd 2000. In this version Stephen, taking the place of John Cleese, played the part of Modern Man, Ronnie Barker was Renaissance Man and I was an ignorant smelly serf from the Middle Ages in terrible old clothes. We then played the original version and I was thrilled to see what a great reception it got from the studio audience. Some of them were probably not even born when we first performed it.

In 1999 I was also asked to play one of the Ugly Sisters in an ITV production of *Cinderella* which actually went out on the same day as *The Nearly Complete and Utter History*. The other Ugly Sister was played by Paul Merton. Frank Skinner and Harry Hill were also in the cast and Samantha Janus was our Cinderella. Paul and Frank were schoolboys at the time I was doing my sitcom called *Sorry!* and, to my amazement, they still actually remembered episodes of it – and even some of the lines.

Paul really wanted to do the "slosh" routine – also known as "decorating the parlour" – for our pantomime, just as I had done it when Stanley Baxter and I were the Ugly Sisters in *Cinderella* in Glasgow and Edinburgh back in 1966 and 1967.

I actually found an old film of Stanley and me doing it then, so I could show it to Paul. I also remembered how important it was to get the consistency of the slosh right, so, for this new version, I went out to the chemists and bought some sticks of Erasmic shaving soap, took them home, grated them into some warm water and whisked it up. I was doing it at home because I wanted to get the recipe absolutely right before I showed anybody. The next day they couldn't believe it when I turned up to rehearsals with my plastic bowl, my sticks of Erasmic, my whisk and my kettle.

Paul, like Ben Elton, loves the theatre. Most of the young performers do. They adore variety and they love the old comics. They went – or they were taken – to the Palladium and the Finsbury Park Empire and they loved to see people like Max Wall and Max Miller and Ken Dodd and Frankie Howerd, but now they are performers, this whole side of entertainment has been sadly denied to them. By the time they were old enough to take it up, the whole world of variety theatre had gone. Now there's just the Comedy Store.

I feel I was so lucky to have been brought up to experience so much of theatre history, and the greasepaint and the hessian of the backcloth and the sets, and the authentic backstage smells – a cocktail of paint, glue, dust, old curtains and stale chips and mouse droppings. These are things which the young comedy performers of today have never been able to enjoy. Of course, it's different for straight actors.

I don't feel there is any gulf between myself and the new generation. Ever since Anne and I have had a house near Edinburgh we have always gone to the Festival Fringe and so I have seen a lot of these performers growing up. I saw people like Jack Dee, Patrick Marber, Jim Tavaré and Bill Bailey before they became famous – and many others who remained unknown. We feel easy in each others' company and they know I appreciate a great deal of what is going on now.

Jim Tavaré is the tall one who wears white tie and tails and performs with a double bass. It's a very good act with musical jokes and there is a bit of a French flavour about it. I bumped into him a few years ago at the Edinburgh Festival and he said: "I've had an idea; if I get hold of a chair like the one you use for your monologues, will you come along to the theatre tonight in a sweater, sit in the chair and start telling a story?"

I agreed, of course. The plan was that, when the curtain went up, the audience, expecting to see Jim Tavaré with his double bass, would discover me instead, sitting in my chair. Jim said: "You can do as much of your monologue as you like – three minutes for four minutes, or whatever – and when you think you've done enough, touch your glasses or start talking about the producer, to give a signal, and then I'll come on."

So I sat there and the curtain went up and I got this huge welcome. It was really terrific and it went on and on. So I started to do my monologue and eventually touched the frame of my glasses to give the signal, and Jim came on the stage and said: "Excuse me, you're in the wrong theatre."

Well, he got a slightly hostile reception from the audience for interrupting me in mid-flow. Well, perhaps "flow" is the wrong word to describe one of my monologues – "arduous journey" might be better; a bit like going on a Virgin train when you don't just worry about ever reaching your destination, you worry that you have forgotten what your destination was meant to be. Where was I? Stopped just outside Penrith station with a defective locomotive. No, I wasn't. I was in my chair, on the stage in this fringe theatre in Edinburgh. At the Festival. Although, I have to say I'm still worried about those poor people stuck on the train outside Penrith. I expect the buffet car is closed, as well. So they won't be able to avail themselves of a selection of hot and cold snacks and beverages.

No, there I was in my chair and Jim Tavaré came on and said: "Excuse me, you're in the wrong theatre." And that was supposed to be the joke. Only it wasn't going down all that well. So I said to Jim: "Oh, sorry, I'll leave it to you," and I kindly left the stage. Then Jim tried to get on with his act. At this point I felt a bit guilty about leaving the audience in mid-monologue like that, after they had been so sweet, so I went back on and picked up the chair, saying "Sorry, I forgot this," and I went off again. Then, to make it clear that this time it really *was* goodbye I said something like "See you next year" and walked out of the theatre.

Driving 18 miles home to East Lothian, still in my sweater, I kept thinking about Jim and the job he would have with that audience. He rang me the next day and said the whole thing had backfired on him. What he thought was a rather sweet idea led to him having a 20-minute struggle to win them back. I felt sorry for him, but it did me good to discover that, as a comedian, I could still be considered a bit alternative.

I am interested in the young comedians, but I suppose I am more interested in their writing (and in their attitudes) than in the actual style of their performance. Let's face it, *they* are not all that interested in the style of their performance either. It's not something that matters to them. This is because they haven't really had any training in what you might call the physical side of the theatre. They are not in any way theatrical in their body language. They're not interested in line or elegance or a sense of physical calm, not at all bothered with the sort of theatrical arts Evelyn Laye taught me in the Dinely Rehearsal Studios when I was in my 20s.

They don't feel they need to bother with all that. They walk on, stand at the mike, deliver and walk off again. Eddie Izzard is the exception. He has a great elegance of movement and his transvestite streak makes him look glamorous, with his highlights and his orange velvet jacket and everything. You feel that he is prepared to be "show business".

Most of the others are not interested in putting on their Sunday best for the audience. It is not important to them, but it is very important to me, because I see myself as a theatre person. I have a dinner jacket which I would not dream of going to dinner in, or even sitting down in. I would only wear it for work, to stand up and perform in. I have been trained to dress up for the theatre, to do my turn.

I believe that part of making people laugh or feel entertained is to make them feel they are looking at something which is not necessarily glamorous, but is special, or "sparkling" in some way. That in itself is uplifting. It's like lovely, well-made sets making the comedy better.

When I go on stage I like to feel that people realise that here is someone who knows the stage and knows his way about. I also think that when they see me in the flesh this is the best they have ever seen me. I want them to feel safe in my hands.

I suppose this is part of being a vaudeville performer, although the species is in danger of becoming extinct. I feel I belong to vaudeville, and I also think Billy Connolly does, in his way, and Harry Hill as well, when you see him in the flesh.

The thing I really admire about the young performers is their imagination and their sheer bravery. They take such chances. Ben Elton told me that he would rehearse for half an hour at home and then go out and perform in front of an audience for an hour and a half, not even knowing if the material was going to work. Performers like Ben give their material such a lot of oomph and energy that they can get it off the ground and carry the audience with them and, through sheer force of character, they *make* it work.

I'm a different kind of animal. I know in advance, in most cases, what I can say that will make people laugh. If I see it on paper I know whether it will work or not. Sometimes I will take chances with a bit of material that I really like, which may or may not get a laugh, but mostly I like to be sure of the reaction I am going to get.

It has become a fashionable and glamorous thing to be a comedian, so a lot of people have come into comedy who are not, in spirit, comic. You have an awful lot of people saying outrageous things and having off-the-wall attitudes, but deep down they are not comedians. It jars; the act never quite gets into gear. They have clever thoughts and some funny angles on life, but not a funny bone in their body. They just want to be comics and that's as far as it goes. They are not physically funny. For them, just wanting to be is enough. It's impossible to explain what I mean by physically funny; you know it when you see it; when a Tommy Cooper or a Frankie Howerd walks on to the stage and people start laughing before he has said a word.

The other thing about the new breed is that most of them have only ever been solo performers. They were almost born being solo performers. In the past, you had to fight your way through the crowd to do something on your own. You might start out as a band singer and then perhaps do a funny announcement for two of the numbers and then somebody thinks maybe you could do a bit less of the singing and a bit more of the funny announcements, and, before you know where you are, you've got eight minutes on your own.

You would probably start in concert parties and after that you would try and get on to the number one halls, like the Chiswick Empire or the Metropolitan Edgware Road, or the Finsbury Park Empire. If you were booked for a number one hall, you did an eight week tour and you did a seven or eight-minute spot. If you went over that time there would be a knock on your dressing room door and they'd say: "You've got to get a minute and a half out of your act. You were eight and a half minutes tonight, and it's supposed to be seven, and that's all you're getting." Even the big top-of-the-bill performers like Max Miller only did 22 minutes. The timing was always strictly controlled.

Nowadays, people become soloists straight away. They go to the Comedy Store and do 20 minutes. Just like that. In our day, someone would say: "Hang on a bit; you have to be in the business a little longer before you can even come on and make an announcement."

In recent years I have done quite a lot of corporate entertaining, taking part in sponsored golf tournaments, standing up at trade association dinners, taking the microphone at awards cere- monies, doing a spot at the Spot Welders Federation Annual Dinner and Dance. It can be quite rewarding financially and I don't find it too hard; it's only one night out of your life, whereas theatre work is eight performances a week. Sometimes you get a difficult audience when the event is badly organised or you're going on too late in the evening and they are pissed, or bored or fed up – or all three.

Not all that many performers do the corporate circuit. Bob Monkhouse is probably the greatest exponent; he puts an awful lot of work into it and is very, very clever. Jimmy Tarbuck is also a regular, and Terry Wogan does a certain amount as well.

I don't mind playing the company game a bit; I don't mind being there as part-gentleman, part-comedian, part-friend, part- whatever-you-want. They know there is no risk in having me there; I'm perfectly house-trained, I won't bark at the clients, I'll be quite friendly with the ladies, I'll sit down and have the meal with them, then I'll get up and entertain them. It's all part of good manners.

A certain amount of homework is necessary. If I am going to address the dynamic sales force of Amalgamated Corn Plasters plc at the dinner after their three-day seminar at the Hotel Slip- Road Excelsior, on the outskirts of Nuneaton, I'll take the trouble to find out a few names of the people involved to include in my act – they are always keen to have somebody's name taken in vain – and I'll also make some remarks about the Nuneaton area. One thing I won't do is tell any corn plaster jokes, because it is a safe bet that anyone in the corn plaster business will know them all already. And it would be wise to steer clear of the verruca gags as well.

It is a peculiar thing to show up at some distant hotel at some time in the evening, to be met by the chairman's p.a. whom you have never met before and by two chaps you don't know from Adam, who are the chairman's assistants, and then go and sit down at a table with 12 people you are seeing for the first time, before standing up to address 500 total strangers. Many people would find this stressful, but you find a way of turning up and just doing it.

The important thing is to keep your curiosity. Every time I do one of these jobs I am seeing a side of life that I would not otherwise see, meeting people I would not otherwise have a chance to meet.

Quite often I am asked to play golf with some important corporate clients at Wentworth, say, and then may stand up at the prizegiving in the evening. I play quite a lot of golf here and abroad, at events organised by big banks and insurance companies and so on. That can make it a long hard day. Playing 18 holes of golf can take four hours and, when you are with people you don't really know, it can take a lot out of you. I try to be a pleasant partner, but it is a long time to be with a stranger you might not necessarily get on with. You've got to keep it going, socially, all the time; you have to be easygoing – or at least pretend to be easygoing.

Luckily, I find the corporate world fascinating. I recently found myself playing golf at one of these events with a chap who had started selling mobile phones from a little shop and had recently had his business taken over by an American company for £37 million. It helps that I am interested in people and in hearing the story of how they got into mobile phones or started their hotel business – or what first attracted them to the world of corn plasters.

It is also a form of self-protection; if you ask a lot of questions there isn't so much time left for you to be answering them. I would sooner be informing myself about, say, the mobile phone business or the economics of running a hotel, than regurgitating the same old answers to the same old questions, such as "Don't you see Ronnie Barker any more?" or "Are you doing anything these days?" Nowadays, if people don't see you on television every week, they think you must have gone into retirement, even if you are doing theatre or cabaret every night.

Sometimes a big computer firm, say, will sponsor a golf tournament and they will want me to be there and to be at the lunchtime buffet and mingle with the staff and the clients, then make a speech in the evening. Actually, though I say so myself, I am a skilful mingler. You need to keep on the move, but never appear to be in a hurry. In a crowded room, it is a matter of mastering the sidle and the flit while never resorting to the dart. I've sometimes thought mingling could be an Olympic event, with points awarded for introduction technique, small-talk expertise, number of encounters – and nimbleness in side-stepping. Points are deducted for introducing yourself to some person and not realising you met them just a minute and a half ago – and discussed corn plasters in depth.

There are also arts festivals and literary festivals that I go to in the summer, so you could also say that I have become quite a connoisseur of marquees. There is a fascinating range of smells in marquees, a variety of odours of trampled grass and a subtlety in the mustiness of the canvas. I have a "nose" for them; I can just pause by the entrance inhale and say: "Ah yes, this one was last used for quite a smart wedding reception and the rain started five minutes into the best man's speech." Or: "A pleasingly

robust little marquee – ideal for the church fete or flower show."
Or perhaps: "A very corporate model; smooth and well
rounded, with a distinct bouquet of Havana cigar in the fabric."

All these functions give me a wonderful opportunity to
observe the rich tapestry of British life, and my experience of
getting up and performing at all these events has also made me a
one-man hotel guide.

With the exception of some of the better hotels in the West
End of London, the food at the dinners can sometimes be a bit
grim – some sort of polystyrene mousse to start with, followed
by latex chicken and rubber blancmange, or perhaps something
like a soufflé with blob of meringue on top. My usual habit is to
have a bit of the starter – it will probably be a sliver of smoked
salmon wrapped round some crab mousse – then just the
vegetables from the main course, one glass of white wine and a
cup of coffee and that's it.

Over the years I have developed a system for myself at these
functions – a few do's and don'ts for the do's. I find that if I am
in the room with everyone for the whole meal, or at least for
most of it, chatting to the people at the same table, I have a
better understanding when I get to my feet, of what the room is
"about" or what the audience is like. Somehow an atmosphere
percolates through to me. The people there feel I am friendlier
because I have been with them through the meal (through thick
and thin) and I am not in any way snooty, arriving at the last
minute or jumping out of the cake. They like me better because
I've been with them first and it also gives me a chance to pick
up some more names to use in my act.

If I am due to do my spot a little later in the evening, say at
half past ten, it is more like a cabaret act, so I take some music
with me and a piano player, or perhaps a trio. It makes the whole
thing a bit more theatrical and it's also company for me. I can
stroll on with the band playing – otherwise that walk can be long

and lonely and all I hear are my heels clicking on the ballroom floor.

It helps to have the trio there; I can refer to them and it cheers me up to know that I can turn round and see a smiling face. It is usually the same pianist and he supplies the bass player and the drummer who have often played for me before. They are extremely good musicians, so they help to make the act stylish and smart.

I don't do much singing, just the odd song and some of the songs are a little bit odd. They are the sort of things I would expect the American comedian George Burns to sing and numbers that few people have heard before except me, like "Excuse Me" and the slightly better known "Lulu's Back in Town". I also sing a Cole Porter song, "Black and White Baby", about a girl who insists that everything has to be black and white, from her black and white coat and her black and white hat to her black and white doggie and her black and white cat. The trouble is that Cole Porter put only one verse and one chorus of it down in black and white, which was not very helpful of him. So I sent it to Dick Vosburgh, who wrote many of the musical numbers in *The Two Ronnies* and is brilliant at this sort of thing, and he added some more lyrics. Now you wouldn't know which bit was Porter and which was Vosburgh. I'll give you a clue – this bit is by Vosburgh:

She got in a fight with a black and white guy,
She gave him black and white teeth and a black and white
    eye,
So they rushed her off as quick as a wink
In a black and white maria to a black and white clink.
She said 'Why, sorry my loves,'
And, with her black and white gloves,

Made a most disgusting sign.
Oh how her family weep,
Cos she's the black and white sheep,
That black and white baby of mine.

One fairly reliable general rule about addressing these functions is that if there are ladies in the room it will improve the quality of the audience. It will be more attractive to look at and more attractively behaved. A lot of gentlemen on their own can be quite hard work and quite boring.

I love the portentousness of the names of hotel function rooms – the Sandringham Suite, the Emperor Lounge, the Lincoln Apartment, the Madame de Pompadour Annexe, the Oedipus Complex – and I love the architecture of some of them with the ceiling mouldings which look as if they have been iced by some megalomaniac *patissier* with a thing about gold. Some of the rooms are much easier to work in than others; it is a matter of proportions; the look of the room, the feel of it, the height of the ceiling, the atmosphere; sometimes it's something you can't define.

There have been two major disasters. The first occurred years and years ago in the days when I was still doing *The Two Ronnies* and I went to the Grosvenor House Hotel, in London, to entertain the salesmen for some office supplies company. For a start, it was in the ballroom at the hotel which, in my opinion, is a death-trap for comedians because it is about the size of the parade ground at Sandhurst.

Blood was spilled. These salesmen were all men and they had been there all day with the drinks paid for by the company. By the time I got up to do my bit it was like a Roman orgy without the good bits. The East Midlands assistant area manager was bashing the up-and-coming West of England sales executive over the head with a bottle, most of the North West regional sales force had got East Anglia by the throat, London and the South East was hitting all its targets in the South Wales area with plates and anything else that came to hand.

Pan's People, the glamorous girl dancers who often appeared on *The Two Ronnies,* were also part of the entertainment that night and I thought they were going to be torn limb from lithe limb.

I was supposed to speak for 40 minutes, but I think my act came down to 12 minutes. I gabbled. This is what happens when you're struggling; you don't feel like giving them the pauses and the neat little asides. You just want to get to the end.

Nobody in the ballroom was listening to me anyway. It was like standing up and telling jokes to Genghis Khan's pillaging hordes as they advance towards you.

On the other disastrous occasion, I was doing a New Year's Eve cabaret at an hotel in Bahrain in 1977. The dining room, which held about 500 people, was packed with Saudis who had come over the border just so that they could have a drink. They had not really come to hear my story about the parrot. As long as they could have a drink they didn't really care about this parrot and the way it was so impossibly rude and insulting all the time that its owner shut it in the deep freeze for three days.

They didn't listen to a word I was saying. I don't think they actually *understood* a word I was saying. So they would not have got the bit about the man finally relenting and taking the parrot out of the deep freeze, thawing it out, finding it was still just alive and suddenly behaving extremely well and acting in a fawning and ingratiating manner. All that would have gone completely over their heads.

These people in that Bahrain hotel dining room did not really know what they were there for, did not know nor care who I was and were half plastered anyway. The only thing that kept me going that New Year's Eve, as I was standing there, dying on my feet, was the knowledge that on New Year's Day the British newspapers would be announcing that Ronnie Barker and I had been awarded the OBE. One each, actually.

And, after its release from the freezer, the de-frosted and beautifully behaved parrot turned to its owner and said, "By the way, what did the chicken do wrong?"

Doing these cabarets is a bit like bullfighting; you never know what it is going to be like and how the audience will be. Even Bob Monkhouse, with all his practice and expertise, must have had some horrible experiences. If you do three bad ones on the trot it dents your confidence. When it does go wrong you feel you are the only person in the world it has ever happened to. You feel that all the other comedians all around the country at this very moment are getting huge laughs. Suddenly tonight you are no longer a funny person; you are very ordinary; you are not meant to be doing this, standing here. It all seems to evaporate. You say to yourself: "Am I the same person I was last week?" It's terrifying.

For this reason, it is nice to go back to the proper theatre from time to time, where all the people are actually facing in the right direction, and you can cheer yourself up again.

I've been back to Bahrain since then. I fact, in the late 1980s or early 90s I went on two or three tours in the Gulf states, doing cabaret. There is quite a circuit out there where the ex-pats gather in places like the Bahrain Country Club or the Abu Dhabi Country Club or a similar establishment in Oman. When I did these tours, Anne came with me and they were organised by a wonderful Geordie called Bill Thompson. Bill was an optimist. Everywhere we went, he travelled with about 13 beautiful suits, on their hangers and lovingly wrapped in polythene. He couldn't wear any of them, because he had thickened out a bit since he bought them. Still, he took them with him everywhere in the fond hope that one morning he would wake up and suddenly find the suits miraculously fitted him.

There were usually about six of us in the party and Bill would always promise us that we would fly First Class, or, at least Club Class. Then he would sometimes have a way of chivvying us to get to the airport about 40 minutes before we really needed to and we would see him in earnest discussion with some official, with a lot of passionate arm waving on his part, and I wondered if once or twice he had bought ordinary class tickets and then counted on his charm and persuasiveness to get us upgraded. Bill was very sweet, but did have his own particular way of operating. He tended to get his way. On one of these tours I found myself one night doing my act out of doors on a covered-over hotel swimming pool near a motorway. Every time I got to a joke, a gigantic lorry would roar past on the motorway, throwing up dust and drowning the most important line. I told Bill that I would never again perform out of doors and I even had this put in our agreement.

On the next tour, Bill and his wife took Anne and me out to a wonderful dinner at a very grand restaurant and, as we were getting to the coffee stage, he said, "Ronnie, I have a favour to ask you."

"If it's about doing my cabaret out of doors, the answer is no," I replied.

He pleaded. He said that all the ballrooms and all the function rooms were booked. He begged. There was nowhere else to go. He had tried everything; he was at his wits' end.

"I'm sorry, but I won't do it," I replied.

Then Bill did the most extraordinary thing. He started crying. This was not just a bit of sniffling; it was the works. He sobbed;

tears rolled and rolled down his face – he was clearly genuinely upset.

Although I was overawed by this show of emotion, I still refused to change my mind. The evening ended awkwardly and Anne and I went to our room, leaving Bill and his tear-stained face. When we were alone, Anne said she thought I ought to agree to just this one outdoor performance. "You can't let poor Bill go on worrying and being unhappy about it all night," she said. So I relented, and Bill got his way. Again.

On one occasion Anne and I were in Bahrain, having come back from Hong Kong where I had been doing a turn at the opening of a golf course near the new airport. We were on a stopover between Dubai and Abu Dhabi and we were lolling by the hotel swimming pool, looking and feeling wappit (which is Scottish for exhausted) when a friend of ours, who used to run the Bahraini royal family's flying squadron, piloting them wherever they wanted to go, came over to my sun lounger. He said that the Prime Minister – I'm pretty sure it was the Prime Minister – was a terrific fan of mine and would we like to go and visit him?

"I am terribly sorry," I said, "but we only have an hour before we have to go and catch our flight, so could you please apologise and make our excuses to the Prime Minister?"

Our friend went away to make a phone call and shortly afterwards he returned with a proposal: if the sheikh – because he was undoubtedly a sheikh – was driven to the hotel car park and sat there in his car, would we be prepared to walk over there and speak to him?

We said we would, and our friend went away again.

Then another message came back. The sheikh had decided that he would actually come into the hotel and that we would meet him in one of the reception rooms. So Anne and I, dressed in our towelling dressing gowns and flip flops, damp-haired and dishevelled, were ushered into this splendid room to find the sheikh already standing looking very handsome, rather like Haile Selassie, and dressed in a beautiful cream silk robe. There were three thrones in the room, rather like the scene you see in newsreels when Presidents go to visit Arab leaders. The sheikh sat on the middle throne and Anne and I were on either side of him. There were nine or ten armed guards in the room, standing to attention, lining the walls.

He started by asking about our daughters Emma and Sophie and about their weddings because he had actually read about them in *Hello!* magazine and then he went on to talk about *The Two Ronnies* and about my sitcom *Sorry!* He had seen all the episodes of *Sorry!* and could actually recite most of the plots. After about 20 minutes, the sheikh waved over an officer from the armed guard who stepped forward with two little boxes containing gifts for Anne and me. He gave Anne a Bahraini pearl bracelet and I got a Rolex watch. We were really touched that he had been so sweet and appreciative.

I believe that going to these corporate functions and entertaining the guests keeps me sharp and fluent. I need to perform and to keep in practice, even if it means I occasionally get a really tough audience.

My act, on these occasions, is a version of the monologue I used to do in *The Two Ronnies*, but it is more flexible and I adapt it according to the feel I have had of the audience during the dinner – and even according to their reaction as I go along. I have a variable opening routine so that I can drop in local or topical references. Then I have "chapter headings" on pieces of paper and words and phrases in my mind, and I can skip back and forth between topics.

For example I might do a bit on "my neighbour who went to conquer Everest", then switch to "bank manager with the embarrassing nervous tic", take in "recipe for a blissfully happy divorce", leave out "how to escape from an enraged elk" altogether, and then return to the summit of Everest.

There again, I might start with the bit about the baby polar bear asking its mother, "Mummy, am I really a polar bear?" then go straight to the memory of my childhood on Christmas Eve when Daddy crept into my little room in his Santa Claus outfit and stole my socks.

This chopping and changing with the material gives me a *frisson* and a sense of danger and gives the whole piece a feeling of freshness and accident – and, because of my particular rambling style, it actually appears more accidental than it is.

And, in the course of the speech, I can do little bits of business: I can pick up a glass of wine, talk a little bit while holding it, then take a sip from the glass of wine, say that reminds me of the case of a serial poisoner in Basingstoke, and then go off at another tangent. All the time, I am making decisions on my feet.

I have always believed that the bit of talent you are born with is not enough to see you through your life; it has to be decorated, or added to, through learning, training, experience and practice. I am basically a comic actor and the storytelling side of me is something I have had to work on. People like Billy Connolly and Jimmy Tarbuck are natural story tellers; they were making people laugh long before they became professional performers and they just carried it on into their show business careers. Most of the comic monologists were entertaining their friends before they were required to do it in front of an audience. It was not like that with me.

When I stand up and do my piece at some event, I feel it is like firing a piece of porcelain; I am putting myself through the furnace of danger to give myself a sort of protective shell to make myself appear more at ease.

I need that feeling of living dangerously, and nowadays I believe I'm doing the act in a slightly different way. A little bit more of *me* is coming out, more daring perhaps, more of not minding what I say. The really important thing is that I am still learning.

CHAPTER FOURTEEN

A sort of Epilogue

In the days when I was a young aspiring actor in Edinburgh, making my way to the Glover Turner Robertson school, in George Street, for drama coaching, or waiting outside the stage door of the Lyceum theatre for one of the stars to come out, I often pictured myself as the sort of performer who would wear a Scotts lightweight felt hat.

This was the fashionable headgear my father so admired and this was what the actor Peter Graves wore when I saw him in Noël Coward's *Present Laughter* with Margaret Lockwood. That hat represented everything I wanted to be. It was sophisticated, stylish and urbane. It was the hat for a man who took trouble about how he presented himself to the rest of the world.

And I did actually put on a Scotts lightweight felt hat when I auditioned in front of Clive Dunn for a part in *Take It Easy,* the summer show at Cromer which was one of my first proper jobs in showbusiness.

Since then, I have worn a good variety of hats in my time and, perhaps because Aunt Nell and Uncle Alec were both tailors, I have always been fascinated by the materials clothes are made of – and by hats.

When I first came to London as a young RAF officer doing National Service I was told that anyone who knew anything about hats went to Bates, in Jermyn Street, because they made the most dashing kind of headgear. So I went to Bates.

And there is Lock's, down in St James's where I have also been a customer and where they make the most wonderful bowlers. There is a particular jauntiness about the curly-brimmed bowlers from Lock's. My dandified cousin, Bunny Roger had one, I remember, which was especially curly and the material of it was slightly fuzzier than usual, which made it very eye-catching.

I have a selection of check caps for playing golf in, specially in Scotland where you need protection from the wind. I also have eight-piece caps, made by Bates and by Lock's. They are expensive, but you can get them to make hats to match your clothes. I got an Italian black coat in the sales at Fortnum's and I got Lock's to match the material. I also have a dashing felt hat made in Italy, by Borsalino.

Being small I am rather limited in what I can buy on impulse. Buying clothes usually takes a bit of planning ahead. One of the few things that I can get for myself, simply off the peg, to lift my spirits in the course of a day is a cap. Or perhaps a sleeveless pullover. If I need a suit I go to have it made by Dimi Major and when I want a shirt I go to Turnbull and Asser, just off Jermyn Street, in London, where they have been looking after me beautifully for years. If I ever get to heaven, I expect to find a Jermyn Street there.

I used to get my shoes from the boys' department in Harrods, which was perfectly all right as long as I remembered not to go there in the school holidays. And the advantage of buying my socks in children's departments is that there is no VAT on children's clothes.

When Ronnie Barker and I were made OBEs in 1978 I went to get my top hat for the Investiture from a shop called Patey's, near Newington Butts, in South London. They make the top hats for you – black silk hats or grey toppers, so you have one that doesn't just go on, but actually *fits* you. This is an extremely rare thing, as any man who has ever been to a formal wedding in a hired outfit will know. The grey topper usually grips you brutally at both sides of the head, but then leaves a big enough gap at the front and back for nesting house martins to fly in and out. Or else it feels as if you have an iron bar fixed to your forehead, while soft breezes waft about the tops of your ears.

It is wonderful to go to Pateys and to smell the lacquer and the glue, to see the wooden blocks they make the hats on and to put on that amazing metal gadget they use to measure the precise dimensions of your head.

So I wore my Pateys top hat for the Investiture. There is a fine photograph of Ronnie B and me, walking away from the camera, wearing our hats, and I am holding the little box with the OBE medal behind my back.

It was a lovely occasion. You all queue up to get your medals from the Queen, like lining up in a canteen, but the rules of alphabetical order were bent a bit so that Ron and I could take our bow, so to speak, together. Our families came, too, of course; Emma and Sophie came in matching coats and skirts and patent leather shoes and velvet berets – everything they hated normally. Afterwards we all had a celebratory lunch at Walton's restaurant, in Walton Street.

My dad always took a lot of care over what he wore. He had his shoes hand-made for him by a shop called Peebles, in

Grassmarket, in Edinburgh. He would pay eight guineas – more than a week's wages – for a pair. They were always kept with trees in them and my dad was always polishing them and they lasted a lifetime. He believed in that sort of thing.

I think it is a wonderful thing that these old specialist shops, like Lock's and Patey's, survive, and that these trades manage to go on. The names stick in my memory, like Dymock and Howden, the grocers in my youth in Edinburgh, and Jacquot, the cake shop in St John's Wood High Street, in my early days in London. Nowadays, I love to go to Paxton and Whitfield, in Jermyn Street, for cheese and oatcakes.

When I go to Patisserie Valerie at Sagne, that wonderful cake shop in Marylebone High Street I still marvel at this daily turnout of high quality and I am still thrilled that there are people who are still interested in doing this sort of thing and taking all this trouble. I watch in awe as they lift the cakes with the tongs, put that little bit of greaseproof paper round the *mille feuille* and place them all so tenderly in the lovely boxes. Then there is that wonderful final flourish when they tie up the box with ribbon, then scrape the scissors along the ribbon so it curls up. I feel like shouting "Bravo!" Or perhaps even "Encore!"

I have been so lucky to have worked with people who have shown the same capacity for taking pains and getting everything just right. People like Danny La Rue, and Ronnie Barker, of course, and Mary Husband who did the costumes for *The Two Ronnies,* and Bobby Warans, who took such care in dressing the set, and all the writers, and particularly Spike Mullins, the master craftsman of my monologues, but also Ian Davidson and Peter Vincent, who made such an excellent job of writing *Sorry!* and who I still turn to for some of my material.

I have tried to match all the attention to detail of these people, and all this care over presentation, in my own work, so that I

am, I hope, like some sort of well established tradesman –
"R. Corbett, purveyor of high class vaudeville."

These are also the values that my father lived by. I think of
him in the bake-house in Edinburgh, lovingly and patiently
preparing the vanilla slices, the iced buns, chocolate cakes,
cherry cakes and beautiful Madeira cakes; I remember him at
home and the endless pains he took in making a wedding cake
for a friend or relative, or creaming the butter for the filling for
a sponge cake and flavouring it with chocolate or coffee, making
sure it was exactly the right consistency. When I think of him
doing these things, it occurs to me that, in a way, I have made a
life in the same sort of business.

INDEX